SIKH REVIVALIST MOVEMENTS

SIKH REVIVALIST MOVEMENTS

THE NIRANKARI AND NAMDHARI MOVEMENTS IN PUNJAB IN THE NINETEENTH CENTURY

(A Socio-Religious Study)

Surjit Kaur Jolly

GYAN PUBLISHING HOUSE
NEW DELHI-110 002

SIKH REVIVALIST MOVEMENTS

ISBN: 81-212-0695-2

Published in 2000 in India by
Gyan Publishing House
5, Ansari Road,
New Delhi-110 002
Phone : 3282060, 3261060
Fax : 3285914
E-mail: gyanbook@del2.vsnl.del.in

Laser Typesetting at: Power Photocomposers, New Delhi-110 002
Printed at: Chawla Offset Printers

To

My Dear Parents

Arjan Singh Harbans Kaur

Contents

Appendices

Plates

Preface

The nineteenth century had witnessed the emergence of a number of socio-religious movements in different parts of India. From Punjab to Bengal there seems to have been a wave of social awareness and protest against the degenerating and dogmatic socio-religious behaviour of the people. The main object of all these movements was to give a vision to the society to appreciate the basic spirit of the religion in a proper perspective. Farquhar has rightly remarked that "the old religions are the soil from which modern movements spring".

The social reform movements usually have their root in the basic religious principles. Any deviation from it, makes the society dogmatic and ritualistic. The call of these movements was again and again to return to original religious principles. According to Annie Besant "any movement to be strong in India must rest on a religious basis and so interwoven with religion is the very fibre of the Indian heart that it only throbs with full response when the religious note has been struck which call out its sympathetic vibration".

The nineteenth century presents a picture not of political upheaval only but also of major changes in the socio-religious life of the country. This period also had the impact of the influx of Christian missionaries and the western culture and education. Thus in a way, the nineteenth century was an important period in the history of the Indian culture. It was effected by a number of factors which had posed serious challenges to its age-old customs, beliefs and traditions.

In Bengal Raja Ram Mohan Roy founded the Brahmo Samaj in 1828 A.D. and he was regarded as the pioneer, in organising the socio-religious reform movement. This movement has been rightly called as a first important attempt in giving an intellectual rationalism and enlightenment to the modern India.

Prarthna Samaj, an offshoot of Brahmo Samaj, was founded in Bombay in 1867. It's founder Madhav Gobind Ranade was a well known social reformer of Maharashtra. It had a number of branches in Madras and Gujarat. The contribution made by it mainly related to the welfare of women. It protested against the caste distinction, which is too well known to be repeated.

Dev Samaj was yet another offshoot of the Brahmo Samaj. It was founded in 1887 under the leadership of Shiv Narayan Agnihotri at Lahore. Being essentially, a believer in the institution of Guruship of worship of their Gurus as *Avtars* (incarnation of God), the Dev Samaj failed to become an effective reform movement and ended in a petty cult.

While the Brahmo Samaj and its offshoots were considered to be ahead of their times, the orthodox Hindus were impelled to form a rival organisation named Dharam Sabha. Its founder was Radha Kant Dev, a well known figure of Calcutta. They were anti Brahmo Samajists.

One of the important socio-religious reform movements of the nineteenth century was the Arya Samaj. It had contributed materially to the awakening of the Hindu society, and to the need of social and religious reforms. Arya Samaj was founded by Swami Dayanand on 7th April 1875 in Bombay. The watchword of the Arya Samaj was 'Back to the Vedas'. It strongly protested against the ritualistic practices among the Hindus and the unchallenged authority enjoyed by the Brahmins. Perhaps nothing would explain the teachings of Arya Samaj better, then what has been summed up by Annie Besant. "The repudiation of the authority of the Brahmins, the denouncing of the infinite number of meaningless rites and worship of the image of different gods and goddesses which split the people into numerous belligerent sects and crusade against the mass of religious superstitions which kept for many centuries the Hindu mind in a state of mental and spiritual degradation. These were the progressive elements in the Arya Samaj".

In 1889 Lahore witnessed another reform movement among the Hindus called Sanatan Dharm. Perhaps it was the most prominent of the formal association of the orthodox Hindus. The aim of this movement was to impart moral religious instructions and to promote and preserve old orthodox Hinduism. Since the principles to which these movements subscribed had their roots deep in the soil of Indian culture, it could spread more easily and with larger appeal to people.

The second half of the nineteenth century witnessed two important Hindu movements, the Theosophical Society and the

Ramakrishna Mission. Both of them aimed at serving the humanity as a whole and tried to create some meaningful sense to the religious teachings by their rational interpretations. Thus they were comparatively more realistic in matters of the religious teachings and the social needs. It made them more liberal in their outlook with greater emphasis on universal brotherhood.

While on the one hand a number of intellectual and religious reform movements had shaken the Hindu Society with a view to making it free from degenerating elements, the Muslims, also tried to strengthen their community. During the period the earliest of the reform movement among the Muslims, was the *wahabi* movement started in 1820 by Sayad Ahmad Khan of Bareilly. He toured all over Northern India demanding that Islam be purged of all idolatrous practices. In their religious sphere, the *wahabis* laid stress on the original teachings of the *Quran* and sought to remove the practices which did not have the sanction of the Holy book. One of the important aspects of their teachings was that they stood for the propagation of widow marriage and discarding of ostentatious ceremonies and other wasteful expenditure on social occasions.

One of the important development in the outlook of Muslim thought, during the period under review, was the gradual impact of the western education and ideas that led to the socio-religious awareness. It was indeed with the efforts of Sir Sayad Ahmad Khan that the Muslims in India started viewing their socio-religious problems and discarding the orthodox and traditional thinking.

Mirza Gulam Ahmad the founder of the Ahmadiya movement proclaimed himself to be the 'Mahadi'. With the passage of time the movement assumed a distinct character and became a sect of Islam. The movement did not make much headway in India, but in Punjab Mirza Gulam Ahmad left quite a number of followers. The Ahmadiyas came into clash with the Sikhs because their founder had declared that the first guru of the Sikhs—Nanak was neither a Sikh nor a Hindu but a Muslim and his mission was nothing but another version of Islam.

One may disagree with the view that Nanak was a Muslim, but it can not be denied that the impact of Nanak's teachings on Punjab remained unquestioned for centuries after his death.

Like other regions of India, Punjab during the nineteenth century was also experiencing some simmering discontent in its socio-religious life. This led to the emergence of two important

Movements—Nirankari and Namdhari. They aimed at eradicating the social evils in the Sikh society. These very movements are the subject of the present study. While considerable work has been done on various other movements of similar nature in the different parts of India during the nineteenth century, relatively negligible studies have been made of these movements, especially of their contributions to the socio-religious life.

As regards the Nirankari movement perhaps the only work, worth mentioning is that of John C.B. Webster entitled *The Nirankari Sikhs.* It can only be said as a good short survey of the Nirankaris from their inception to the contemporary times. It helps to know, though briefly, the major contributions of the Nirankaris in the field of socio-religious reforms.

Webster has utilised the English translation of the Punjabi sources in this book leading to certain omissions. He had devoted about ten pages to the activities of the Nirankaris during the nineteenth century, which is hardly sufficient to know about them and their activities in some detail.

Webster in the introduction has referred to five major sources of the Nirankaris i.e. the *Hukam Nama, Parwana of Sahib Ratta Ji* (1873 A.D.), *the Will of Ratta Ji (1903) Prem Prakash* and two letters and a telegram of Baba Hara Singh and Gurudit Singh. He has also referred to the flag (*Nishan Sahib*), ornaments and canopy of Sahib Ratta Ji and a few practices of Baba Darbara Singh. He has rightly indicated that more Nirankari sources were written in the twentieth century. Thus a person working on the nineteenth century has to naturally face the paucity of sources. I have tried to explore as far as possible all the material published, unpublished, archival and personal collections, available on the subject.

After going through the pages of their history written and unwritten I have drawn certain conclusions. The socio-religious reform activities of the Nirankaris were certainly in the form of a movement and she is inclined to disagree with the views of Webster who does not consider it a movement. In this connection the following observations of Webster need special attention.

> "Although it has been customary for historians to refer to the Nirankaris as a movement, this practice is open to serious question. A social movement has been defined as a collective attempt to bring about change in certain social institutions or to

create an entirely new order and as socially shared demands for change in some aspect of the social order. These definitions would imply that a movement (i) involves collective effort, (ii) is assertive, perhaps aggressive, in seeking to bring about change, and (iii) has some impact or influence even if it is not successful in changing any part of the social order. Of these three characteristics of a movement, only the first would apply to the Nirankaris, as they have had a collective life, although in a loosely organized form". Webster further adds, "there is no evidence that they sought to change the social order, in whole or in part, and, indeed, their influence or impact upon the social order has been negligible. Thus they could not be called a social movement".

Looking through Webster's own standard of judgement about the characteristic of this movement, his conclusion in this regard appears to be pre-conceived. The activities of the Nirankaris were a collective effort, assertive and sought to bring about a change and certainly had considerable impact and influence on the social life of the Sikhs. This aspect has been discussed in detail in the book.

It is strange that Webster is not inclined to consider it a movement. According to him, after Baba Dayal and Baba Darbara Singh, the Nirankaris were very peaceful and quite. What he means by "very peaceful and quite" is not clear. Any movement cannot have similar vigour and assertion throughout and the contemporary conditions, to a great extent determine its nature and course of action. There could be hardly any doubt that the Nirankaris remained effective throughout the nineteenth century and had influenced the contemporary society through their teachings. It certainly had all the characteristics of an important social movement. Webster has raised a few important issues about the Nirankaris which need to be contested. He said:

(i) "However their attempt to change ceremonial were directed primarily at those associated with them rather than at the wider Sikh community".
(ii) "Their impact upon the religious institutions of the Sikh is by no means clear".
(iii) "The Nirankaris are a cult which has been defined as a particular system of religious worship especially with

reference to its rites and ceremonies and a group having a sacred ideology and a set of rites centering around their sacred symbols as such".

As regards the first point it would be misleading to conclude that the teachings of the Nirankaris were only for the Nirankaris. In fact his message was for the whole society and particularly for the Sikhs and the primary objective of the Nirankaris was to reform the society. There could hardly be any justification in attributing their teachings for any particular section of the Sikhs.

Opison writing in 1861, observed that the number of the Nirankaris was several hundreds in the city of Rawalpindi and in the neighbouring villages. According to Census Report Punjab (1891), they were to the tune of 50726 in the British territory and 9385 in the native states. It explains the extent of increasing influence of the Nirankaris. One would hardly find any justification in Webster's doubting these figures abnormal or exaggerated or highly inflated. Even after giving due margin to inflation of these figures there could hardly be any doubt that the increase of the Nirankaris in number within thirty years was substantial. This explains the extent of their influence during the period.

The main object of both the movements was not to establish a separate religious group, sect or cult. Any such attempt would have been the negation of their very teachings—'Return to Nanak' or restoration of Sikhism to its original spirit. Therefore, the question, of their being anything else than the Sikh, indeed a true Sikh, does not arise. However, the various aspects of this movement have been discussed in this book.

As regards the Namdharis, it may be mentioned that their movement has attracted relatively a little more attention of the scholars than that of the Nirankaris. Some of the important works on the Namdharis which deserve mention are *Kuka Movement* by Fauja Singh, *Kukas* by M.M. Ahluwalia, *Kookiyan di Vithya* by Ganda Singh, *Baba Ram Singh Namdhari* by Jaswant Singh Jas, *Namdhari Itihas* in two parts in Hindi and Punjabi by Nahar Singh, *Karanti Kari Satguru* by Nidhan Singh Alam, *Satguru Bilas* an unpublished work, besides some article published in the *Sut Jug*. Yet another work on the Namdharis obviously needs an explanation. All the works referred to above have seen the Namdhari movement from a particular angle. For example, the outstanding work on the subject by Fauja Singh is essentially a work on the political role of the Namdharis. The work of Ahluwalia is important in the sense that he has reproduced verbatim portions of some sources in course of his narration determining the political activities of the Namdharis. In a way it is more a collection of different sources arranged in a fashion that it projects a picture of the political role of the Namdharis. Ganda Singh was perhaps the first scholar to write about the Namdharis as early as 1946. He has utilized the original letters of Baba Ram Singh. Being the pioneer work it could be considered at best the first authentic survey of the Namdhari Movement without taking up any of the aspects in greater detail. The work of Jaswant Singh Jas entitled *Baba Ram Singh Namdhari* is a biography of one of the important reformer of this movement, and as such is useful in a limited sense. Another work *Namdhari Itihas* by Nahar Singh is an important work and gives some idea of the history and development of the movement, but it could hardly be considered a research work.

The works mentioned above certainly help to understand the political significance of the Namdhari movement. In the present work, an attempt in particular, has been made to examine the role of the Namdharis in reforming the socio-religious life of the society during the nineteenth century.

As Punjab witnessed the emergence of two important movements—the Nirankari and the Namdhari in the nineteenth century with almost identical objective, they obviously need a comparative study.

An earnest and sincere effort has been made to present a comparative study of the Nirankaris and has tried to present a comparative study of the Nirankari and the Namdhari movements in Punjab during the nineteenth century and has emphasized on their socio-religious activities, besides their attempts in restoring the Sikh society. This aspect has so far remained neglected.

My interest to do something solid in the field of Sikh history urged me to take up this subject for research. I worked hard for this manuscript to go through various sources available on the subject. Extensive field work has been done, consulting the material available in the personal collection of Baba Gurbux Singh Nirankari and Baba Jagjit Singh Namdhari. I had the opportunity to discuss at length the research work with eminent scholars like Professors Ganda Singh, Fauja Singh, P. Saran, Mahinder Singh, T.R. Sareen, M.M. Ahluwalia,

Nahar Singh and Bhai Jodh Singh. I yet remember the opportunities offered to me by Dr. Ganda Singh who was quite aged at that time. I cannot forget the bus journey from Chandigarh to Ludhiana with Baba Gurbux Singh to keep an appointment with Dr. Bhai Jodh Singh an eminent scholar in Sikh history. He was bed-ridden reduced to skeleton but the spirit and voice was truly like a Khalsa. He gave me enough of time to discuss certain issues which were disturbing my mind. I feel grateful to them for their valuable information and help.

I owe a deep debt of gratitude to the authorities of the National Archives of India, Punjab State Archives, Patiala, Sikh Reference Library Golden Temple Amritsar, Guru Gobind Singh Bhawan Patiala, Library of Teen Murti, Indian Council of Historical Research, Central Secretariat, Delhi University Khalsa College, Indian Institute of Public Administration and Guru Nanak Foundation at Delhi. In order to ensure that all available material in India and abroad is fully studied and utilized I got an opportunity to visit the United Kingdom and consulted the material available at the India Office Library, the British Museum, the School of Oriental and African Studies. I am thankful to them for providing access to the valuable records.

My family deserves the greatest appreciation for their cooperation. I still feel sorry for my children whose innocent childhood was at times deprived of mother's full attention when I used to go out of town for several days for research work. At the same time there is a deep sense of satisfaction as my daughter Sonali has not only done Masters in History with double Hons. and commendable awards of excellence. She herself has authored a book on gender studies "Gender: A Cross-Cultural Perspective" at this young age. I am extremely thankful to my loving children Arshi, Amit and Nirr who have been always inspiring me to take up more challenging ventures.

No acknowledgement would be complete without my gratitude to my husband Mr. U.S. Jolly who is Commissioner in Delhi and has always remained a constant source of inspiration and strength for me.

SURJIT KAUR JOLLY

New Delhi
22 October 1987

1

Introduction

Punjab, initially was like a triangular piece of land lying between the Indus and the Yamuna. It was bounded in the north by Himalayan ranges, on the west by the Suleiman and the Kirthar ranges, on the east by the river Yamuna and in the south by the Sindh and the Rajputana deserts.[1] The climate of Punjab is one of extremes.[2] Even in the fertility, there is no homogenity. There are tracts of land in the Buri and Bist *doabs*[3] which are very productive and densely populated while soil around Ambala region looks like deserts and busky jungles.

Thanks to its location at the border of India the people of Punjab have always kept themselves armed. By the grace of nature they were all placed in a locality which enjoyed a prominent position and served as the gateway to India. Every invader from the North had by its possession sought the road to fame.[4]

It was because of the peculiar geographical position that the people of Punjab were so virile and warlike. Its boundary was subject to variation depending on the political developments. "Punjab as such is the Sikh gift to India. It is Sikhs who placed it on the political map of the world as an independent entity in the 18th and 19th centuries when they freed it from the Mughals and the Afghans and gave it the geographical boundaries from Tibet to Baluchistan and from Khyber Pass to the neighbourhood of Delhi.[5]

Punjab remained predominantly *inhabited by the Sikhs.*[6] They were the followers of Guru Nanak.[7] His religion was a programme of action to integrate the people in the bonds of harmony, love and respect for one another. When religion declines it always becomes an aggregate of superstitions, rituals and ceremonies. Guru Nanak and his successors understood this phenomenon and aimed at giving to the people a simple natural religion which should be free from meaningless and expensive rites and rituals. He opposed the priestly classes who exploited the masses for their own selfish ends. Thus, there was a need to revive the basic and universal principle of a religion.

Nanak wanted to give the people a spiritual light through his message of love and brotherhood. He wanted to make them aware of their own worth and virtue. To achieve this object he established institutions to preserve true Sikh traditions. There were the institutions of *Sangat*[8] and *Pangat*.[9] These institutions strived ceaselessly against any distinction of castes, classes high and low, touchable and untouchable, "Wherever he went he left behind him a *Sangat* or association of his followers with an injunction to build *Gurudwara*[10] or temple for the purpose of meeting and singing His rymns together."[11] Subsequently, these places became the laboratories for both, the demonstration and practice of his teaching.[12] Thus, the role of the Guru in this respect was that of preaching the masses to awaken them to the realities of the spiritual heights. This naturally brought Nanak in conflict with the orthodoxy. He admonished the Hindus as well as the Muslims, who were engrossed in mud-slinging on each other's religion. The Brahmins dubbed the Muslims as *Malecha*[13a] and the Muslim Mullahs termed, the Hindus as *Kafirs*.[13b] Guru Nanak who was certainly not a political leader, wanted and tried to provide religious and spiritual solace and light to the degenerating social life.[14]

It is well-known that on the event of Nanak's demise the religious life in Punjab had two distinct waves of thoughts—the orthodox and the liberal. It was the latter which Nanak wanted to strengthen.

In September, 1539, a few days before his death Guru Nanak summoned Lehna and his other followers and initiated Lehna as Guru.[15]

The period of Guru Angad (1539-59), was the most crucial one for an infant movement which was started by Guru Nanak not long ago. In fact, his teachings had, yet, to take the shape of a movement and for it was needed a more dynamic man to give the religious ideology of Nanak a thrust and a direction. Guru Angad succeeded in giving the movement a distinct and definite character. By popularizing Gurumukhi[16] script for propagating Nanak's teachings and implementing them as practices, he saved the young movement and its followers from again merging into the vast sea of Brahmanism whose vitals had already been eaten up by the Brahmins themselves.[17]

The fact that asceticism was alien to the creed of Nanak was explained to the Sikhs by Guru Amar Dass the third Sikh Guru. He took another step in the direction of social equality by the construction of a *baoli* [20] at Goindwal whose water was openly available to everybody.

To have better organization and consolidation of the Sikhs he divided his whole spiritual domain into twenty-two *Manjis*.[21] The charge of each *Manji* was given to a devoted Sikh who acted as the lieutenant of the Guru. The Guru established another organization called 'Piri' system.[22] The incharge of *piris* were ladies who used to spread the preaching of the Gurus among the women. Thus, it seems that there was a systematic attempt to propagate the principles of Sikhism among the masses. One of the most enlightened social reform of the Gurus was to condemn the religiously sanctified practice of *Sati*.[23] Discarding the *purdah* was, yet, another social reform, which they preached.[24] All the rituals connected with birth and death were condemned by Guru Amar Dass. He had said "after my death sing God's praises, call God instead of a Pandit, read God's words instead of Puran".[25] This indicates the attempt made by the preachers of Sikhism to get rid of the religious rituals and save the society from the traditional Brahmanical practices.

It was stressed that the marriage ceremony should be simple and inexpensive. Only recitations of *lavan*[26] was prescribed. All other rituals enjoined by the *Brahmins* and the *Varanashram dharama*[27] were rejected. By the time of fourth Sikh Guru Ram Dass (1534-1581), Sikhism had made a distinct identity of its own. It seems that the Sikh religion, since its beginning gave equal emphasis to both the religious uprightness and social awakening. Thus, the Sikh movement essentially viewed the social problems in totality.

Amritsar was developed and established to be a centre of Sikh activity. A distinct setup could be seen with the appointment of the *Masands*[28] and a central treasury by authorising the *Masands* to collect a part of the income of every Sikh from their respective areas and then send the same to the Guru. "The Masands were full time religious preachers who in addition to the propagation of the Sikh faith were also required to collect the subscription from the devotees in their respective areas."[29] It was felt necessary to give a proper organisational set up to the Sikh religion and provide a perpetual source of income for the religious activities of the Sikhs through approved centres of religion—*Gurudawaras*.

Under Guru Arjun (1563-1606), Harminder Sahib at Amritsar became the Mecca to the Sikhs. Most remarkable thing of his pontificate was the compilation and editing of the Adi Grunth[30], which is the only scripture of the Sikhs. "It was the crowning achievement of the Guru"[31] It is significant to note that it was the first religious book which contained the writings of men of different communities and religions. Sixteen of them were *bhaktas*, four *Sudras*, two Muslims, four Brahmins, one Jat, one barber and two of unknown castes. On receiving certain complaints that Guru Arjun has reviled the Muslim and Hindu prophets in his Grunth, Mughal emperor Akbar had visited Goindwal.[32]

In short "the disciples of Nanak condemn idol worship ... they do not read *mantras* of the Hindus, they do not venerate their temples with idols nor do they esteem their Avtars".[33]

The death of Akbar gave a blow to the secular note noticed in his religious policy based on the principle of toleration. His dream of a nation and a secular state was lost. Naqshbandis were getting momentum and became influential at the Mughal Court.[34] The attitude of the Mughals towards Sikhs changed. Meanwhile prince Khusrau rebelled and fled to Punjab. The Guru was alleged to have been sympathising with him.[35]

After an enquiry into the allegations, emperor Jahangir ordered, "having confiscated his property he should be tortured to death".[36] The execution of the Guru transformed the peaceful Sikh movement into one with a more forceful militant character which could combat all sorts of injustice thus, symbolizing a wonderful combination of bhakti (spirituality) and shakti (power).

The young Guru Hargobind succeeded his father with two swords girded round his waist; one to symbolize spiritual power and the other temporal. He said "My rosary shall be the sword belt and on my turban I shall wear the emblem of royalty."[37] Then onwards the Sikh Gurus became an eyesore for the Mughals. A further change in the outlook of the Sikhs came when Guru Gobind Singh (1666-1708), did away with all the vestiges of Brahmanical distinction of caste and creed, high and low by creating Khalsa.[38]

After the initiation of the first five. Guru himself was initiated in the same manner wearing the same symbols.[39] The creation of the *Khalsa* was in fact a proclamation of an independent entity of the Sikhism. This freed them from the age old dependence on the traditional priests and saved them from exploitation.[40]

Amar Dass prevented the infant community from reducing it into a sect of 'quietists' or ascetics. Arjun's contribution was still more important as he gave his followers a written code and civil organization. Hargobind added to it the use of arms and a military system. Gobind Singh bestowed upon it a distinct political existence and inspired them to be socially free and independent.[41]

After the death of Guru Gobind Singh,[42] the Sikhs stood firmly to the test of time. They had to bear the tyranny and tortures of Mughal rule but nothing could deviate them from the path of piety, truth and righteousness. Emperor Bahadur Shah I had issued an edict on December 10, 1710, for a general massacre of the Sikhs. "During the governorship of Zakaria Khan and Mir Muin-ul Mulk (Mir Manoo) conditions went to worst. Now even the Sikh women and children were also seized".[43] With the decline of the Mughal authority, the Afghans attack increased. In February 1762, Ahmad Shah Durrani inflicted heavy losses on Sikh lives. But very soon the Sikhs recovered from the losses and by 1764, they were able to free the entire Cis-Sutlej Punjab from the possession of the Afghans.[44]

The *Khalsa* during the 18th Century consolidated their position and changed their outlook. When Ahmad Shah Durrani left for Afghanistan by the end of March 1765, the *Khalsa* met at Amritsar on the occasion of *Baisakhi* and decided by a *Gurmatta*[45] to march upon Lahore which they were able to occupy. Capturing the capital facilitated the occupation of the whole of Punjab. In order to meet the danger of the Mughal and Afghan persecution, the Sikhs were forced to organize themselves into small military bands or *Jathas.*[46] Then these bands were leagued together into twelve divisions each with a distinguishing title and banner, but varying in strength. These divisions in due course of time were called '*Misls*'[47] and from 1767 to 1799, the whole of Punjab was held by these *misls.* Consolidation of Punjab by the Sikhs was completed by 1799, when foundation of a Sikh empire was laid by Maharaja Ranjit Singh.[48]

Surprisingly even during the *Khalsa Raj* in Punjab, there could hardly be any growth of Sikhism. Sikhism was in fact a product of struggle for survival. To them the religion remained an inspiring force in facing all the odds. But once the political stability was established apparently the religious values for which they fought started decaying.

Several causes are attributed to their decline, which relate to the political, religious and socio-economic life of the contemporary Punjab.

(I) Political

The nature of Ranjit Singh's Government was cosmopolitan. It was a popular and secular government. Most of its ministerial offices were held by non-Sikhs. Brahmins from Uttar Pradesh and Dogras from Jammu had assumed more importance in the Maharaja's council.[49] Infiltration of the foreign elements in the royal court paved way for the Brahmanical superstitious practices. These people also brought with them the worship of Hindu gods and goddesses and the performance of Brahmanical rites in a Sikh state while idol worship is essentially forbidden to a true Sikh.[50] This created an anomalous situation.

The increasing influence of the Brahmins and the Dogras at the Maharaja's court gave a great setback to Sikhism.

The impact of the Brahmanical practices at the court[51] had its influence on the life of the masses.[52] Moreover the Maharaja extended huge offerings to the temples and Gurudwaras, but for the promotion of real values of religion nothing was done.[53]

Sikhism received a rude shock once the rule of Ranjit Singh began and pristine purity of the Khalsa was lost. Sikhism was just reduced to a thing of 'hair and beard'. The Sikh aristocracy had fallen into all possible vices. Gradually they had acquired enormous wealth and power. Many of these newly rich were taken to the pleasure of drink and debauchery. Simplicity and purity taught by Guru Nanak and his successors was almost lost. Belief in astrologers and other superstitions were again getting dominant in the royal court. Ruchi Ram Sahni remarks, "After Maharaja Ranjit Singh, when kingship became a thing of jewels and clothes, Sikhism too with the higher classes became a mere fashion of the turban and the beard until a people with sterner ways and better discipline struck the scepture from their hands".[54]

(II) Religious

Besides the political condition, religious causes were also responsible for the decline of Sikhism during the eighteenth century. For long Sikhism was left to grow of its own and perhaps little was done to strengthen it. The *Gyanis*[55] or learned man of the faith who knew the *Granth* and interpreted it, had gradually lost the essential vigour to emphasize the fundamental spirit of the faith. This naturally drifted it towards Brahmanism which had the strong quality of assimilation of the allied faiths. The growing new faith which came under the influence of Brahmins soon succumbed to its traditional ways of idol worship and belief in caste and creed distinction.[56] Thus, it could not escape the influence of the socio-religious principles of Brahmins. It is not surprising, therefore, to find the Ganesh idol[57] on the entrance of the house of the chief Grunthee[58] of the Darbar Sahib under Ranjit Singh.

It establishes as to how far the houses of the Sikh priests "were not free from the clutches of Brahminism". This was to the "extent that at the Akal Takht—which is supposed to be the throne of Timeless God and which is free from the chains of birth and death—there was one picture of goddess Durga or Chandi in which Guru Gobind Singh was sitting before the Devi".[59]

The above evidence bears testimony to the fact that by the time of Ranjit Singh, the basic principles and teachings of Sikhism were under the profound grip of Brahminical rituals and dogmas. Such a situation was possible only with the sense of indifference on the part of the Nihangs and the Sikh priests.

(III) Christian Churches

With the advent of the Britishers in India the Christian churches and the missionaries had intensified their efforts for conversion. After the annexation of Punjab Britishers, their activities posed more serious threat to the Sikhism in this region like other parts of India. Various socio-economic temptations had helped their programme of conversion. On the one hand Sikh mission was getting weak and on the other advent of Christianity was there, it has been described well by an officer of Bengal Army.[60]

Furthermore the degeneration of the priestly class had greatly shaken the moral strength of the Sikh religion and the vices that had crept in it, shook it to its very foundation. If the Sikh religion was losing ground, it was essentially because of its deviation from its basic teachings and practices. Such a condition naturally prepared the ground for some sort of efforts to revive the true principles of Sikhism.

Nirmlas and Udasis

After the death of Banda Bahadur and to the establishment of Sikh rule in Punjab, the Sikhs were subjected to persecution and had to take shelter in the jungles and deserts of Rajputana. During this period the religious institutions of Sikhs were guarded by *Nirmlas*[62] and *Udasis.*[63] They were highly respected men of high moral character and integrity. But incidentally both of these sects had Brahmanical leanings because their orders believed in asceticism. Most of people, among these *Udasis* and *Nirmalas* were great scholars of Sanskrit and Vedantic literature. They could not strictly persuade people to follow the puritan way of life as taught by Nanak and his successors. Against the advice of Guru Nanak they were using the offerings and grants for their personal ends. They even started getting themselves married and subscribed to the rituals relating to birth and death.

Udasi and *Nirmala* saints in course of time became *Mahants* having their own *deras* and *akharas* etc.[64] Rich tax free *Jagirs* endowed to the *Gurudwaras* became a source of their personal income. Gradually "the Mahants and their Chelas began to live a life of luxury and dissipation verging on depravity."[65]

While *Sikh Gurus* were addressing on *Akal Purakh*[66] and

'Nirankar'[67] (or one God) in their hymns and works, their followers were looking towards the Brahmanical gods and goddesses with reverence. Kavi Sodha writing in the praise of Amritsar titled, *Sri Amritsar Mahima*, starts the work by adoring *Ganesh* and *Sharda*, any new work *Sharda* is associated with learning and education. Similarly another source *Ustat Sri Amritsar Jiki* written by Kavi Sant Dass Chibber and Narayan Kav begins with the praise of *Ganesh*.[69] Puran Singh writing in 1823 (Samvat 1880), also adopted the same practice. After writing about himself he starts with *Ganesh* and *Devi*.[70]

Bedi and Sodhee Families

The *Bedi* and *Sodhee*[71] families were also responsible for the decline of the Sikh religion. *Gurus* of the faith originally belonged to these families so, naturally, for the common people they were a source of inspiration. People looked to them with reverence and devotion. These *Bedis* and *Sodhees* assumed high positions apart from their basic religious duties. Their main interest shifted from spiritual to material considerations, "The effect of this *territorial aggrandisement* was that the missionaries and high priests of Sikhism of yore had abandoned their noble work and devoted themselves wholly to the management of their newly acquired possessions".[72]

Baba Khem Singh Bedi rather had a good following in the Dhani Pothohar area in the north-west of Punjab. But, he was also leading his followers towards Brahmanism. He wrote to his followers to follow all the rituals enjoined by Brahmins and Vedas at the time of various occasions in life.[73]

According to Farquhar there was an other cause of degeneration of the Sikhs. "The transformation of the Church into an army produced another evil result living preaching ceased among these Sikhs and their religious life began to go down, Hinduism began to reappear among them".[74]

The society in Punjab had many a socio-religious superstition. And the Sikhs were no exceptions to it. It is noticeable from their growing practices of infanticide and *sati*. With utter disregard to the instructions and teachings of the Gurus insisting on the practice of equality, irrespective of caste, creed and sex, the position of women had deteriorated in Sikh society.

Killing of the daughters at the very time of their birth was widely prevalent in Punjab. Guru Gobind Singh had strictly opposed it and had forbidden this evil practice among his followers. In one of his *Rehatnamas* he says "with the slayers of daughters who ever has inter course, him do I curse, who so ever taken food from the slayers of daughters shall die unabsolved."[75]

Sati was another evil prevalent in the Sikh society. The women were forced to be burnt alive on the pyre of their dead husband. Guru Amar Dass took note of this inhuman practice and forbidden the Sikhs from following it. But the practice of *Sati* was so deep-rooted in the contemporary society, irrespective of class and sect that even many queens of Ranjit Singh had burnt themselves alive on the pyre of the Maharaja.[76]

Sikhs were worshipping the Sakhi Sarvar, Nigah, Sheikh Haider, Pir Binoi, Bhairon and Guga, etc. Visits to *samadhis* and *mazars* were common. Guru Gobind Singh while creating the *Khalsa* ordered the Sikhs, "Let no one associate with much less offer presents to those who worship Sarwar, Guga and similar pirs."[77] These practices, in a way led to idol worship, which was essentially forbidden in the Sikh teachings.

By creating *Khalsa*, Guru Gobind Singh aimed at abolishing all signs of caste, etc. While the Sikh community was expected to change their outlook and become a casteless society believing in the principles of brotherhood, in practice the caste distinction gradually re-entered their social fabric with greater vigour. Referring to it, Cunninghan says, "The truth is that the Sikhs have only partially rid themselves of caste. They were able to suppress the instinct so long it endangered their existence, but when they became paramount in the Punjab and Khalsa was sufficient for its own needs the old exclusive Brahmanical spirit returned, the influence of Ranjit Singh's Court increased this retrogressive spirit."[78]

The rise of the *Misl* had opened new vistas of jobs, and a status in the society for people in Punjab. A number of Hindus accepted Sikhism. But they, by their instinct could not disassociate themselves from Hindu customs and prejudices. Among them the caste prejudices and the cow worship retained their importance. Incidentally the Sikh aristocracy which was largely drawn from the Jats, began to look upon itself as the *kshatriya's*, and performed all the customs with pride.[79] It helped in the re-assertion of the caste system among the Sikhs.

The socio-religious life of the eighteenth century Punjab presented a gloomy picture. The efforts of Guru Nanak and Guru Gobind Singh, which aimed at making the Sikh society, religiously rational and socially wide-awake, had now almost fallen to ground. The fast degenerating political, social and religious condition was at the verge of a collapse. Some new efforts were needed to give a vision and direction to the Sikh society for reorganising its socio-religious outlook. The Nirankari and the Namdhari movements were perhaps the need of the time.

REFERENCES

1. For details see *History of the Sikhs* by Khushwant Singh, Vol. I, p. 5. *J. Dewson Classical Dictionary of Hindu Mythology and Religion*, p. 183.
2. In winter the cold in certain areas of Punjab is severer and more rigorous than in almost any other region of India. The temperature falls even below 18°F whereas in summer it rises at certain places to even 120°F. Whereas Himalayan tract enjoys rainfall of 80 to 120 inches, the sub-mountain regions of Sialkot and Hoshiarpur and Pathankot from 30 to 40 inches and in the Western plains average rainfall is not more than 10 inches.
3. There are five doabs in Punjab—Sindh Sagar Doab, the Jetch or Chaj doab, the Rechna doab, the Bari Doab and Bist doab.
   See for details *History of Sikhs* by Khushwant Singh, Vol. I, p. 5.
4. *History of the Punjab Preface Part* p. ii, Syed Mohammed Latif.
5. *Bibliography of the Punjab*, by Ganda Singh Introduction p. 6.
6. *Sikhs*—Seems to be derived from the Sanskrit Sisya, disciple or Siksa, instruction in Pali Sikkha or followers.
   Sikhs are the follower of Sri Guru Nanak Dev who consider ten Sikh Gurus to be of one spirit and whose religious book is Adi Grunth. For other details in this connection see *Encyclopaedia of Sikh Literature*, p. 154.
7. Guru Nanak was born in Punjab on April 15, 1469 in Rae Bhoe Ki Talwandi now known as Nankana Sahib in the Seikhupura District of West Pakistan. "He mounted a huge tower in his mind and looked out the spiritual state of his countrymen and behold one half sunk in the sloth and degradation of a ceremonial worship and the other half pressed in deed by a great spiritual truth but blinded by fanaticism and false zeal".
   The Calcutta Review, Sept., 1859 Vol. LXV, p. 85.
8. *Sangat*—Congregation of flowers. W. Oven cole Piara Singh, *The Sikhs, their religious beliefs and practices*, p. XXIV.
9. *Pangat*—Literally meaning one row or line. It required followers to sit in one line while partaking in free kitchen. *Guru Shabad Ratnakar Manakosh*, p. 179. Also see Fauja Singh—*Development of Sikhs under the Gurus* (Guru Nanak Quin Centenary Celebration Series, Punjab University, Patiala, p. 6.
10. *Gurudwara*—The word Gurudwara is a compound of the Punjabi words Guru and dwara literally meaning the Gurus Gate. See Bhai Kahn Singh's *Mahakosh*, p. 496.

11. *The Gurudwara Reform Movement and the Sikh Awakening*, p. 1. Ruchi Ram Sahni.
12. *Guru Nanak's impact on history—Guru Nanak*, p. 90. Ganda Singh.
13a. *Malecha* literally means unclean generally used by Hindus and Sikhs against Muslims and Britishers.
13b. *Kafir*—is a word which is considered in Islam as the non-believer of the faith.
14. Guru Nanak was aware of the degenerating political atmosphere which led to the degeneration of society also. "Decaying rule of the Lodhis, poor administration at the central, provincial and local level and the invasion of the Mughals. He was intensely moved to see the pitiable condition of his countrymen especially of the women folk at the hands of the Mughal invaders."
See for details *Rise and Fall of the Mughal Empire* by R.P. Tripathi, pp. 20-22.
15. He placed five coins and coconut before him and bowed at his feet. The ceremony has been described as "the Coconut is said to represent the created universe, the hair on it being the vegetation the coins are the five elements air, earth, fire, sky and water—thus to new Guru was offered the world of the nature and the world of the man of his protection."
The Sikhs Their Religious Beliefs and Practices, p. 16.
16. *Gurumukhi*—It is Vernamala (Alphabate) have come from *Sarda* and *Tankri* and was originated by Guru Nanak and not by Angad as popularly known. Guru Angad only popularised it. *Gurshabd Rotnakar Mahankosh,* p. 313.
17. *Udasi* is a sect of Sikhism started by Shri Chand, son of Guru Nanak, who believed in the renunciation of the world. The word Udasi is derived from the Sanskrit word *Udas* meaning grief, dejection. Sect owes its origin to Baba Sri Chand eldest son of Guru Nanak who adopted a peculiar type of dress and formed a new class of Sikh preachers. Gurshabd Ratnakar, p. 7. Generally it is mistaken that Baba Sri Chand Udasi preached renunciation actually that was just his own way of devotion to Guru Nanak to marry and have a family—Sikh Gurus used to visit Baba Shri Chand and have discussion with him on certain matters.
See for details *Udasi Sikhan di Vithiya* by Randhir Singh, Also see *Ithias Baba Sri Chand & Udasi Samoradai*, Isher Singh.
18. *Dutu*-Datu and Dasu were two sons of Guru Angad and wanted to have hereditary claim on Gurgaddi.
19. *Transformation of Sikhism* by G.C. Narang, p. 32.
20. *Baoli*—It is a well with a staircase to reach at the bottom. *Gurushabad Ratnakar Mahakosh*, p. 644.
21. *Manji*—It literally means couches on which the Gurus used to sit and communicate instructions to their audiences. Macauliff, *Sikh Religion,* Vol. II, p. 151.
22. Piri—It is a sort of small couch on which ladies lieutenants of the Gurus used to sit for imparting the teachings of Gurus.
History of the Sikh Gurus by S.S. Gandhi, p. 194. Also see *Twarikh Guru Khalsa* by Lal Singh.
23. *Sati*—This practice demonstrated that women had no independent and separate entity and her salvation lies only in living with her husband and finally committing herself to fire-alongwith her deceased husband. This was indeed the traditional socio-religious custom prevalent in orthodox Hindu societies.
Payne—*Short History of the Sikhs*, p. 31.

The Guru says "the women burn themselves on the Pyre of their husbands but if they love their spouses well they suffer the pangs of separation even otherwise".

"सतीयां से ना आखीअन जो मड़ीया लग जलन
सतीया सेई नानका जो, बिरहू अगं जलन !

24. It is mentioned that when the ruler of Haripur and his queens came to have his pure and sacred *darshan* they were asked to discard pardah first if they wanted to meet him. This explains the attitude of the Guru towards the 'Pardah' system. Macauuliff *Sikh Religion*, Vol. II, p. 151-53.
25. He had forbidden his people for making barely roles bread in leaves Hindu obsquicks, lamps etc. as is the general practice among the Hindus according to Brahmanical rituals.
Var Soohi Mohala III Adi Grunth.
26. *Lavan* (the Sikh Epithalamium). It is that part of marriage ceremony which consists of tying together the upper garment of the bride and bridegroom and causing them to go four rounds around the Guru Granth Sahib while the hymn is repeated by the Sikh priest or Sikhs themselves.
27. *Varanashram dharma*—Code of conduct laid down by the Shastras.
28. *Masand* were the authorised leaders of local assembly of Sikhs. *The Sikhs, their religious beliefs and practices.* p. XXIII. Masand seems to be a corruption of Masand shorter form of Masand-i-Ali or his excellency the title which Mughal Governors often held.
Also see *History of the Sikh Gurus*, S.S. Gandhi, p. 209.
29. *The Akali Movement* by Mohinder Singh, p. 3.
30. The Grunth Sahib is the central object of Sikh worship and ritual. In all Gurudwaras copies of Grunth are placed under a canopy covered with a clean fine cloth. It is the source and the object of prayer or worship Sikhs revere if because contains the word and teachings of their Gurus. It is a book of Divine wisdom. For the students of History it contains a priceless treasure of historical data on the social, cultural, religious political and economic life of the people in medieval ages.
31. *Evolution of the Khalsa*, I.B. Banerjee, p. 204.
32. "On the 13th Azhar crossed the river Biah-Beas on an elephant at Goinwal while the troops crossed by a bridge. On this day the house of Arjan Kuru (Guru) received fresh lusture by the advent of shehnshaha, *Akbarnama* (Persian) Vol. III, p. 801.
Also see the *History of the Sikh Gurus*, p. 219-220.
33. *Punjab Past and Present*—Volume I part I 1967 Translation of Debistan-I-Mazahib written by Mahabadis who was by faith a zorastrian and a contemporary of VI and VII Sikhs Gurus. Till recently the work was attributed to Zulfiqar Aretistani also called Mubid.
34. *Naqshbandi*—it was a Muslim revivalist movement aiming at pure Islam. In Punjab they were headed by Sheikh Ahmad Sirhindi Mujjad-id-Ali-I-Sani who was a disciple of Khawaja Baqi Billah. They wanted to expand their missionary activities in the Punjab. See for details—*Revivalist Movement* by S.A.A. Rizvi.
35. Jehangir in his memoirs records "A Hindu named Arjun in the garb of Pir and Sheikh had by his ways and means captivated the hearts of many simple minded Hindus may even of foolish and stupid Muslims. He has misled himself about as a religious and worldly leader. They call him Guru and from all direc-

tions poor worshippers were attracted towards him and expressed full faith in him. For three or four generations they have kept this shop warm. For a long time the thought had been presenting itself to me that either I should put an end to this false traffic or he should be brought into the fold of Islam." *Tuzuk-I-Jahangir* (translation) Vol. I, p. 72.

36. *Tuzuk-I-Jahangir* (tr.) Vol. I, p. 72.
37. *The Sikh Religion*. Vol. IV, p. 2. Maculiffe. Guru Har Gobind was succeeded by Guru Har Rai and Guru Har Krishnan (1656-1664) who were called to court of Delhi. Execution of the ninth Guru Tegh Bahadur (1621-1675) brought a sudden change in the development of Sikh principles and Sikhism in particular.
38. *Khalsa*—it meant pure among the men. Encyclopeadia of Sikh religion, p. 280, Bhai Kahan Singh.
    Khalsa was created by giving *Khande-da-pahul* Religious water prepared to baptize *Mahan Kosh*, p. 565.
    It was a novel kind of bptismal ceremony the Khande-da-Pahul which brought about the pure from among the Sikhs who were given the commen sirname of the Sikhs.
39. Symbols—Five K's—Kes (unshom hair) Kangha (comb for the hair) Kachha (Shorts) Kera (iron-bangle) and Kirpan (Sword), *Kuka movement* by Fauja Singh, p. 20.
    They were hence forward to look to the words of the Guru as incorporated in the holy Grunth Sahib as their only guide in their religious and social ceremonies. *Sikhism and the Nirankari Movement.*
40. Cunningham writes "Nanak disengaged his little society of worshippers from Hindu idolatry and Mohmedan Superstitions and placed them free on the basis of religion and moral point."
    History of the Sikhs, p. 65.
41. *The Calcutta Review,* September, 1859, Vol. LXV, p. 85.
    Punjab reports published in 1859 say "If Nanak was the Moses Gobind was the Joshua of the new people".
42. Genealogical Chart of the Sikh Gurus, Appendix 'B'.
43. About the atrocities of Mir Manoo there was one popular saying of the time which express Sikh sentiment at that time.
    "Mir Manoo is our sickle
    we are the fodder for him to now
    the more he reaps the more we grow"
    "मनु साडी दातरी ते असी मनु दे सोये
    ज्यों ज्यों मनु वडदा असी दूने चौने हौये।
44. Qazi Nur Muhammad Ganjba who had accompanied the Shah Durrani was greatly impressed with what he saw of the Sikhs and has in his *Jangnama* paid glowing tribute to their bravery and high moral character.
    According to Dr. Ganda Singh, *Sikhism and the Nirankari Movement.* It was written by Qazi Noor Mohammad Ganjba.
    However Khushwant Singh, *The History of the Sikhs,* p.140 records that it was written by Aliuddin *Ibrat Nama,* p. iii a.
45. *Gurmatta*—To take some decisions according to Sikh principles in the congregations issued from *Akal Takht, Akal Bunga* or *Kesgarh* are binding to all Sikhs. *Guru Shabad Ratnakar Mohankosh*, p. 315.
46. *Jatha*—military bands or a group.

47. *Misls*—The word Misl is an Arabic word which means equal or alike. Cunningham *History of the Sikhs*, p. 106.
48. Extent of "Ranjit Singh's kingdom at the height of its power comprised an area of 1-40000 sq. miles. In the North it extended on the one side to Ladakh and Iskardu on the other to the Sulaiman Hills. In the South East it extended upto the river Satluj and in the South West upto Shikarpur". *History of the Punjab* by K.S. Narang, H.R. Gupta, p. 269.
In the international art exhibition on Maharaja Ranjit Singh organised by the Govt. of Punjab Department of Archaeology and Museums from April 24, 1981 to May 3, 1981 at AIFACS gallery, Rafi Marg, New Delhi. The extent of Ranjit Singh's empire is described "Area of Maharaja Ranjit Singh's kingdom one lakh 7000 sq. miles more than three times the areas of England (5,227 sq. m.) larger than combined area of Itlay (1'162286) and Switzerland (15,944 sq. m.)."
49. "It is also a sad verdict of History that most of these non-Punjabi imported brahmins did their worst to hasten the end of the Khalsa key". A.N. Bali—*Glimoses of Punjab History*, p. 43.
50. *The Sikh Folk Lore Series No. 1*
Tales from the Sikh History of the Rawalpindi
Attock and Peshawar District, p. 101.
The Khalsa Historical and Literacy Society.
'महाराजा रंजीत सिंह के वक्त मिटी सब रीति
आगे पाछे बामन हो गये कीतीबड़ी अनीति
भोला पातशाह नहीं समझे जो चाहुंदे सौ करदें
निज मत दी सभ रीति चलाई नहीं अकालो डरदे''
'At the time of Maharaja Ranjit Singh all traditions and values are lost. He is surrounded by the Brahmins and ignorant Maharaja does not understand them they are doing what ever they want to do'.
51. "The early life and surroundings of Ranjit Singh explain much. The plasic mind of the young body was moulded by men and women from whom he had no lofty religious and moral ideas to imbibe." *Ranjit Singh,* S.K. Sinha, p. 9.
52. How far Hinduism had an impact even on the royal Court can be seen from this example which was recorded by Karam Singh historian in 1907 AD when he was collecting oral records from those people who had lived during the Sikh rule.
Mai Satnamon says that her father-in-law was an Anghitia ritualist of the royal court of Maharaja Ranjit Singh. The ritual consisted of burning of coal in the portable pot (Angithi) made of gold in winter and silver in summer and take it to the Maharaja who first of all in the morning would see this *basantar devta* (God of fire) circumscribe thrice around it and offered two gold coins every day. In recognition of this service king had granted a revenue free and of the value of Rs. 6000/-. After this Maharaja Ranjit Singh used to observe the vision of Cow-hoofs following feast to the Brahmin maidens (kanjks) and used to offer them silken clothes, some utensils and gold ornaments. *Karam Singh Historian di Itihasik Khoi*, p. 317.
53. If Maharaja was giving lump sum of money to Sikh religious shrines if he was imposing marble and gold to these buildings that can be to show the richness, glory and prosperity of his own empire. It certainly added to the

grandeur of the empire but for the causes of the promotion of the Sikh religion as such it was not a good example to have desirable impact on the masses in general.

54. "How can Maharaja keep his position among his brother Maharajas if he does not invite astrologers and pundits to help him in making his coronation or marriage imposing and circumstantial. The Sikh monarchs and grandees have always found it difficult to break Sikhism to their taste. They are therefore, often obliged to go out of the pale of Sikhism when they want to indulge in more ceremony and show". *The Gurdwara Reform Movement and the Sikh Awakening,* p. 33.

55. *Gyani*—The wise or perfect, term some times applied to Sikhs who are at once learned and pious. Cumingham, *History of the Sikhs,* p. 348.
Also see Bhai Kahan Singh—*Encyclopaedia of Sikh Religion,* p. 305.

56. J.N. Farguhar in *Modern Religions Movements in India,* p. 340-41, writes "Idols found their way not only into the homes of the people but into the Sikh temples, caste crept back and all the evils of Hindu social life."

57. See Plate No 1.

58. *Grunthee*—Priest who recites the Adi-Grunth.

59. The author of this thesis had met Bhai Jodh Singh who was an ex-Vice Chancellor of Punjab University and an eminent writer on the Sikh scriptures. He described in detail about the above-mentioned picture which he himself had seen and which was later on removed under the influence of Singh Sabha Movement. Meeting was held on 22.6.1979 at Model Town, Ludhiana.

60. Nihang 'naked or pure' Cunningham, History of the Sikh p. 348. "Soldiers devotees or protectors of the Gurudwaras" Owen Cole and Piara Singh Sambhi. The Sikh their religious practices and beliefs, p. XXIII.

61. The Army Officer of Bengal further records "although priests are held in greatest reverence still you are not to suppose that they are entirely exempt from every vice. In many respects they bear a great similarity of character to British Sailors spending their money thoughtlessly and extravagantly and as fast as they can get it. Chiefly too like as Britishers in the indulgence of women and liquor totally improvident of the future. They sing being greatly devoted to pleasure give away every encouragement to the nautch girls". *A Tour to Lahore (1808) by an Officer of Bengal Army, Punjab Past and Present* Vol. I, Part I.

62. *Nirmala* : The sinless or one who has acquired this title usually administers the pahul to others. *History of Sikhs,* Cunningham, p. 348.

63. *Udas*: as already discussed earlier.

64. *Akali Movement,* p. 5, Mohinder Singh.

65. "The rise of the powerful Sikh misaldars in the later 18th century and the subsequent coming into political power of Ranjit Singh in 1799 A.D. led to the institutionalisation of the Sikh religion. The introduction of complicated rites and ceremonies in Sikh religious practices and the emergence of rich and powerful Mahants." *Ibid*

66. *Akal Purak*—one who is free from time *Gurushad Ratnakar Mahankosh,* p. 27.

67. *Nirankar*—is parbrahm or The Formless who has got no shape. *Ibid,* p. 535.

68. Kavi Sodha '*Sri Amritsar Mohima*' Manuscript village Kale Distt. Amritsar.
"गुरु गणेश अरु शारदा वदे हित चित लाये
जा की कृपा बिलास ते उत्तम भत को पाये"

69. *Ustat Sri Amritsar Ji Ki* by Sant Dass Chibber and Narayan Kav.
 की गणोशाय: नम: अब उसतत की अमृतसर जी की
70. *Sri Amritsar Ji ki by Sant Dass Chibber and Narayan Kav.*
 अथ श्री अमृतसर जी की उसतत लिखयते दौहरा,
 प्रथमें सिमर गणेश को देवी बहुड़ मनाए।
71. *Bedi and Sodhee*: There were the families to which Gurus had originally belonged. *Sikhism and the Nirankari Movement* by Ganda Singh, p. 14.
72. *Namdhari Itihas*, Part I p. 14, Nahar Singh British sources also speak about this tendency of these spiritual leaders, "Maharaja Ranjit Singh subsequently alienated a number of villages to Sodhees and Bedies, the descendants of the spiritual leaders Guru Nanak and Govind, their descendants under the name of the Bedies and Sodhees hold several hundred villages and are among the most turbulent and least of the friendly Jagirdar". *Foreign Deptt. Political Proceedings,* 31st Dec. 1828 A.D. No. 2443.
73. See Appendix 'C'.
74. Modern Religious Movements in India J.N. Farquhar, p. 337-38.
75. *Rahtnama Guru Gobind Singh*
 Cunningham, *History of the Sikhs,* p. 335.
76. "The performance of some of the Brahmanical Rites on the death of Maharaja Ranjit Singh at Lahore on the June 27, 1839 and of Sati or burning alive of four of his queens and seven maid servants on his funeral pyre under the beneful influence of the Brahmin was quite shocking for true Sikhs." *Sikhism and the Nirankari Movement,* p. 17-18.
 For details also see *Thirty five years in the East* by Honigberger.
77. *Sikh Religion,* Macauliff, Vol. V. 158.
78. Cunningham, *History of the Sikhs,* p. XI.
79. Khushwant Singh, *History of the Sikhs*, p. 289.

2

Origin and Establishment of the Nirankari and Namdhari Movements

In nineteenth century, Punjab witnessed the emergence of two important Sikh religious movements—the Nirankari and the Namdhari. Though they had their origin in a comman attempt to revive the Sikh religious principles which had declined in the closing years of the eighteenth century, yet, these movements flourished in two different parts of Punjab, independent of each other. Moreover, they did not grow simultaneously. While the Nirankari movement had their origin in west Punjab at Rawalpindi (around 1808),[1] the Namdhari movement grew at Bhaini, district Ludhiana in the eastern Punjab (1847). Followers of these two movements also had different socio-economic backgrounds.

In order to appreciate the nature and the contribution of these movements in a proper perspective, these are to be studied separately.

I. Nirankari Movement

The word 'Nirankar' or 'Nirakar' means 'the Formless'. This term was commonly used by Baba Nanak as an equivalent of the Diety.[2] "They are called Nirankaris from their belief in God as a spirit without bodily from".[3] The Nirankaris are described as the followers of Guru Nanak.[4]

Baba Dayal—The Founder of the Nirankari Movement

This movement owes its origin to Baba Dayal. According to contemporary sources Baba Dayal's name was Diyal Dass.[5] E.D. Maclagan says "Bhai Dayal Dass the founder of this sect was a Dhaigar Khatri of Peshawar who settled in Rawalpindi as a shopkeeper, some fifty years ago".[6] Unfortunately not much is known about the life and career of Baba Dayal. Here an attempt has been made to present an integrated picture of his life and career. It may be helpful to appreciate the contributions of the founder of this important movement.

Baba Dayal was born at Peshawar.[7] His father's name was Ram Sahai who did money exchange business. Ram Sahai originally hailed from Kabul but had migrated to Peshawar before the birth of Baba Dayal. His mother's name was Ladiki. She was daughter of Bhai Wasakha Singh.[8] Since his father died at an early age, he had more impact of his mother on his personality. She was a pious and religious lady. She inculcated in her child qualities of courage, truthfulness and utmost love for *Gurbani*[9] the words of Adi Grunth. He used to accompany his mother to Gurudwara Bhai Joga Ji at Peshawar. When she used to sweep and clean the floor child Dayal helped her. His regular visits to Gurudwara and the keenness with which he watched the religious ceremonies soon exposed to him the hollowness of the Sikh priests. Religious activities of Sikhs at that time were just confined to reciting the *Grunth* like Vedic *Mantras* without understanding them.

As common those days, Baba Dayal got his education in Urdu, Persian and the language of business which is known as *Lande.* He was taught *Gurumukhi* at home by his mother which in the long run helped him not only in reading the *Grunth,* but also in interpreting it.[10]

His father Ram Sahai Malhotra was running a banking shop at Peshawar. After his death Dayal's relatives were looking after his business but when he came to an age they wanted him to take over his family business. But Baba Dayal did not feel much concerned about the business so they separated him with the hope that he would automatically then manage it. Under the persuasion of his maternal uncle, Milkha Singh, Baba Dayal shifted to Rawalpindi in 1808 and started a grocer's shop.[11]

Sometime in March 1809, his business took him to the town of Bhera, which was then a big market place. At Bhera he stayed with Sant Budhu Shah of the *Sewa Panthi* order, who had a Dharamshala also. Baba Dayal used to discuss with him the matters of religion. Impressed by his devotion and views about Sikhism, Bhai Charan Dass Kapur and his wife Bishen Devi decided to marry their daughter Mool Devi with Baba Dayal. That was the month of *Chettra* generally considered to be inauspicious for marriages among the Hindus. No Brahmin priest agreed to perform the marriage during ill omened days. Baba Dayal was against all these superstitions. Sant Budhu Shah endorsed his view and the marriage was performed with the recitation of *Anand*[12] *lavan* and *ardas.*[13] This marriage has been considered, very significant in history for its simplicity, freedom from Brahmanical rites and devotion to the words of the Gurus. It also added to the reputation of Bhai Dayal as a practical reformer. Example is always better than precept and is a living proof of the preceptor's sincerity."[14]

Origin of the Movement

At Rawalpindi Baba Dayal had started visiting the Baradari Gurudwara which was also known as *Pehshawarian-di-Dharamshala.* By his discourses and *kirtan* at Gurudwara he attracted a number of people. In the morning, he used to perform *kirtan* at Gurudwara Peshwarian and in the evening at *Gurudwara,* Bhai Ram Singh[15]. He taught Sikhs and others to have full faith in *Grunth Sahib* and give up all kinds of superstitions and practise only those rites and ceremonies which were consistent with the teachings and principles of *Guru Grunth Sahib.* His honest and truthful living and his meaningful words soon attracted people towards him. Impressed by his personality and devotion, the like minded people associated themselves with him and in course of time they became his followers. Baba Dayal never associated himself with any *Guru* or *Bhakt* unlike the Namdharis.[16]

Nirankaris believe that: "Satguru Dayal Ji neither got gurgaddi from Balak Singh of Hazro nor of Sindh Shikarpur etc. He got some spiritual power from the same omnipotent God who gave it to Baba Nanak.[17] But according to the *Nirankari Chalan da Chitha* which refer that once Baba Dayal went to the abode of God where Guru Nanak and other ten Gurus were sitting. They ordered him to carry out the missionary activities for keeping the people on the right path as told by *Gurbani* and *Adi Grunth.*[18] *Nirankari Chalan da Chitha* is one of the most important and highly respected book of the Nirankaris. It occupies the position of a sacred scripture in the eyes of Nirankaris.[19]

In due course of time the teachings of Baba Dayal took the

form of a movement. However, no definite date is recorded about the beginning of the movement. It is only through different sources, that one has to infer the approximate period of its emergence.

It is surprising that even Nirankari sources are silent about this aspect. However, they associate the origin of the movement with Baba Dayal's migration to Rawalpindi around 1808-09.[20] Missionary sources also give some clue about it, J.H. Morrison recording in 1854, says that: "After reaching Rawalpindi he came to know about the new sect which was in progress since eight or ten years".[21] This means that the sect must have started some where around 1845 or 1847. J.H. Orbision visiting the Nirankaris in July 1861, records: "This new religion or sect had its origin in Rawalpindi about forty or fifty years ago".[22] It means 1811-12 AD. However according to a modern view it is accepted as 1815, which hardly makes any significant difference.[23]

In fact, what is significant is the break that came in the general stream of the Sikhs and the Nirankaris. Disgusted by the activities of certain groups Baba Dayal shifted his activities out of the city of Rawalpindi.[24]

Baba Dayal's determination to preach his teachings effectively led to the purchase of a piece of land on 3rd December, 1851 AD[25] for building a separate shrine near the city of Rawalpindi. During the course of time this place came to be known as Dayalsar with a big shrine near the river Lei. Here Baba Dayal began to loudly raise his congregrational slogan termed as *Bola,* in the following words, "O dear remember the wonderful and formless God. Everything in physical form is mortal". [26] His main teachings were *'Dhan Nirankar' 'Sat Nirankar' 'Jap Nirankar'*[27] Baba Dayal had given a common platform for the like minded people where they could come and discuss matters with regard to religion and society without any fear. During his life time, the movement was still in its initial stages, but was becoming popular. His followers were convinced that Baba Dayal would show them the spiritual light. They thought: "Baba Dayal is evidently determined to be a great Guru and the leader of a new sect by which his name will be handed down to posterity.[28]

Baba Dayal was succeeded by his son Darbara Singh.[29] He was married to the daughter of Bhai Balak Chand Kakkar. Her name was Shammi. She gave birth to three sons; Baba Kalyan Singh, Baba Jai Singh and Baba Hari Singh and three daughters. He took his initial education in Urdu and Persian. Baba Darbara Singh learnt *Gurmukhi* at home and was a scholar of *Gurbani.* He was more vigorous and energetic in his missionary zeal and effectively reorganized the Nirankari movement. He started reorganizing his followers with a greater enthusiasm and confidence. He visited different areas of Pothohar (around Rawalpindi). It was during his time that the Nirankari movement started taking a positive shape and developed a distinctive objective alongwith an organizational set-up.

While his basic principles and teachings were the same as that of Baba Dayal, he took some special steps to consolidate the movement. He established 40 centres of Nirankaris called *Biras*[30] and each centre used to be under the charge of a *biradar* (local leader).[31] In many villages *Sangats* were established with a *Gurudwara* of their own. He gave to each of them a *Hukumnama* and a multicoloured flag.[32]

Another significant step taken by Darbara Singh towards proper organization and consolidation of the movement was issuing *chitha* or a letter of order and command for the propagation of his faith and teachings.[33] It was published in 1857 and is known as the *Hukumnama,*[34] or the book of ordinances. It was a sort of code of conduct in which all the do's and don'ts for the Nirankaris were compiled. It was to be kept in each and every Sangat of the village and was to be read every fortnight to keep it fresh. "The Hukamanama issued during the time of Baba Darbara Singh carried forward the innovative work of Baba Dayal in this regard and made these innovations mandatory for all Nirankaris".[35]

Baba Darbara Singh associated Nirankaris with all the insignia of royalty. He used to lead the procession on the horseback wherever he went for preaching. On his tours he used to be accompanied by his followers on horses, camels and on foot. Tents and *Shamianas* were taken from Rawalpindi for his tours and there used to be a regular camp. Everything required for *langer* was taken from Rawalpindi.

Baba Darbara Singh was succeeded by Sahib Rattan Chand, popularly known as Sahib Ratta Ji (1870-1909). (He was the third and the youngest son of Baba Dayal). He was married with Sahib Devi daughter of Bhai Ram Chand Kapoor of Kalan-Gujran. He had four children—two sons; Baba Gyan Singh and Sahib Gurdit Singh and two daughters. He knew *Gurumukhi* well and since his childhood he had helped his father in propagating and establishing his mission. When Nirankari Darbar and Dayalsar were being constructed he had helped in it.

Besides the existing centres he established new *Biras, Sangats* and centres. Once a year, he used to visit his followers, when he especially emphasized on the teachings of Baba Dayal.[36] Sahib Ratta was, disturbed when he found that even Nirankaris had started following the old rituals and were not strictly following the *Hukumnama*. He issued a *Parwana* (order) on Samvat 1930 (1873 AD).[37] It was written by Bhai Manna Singh and signed by Sahib Ratta Ji. Several copies of this *Parwana* were made and sent to different *Biradars.* It was made mandatory for all to follow the *Hukumnama* in all religious and social affairs.

Central shrine near Rawalpindi was enlarged and the will of Sahib Ratta Ji shows that by 1906, the Darbar had two houses for visitors, a building for *langer* and a big hall. There were several gold and silver ornaments to decorate the Darbar on annual gatherings.[38] Annual *melas* were held on death anniversaries of Baba Dayal and Darbara Singh. They were of special significance to the Nirankaris. This distinguished them from other general Sikh practices.

From the contemporary sources either of the Nirankaris or the British, one does not come across any practice of initiation, which is found among the Nirankaris. Anybody while keeping the *kesa* (Hair) and by taking the *amrit* of Guru Gobind Singh or even without that the *Sahjdharis*[39] could be Nirankaris. The only thing which was binding for them was to follow the *Nirankari Chalanda-Chitha.* Their ceremonies were to revolve around *Adi Grunth* only for all practical purposes. Baba Ratta emphasized that the Nirankaris must celebrate all the annual functions in future also as it was the only cementing force to keep Nirakaris together. "It gave them a sense of belonging together and being distinctive".[40]

There were no formal steps which one took in order to become a Nirankari. One may be baptized according to Guru Gobind Singh's *amrit* and follow the *rehat* of five K's or might not follow any of them. Even without keeping long hair one could be a Nirankari. "This suggests that Baba Darbara Singh did not see his followers as a separate group or sect drawn apart from the main body of Sikhs and Hindus as much as the collection of people who have decided to reorder their ceremonial life along the lines laid down by Guru Nanak and Baba Dayal".[41]

Thus, it seems that the successive line of *Gurus* of the Nirankaris, the *Hukumnana*, the *Parwana* and the special gathering kept them away from merging into the vast sea of Hinduism. It was indeed an attempt to retain their identity and believe in the principles for which they struggled since the very beginning.

It has been seen in the preceding pages how the Nirankari movement aimed at reforming the Sikh society from the influence of hollow Brahmanical rituals. It strived to restore the Sikhism to its origional principles, based mainly on the teachings of Guru Nanak. It has also been indicated that the area in which this movement grew and expanded was ronghly the area which was termed as the north-western frontier region of India. Incidentally the area which was popularly known as Punjab was not considered part of the frontier. These two regions geographically framed two distinct and different units. But, the teachings of the Nirankaris which grew at Rawalpindi as a base perhaps covered both the regions.[42]

The general socio-religious conditions of both these regions were perhaps identical and some of the attempts to reform it was needed. The Nirankari movement took a lead in that direction and became known all over in the first half of the 19th century.

The second region which was popularly known as 'Punjab' witnessed the emergence of yet another reform movement in the beginning of the second half of the nineteenth century. It was almost on the same lines as that of the Nirankaris. It was the Namdhari Movement. Namdharis were also called as *Kukas*. However, in matter of details the Namdharis were certainly different from the Nirankaris with regard to their principles and practices. Yet their object of reforming the Sikh society was identical.

Namdhari Movement

According to the official records this sect first came into existence in 1847. "The Kuka sect Juggeasees and Hubeasees was originated by a Sikh named Balak Singh of the Arora caste in the year 1847, in the district of Rawalpindi".[43] District Gazatteer of Rawalpindi records that "Kuka sect owe their origin to a Sikh, who resided in Hazro in the Attock Tehsil in the time of Ranjit Singh. One Dal Singh Arora of Hazro had two sons Balak Singh and Manna Singh. There was at that time a Sikh fort in Pirdad a village adjoining Hazro and a Sikh official had his office in Hazro and the garrison of the fort and all the officials connected with Banki Rai, the Sikh civil official incharge at Hazro got his supplies from Dal Singh's sons. Bhai Balak Singh professed the Sikh religion and obtained the name of a holy and wiseman and became a teacher among the people and many of the Sikh garrison at Pirdad became his disciples, and others from the neighbourhood also began to look up to him as their spiritual adviser and head. This garrison was moved from southwards including in it one Ram Singh belonging to a village in Ludhiana. He too was a disciple of Balak Singh and spread his doctrines wherever he went. After the Sikh power passed away Balak Singh continued to teach at Hazro and built a place of reception there, where his disciples and friends assembled to hear him. He died at the age of seventy in 1863 and was buried at Hazro. Ram Singh returned to Hazro two years before the death of Balak Singh and obtained his permission to instruct the people in his doctrine."[43a]

However, the Census reports of 1881-1891, Baba Balak Singh is referred "as an *Udasi* Arora and a moneylender who was guru of Baba Ram Singh".[44] According to one view the sect originated with Bhagat Jawahar Mal.[45]

Baba Balak Singh was born in the village Choee at Attock in 1856 BK 1799 AD in the home of Bhai Dayal Singh.[46] *Tarikh-e Makha Zan-i-Punjab* records that there were mainly thirteen major teachings which were supposed to be observed by all his disciples and followers.[47]

Assistant District Superintendent of Police Mr Green reported "about 16 years ago a Sikh named Balak Singh caste Arora started a new sect of Sikhs at Hazru in the Rawalpindi district. They were named jagiasees (or Habiasees) and made large numbers of converts in the neighbourhood during their founder's life time.[48]

Amongst his favourite disciples were the following three:

1. Kahn Singh who was the head of the sect at Hazru.

2. Lal Singh a resident of Amritsar.

3. Ram Singh was a resident of village Bhaini in Ludhiana. The sect seems to have failed in the neighbourhood of Hazru after Balak Singh's death. It has however, thriven in a remarkable manner in the district adjoining the home of Ram Singh—his more energetic successor.[49]

Baba Ram Singh

Baba Ram Singh was born on 3rd February, 1816, at Village Bhaini Araian District Ludhiana in the home of Jassa Singh Ramgharia.[50] His mother Sada Kaur was a religious lady who loved *Gurbani* and used to recite it and tell the stories of Sikh martyrs to her children. "Ram Singh like Shivaji earlier owned a lot to his mother Sada Kaur who nurtured him in the best spirits and traditions of Sikh religion and history".[51]

Baba Ram Singh had a younger brother Budh Singh who was four to five years younger to him. He had one sister Sahib Kaur who was married to Kabul Singh of Raipur a gunner in the Sikh army. His mother taught him how to read and write Punjabi in the *Gurmukhi* script. It was at Bhaini that Baba Ram Singh developed a passion for *Gurbani,* other Sikh scriptures and Holy book—*Adi Grunth.*

He spent his childhood studying *Gurbani* and learning the art of carpentry. He began meditating since early childhood. When children of his age used to sing folklores and songs, Ram Singh used to recite *Gurbani* which was very impressive and astonishing for the aged people. As was the practice in the rural areas of Punjab, he was married at the early age of seven to Jassan, a gril from Dhseoul village in the same district. His in-laws were from the village Dharour in the same district. Jassan is now reverently and devotedly called by the respectable name of Mata (mother) Jassan by the Namdharis. Baba Ram Singh had two daughters, named Nand Kaur and Daya Kaur.[52]

Baba Ram Singh has been described as being a man of firm decision and character. He was an able bodied person with mild appearance. Deputy Commissioner Ludhiana wrote about Ram Singh to the Secretary of Government of Punjab in the following words. "He is a man of mild appearance and prepossessing manners respectful but not cringing".[54] British officers further report that "no one who has seen and talked with Ram Singh will have failed to observe an intelligence, firmness and decision of character which coupled also with great self-restraint do not belong to a mere religious enthusiast still less to a puppet".[55] He has been described as a remarkable man with profound qualities of leadership. "The founder of this remarkable movement was Baba Ram Singh a great personal charm and magnetism, a seer gifted with many qualities of head and heart usually found in leaders of men."[56]

In 1837 AD Ram Singh joined the Sikh force of Kanwar Naunihal Singh's regiment. His simple and pious religious life had a good impact on other soldiers also. Ram Singh came to be known as 'Bhai Ram Singh'.[57] His regiment came to be known as the regiment of *Bhaktas* (devotees). But he could not tolerate the defeat of the Sikhs at the hands of Britishers in the battle of Mudki on 18th December, 1845 and instead of going to Lahore he came back to Bhaini. At Bhaini he started tilling his land and later on also opened a grocer's shop to meet the general needs of the villagers.[58]

Why Called Kukas

In the beginning Ram Singh's followers were also known as *Jagiasees* and *Abhiasees* but soon the sect came to be known as *Kukas.* [59] The sect was known as that of the *Kukas* or shouters, because unlike the ordinary Sikhs, they permitted themselves to fall into a state of *wajad* or frenzy during their religious exercises shaking their heads and reciting their prayers in a loud voice. According to Khushwant Singh "They also came to be known as Kukas because of their cries (Kuks) they emitted in a state of religious frenzy."[60] They finish prayers with a loud cry of *Sat Sri Akal* or God is Truth. Since Baba Ram Singh emphasized practising *Nam* and *Bani,* his followers came to be popularly known as *Namdharis* or ones who practice the name of God.[61] They were also known as *Sant Khalsa.*[62]

The Namdharis unlike the Nirankaris seem to have laid more emphasis on a proper organizational set-up for promotion and expansion of their teachings. They wanted to take within their fold various sections of the society, especially the common people. This naturally called for a proper network and an effective system at the village level. Such an attempt was often seen as running a parallel administrative organisation. It created some apprehension in the minds of the elite and the Government.

However, it would be unfair to consider their organizational set up as mainly aimed at acquisition of political power. The keenness with which they organised themselves could only lead one to think that they were interested in properly organising their religious and spiritual activities.

The *Baisakhi* of 1914 BK (1857 AD) was decided upon for the formation of Namdhari Panth or Sant Khalsa. A strict code of discipline was laid down for the members of the new organisation which was termed the Sant Khalsa so as to distinguish it from the body of routine Sikhs.[63]

On the *Baisakhi* of 1857 AD Baba Ram Singh administered baptism to five Sikhs and also unfurled the flag of *Sant Khalsa* which was triangular in shape and white in colour.[64] First of all Kahn Singh Nihang of village Chak Malerkotla State (2) Labh Singh Ragi of Amritsar (3) Atma Singh Alamuhar District Sialkot (4) Naina Singh Amritsar District (5) Sudh Singh of village Durgapur District Jullunder were initiated and then several people from the *Sangat* took *Amrit*.[65]

The main centre of the Namdharis remained at Bhaini. It was the native place of Ram Singh. However, people were allowed to perform the ceremony at any place. The only condition imposed was acceptance of *rehat* and *maryada*. This naturally broke the monopoly of a few Sodhi, Bedi and Udasi families living at the major Sikh centres.

The initiation verse of the Namdharis was as follows:

"First consent to death, Give up the desire to live
Become the dust of the earth, then come to me."[66]

Earlier the baptizing was done at *Akal-Takhat, Kesgarh Sahib* Anandpur and Amritsar, etc. Baba Ram Singh tried to simplify the system of baptizing. The big centres of Sikhism were managed by the *Pujaris*. They made changes in the process of baptizing, considering it their monopoly. Ram Singh knew well that any attempt to reform the Sikhs was likely to face a lot of opposition from the priestly class. Things were not easy for him. In view of the great challenge before him he tried to provide some viable alternatives to his followers in the matters of religious teaching and practices.

Baba Ram Singh thought that only Huzur Sahib, Nanded[67] was the place where he could get proper knowledge about the original practices of Guru Gobind Singh.[68] Bhai Ram Singh sent his follower Bhai Rai Singh of village Madihar (District Ferozpur) to Nanded. He was asked to stay there for some days and observe all the religious practices followed there.[69] He was especially asked not to accept any money in the form of offerings.[70]

Official sources record that any man who was initiated by Ram Singh received a rosary and was taught a *gurumantar* or mystic word simply the ejaculation *Wah-Gooroo.* This *gurumantar,* he was supposed to repeat constantly whether he was working, walking or sitting. But while uttering this mystic word he was supposed to repeat it with his lips only and teeth were supposed to be closed. Special emphasis was laid on the administration of *gurumantar.* This secret word was whispered into the ears of the new entrant by the Guru himself. The recipient was not supposed to tell that 'mantar,[71] to others. This used to be an important occasion for the recipient since it established a personal contact between the teacher and the disciple. It "possessed great potentialities for working a psychological change in the heart of the recipient of the Gurumantar".[72]

About the Namdharis, Captain Wall, District Superintendent Gujranwala, wrote in 1866, that the secret sign of the Kuka brotherhood is the ability to reply *Sut Akal Purakh* to the ejaculation *Sat Sri Akal.* Generally a Sikh greets other Sikh by *Sat Sri Akal* and the reply is also *Sat Sri Akal.* Hence the practice of Namdharis which was distinctly different from that of general Sikh could be noticed.

Baba Ram Singh was not satisfied by merely initiating the movement. He understood the importance of consolidation and organization on which the success of any movement depends. He, therefore, appointed several assistants to carry on the missionary work.

One missionary council of six members was established at Bhaini. Schemes were prepared and efforts were made to make his teachings popular. Members of this council were supposed to tour different parts of Punjab and report to Baba Ram Singh about the progress. These people were selected by him and were assigned particular areas. (1) Baba Jawahar Singh was appointed to take care of the Takhtupura and Amritsar. (2) Baba Kahn Singh Nihang was responsible for Nabha, Patiala and Sangrur. (3) Baba Lakha Singh for Duaba. (4) Baba Sahib Singh and (5) Baba Brahm Singh both were entrusted areas beyond Byas and Majha and Baba Sudh Singh was given main Doab.[73]

Baba Ram Singh understood the importance of Congregational worship as it gave an opportunity to come in contact with the masses. Much empasis was laid on *kirtan*[74] as it provided an opportunity for the people of the faith and those who could be attracted to the faith to be together at a place for some time. Here the ideas of the faith could easily be passed on to the people.

Here it may be pointed out that *Kirtan* has got an important place in the development of Sikh religion. Since the very inception of Sikhism Nanak said "let every home be an inn and let there be singing of hymns in thy praise every day".[74a] Keeping in conformity with the long established tradition of Kirtan, Baba Ram Singh appointed regular parties of singers for various parts of Punjab. Thus, the following parties were assigned the job.

1. *Ragi* Shai Ditta and Bhai Fakiriya—District Siyalkot.[75]
2. Bhai Prem Singh Kirpal Singh Bhador—Malwa.
3. Bhai Sooba Singh—Doaba.
4. Bhai Tara and Bhai Pati Attari Wale—Majha.
5. Dhadhi[76] Bhai Pishora Singh was entrusted the whole of Punjab.[76,77]

What was more interesting and important was that he sent orders to his followers in different villages that they were not supposed to offer much, to these missionary parties. They were to offer food and only one rupee for other expenses.

For the convenience and better organization Baba Ram Singh divided his sphere of influence in Punjab in twenty-two divisions[78] which were known as *subas*.[79] In every such division or suba one incharge was appointed. The book entitled *Sri Guru Singh Itihas*[80] written in 1883, provides many useful details in this connection.

Official records speak about seventy *subas* instead of twenty-two as mentioned in other sources. In the Government records of the period there is abundant evidence on their organization. It mentiones, "Not only was the whole Punjab apportioned into about seventy *subas* or provinces through which the Guru's lieutenants actively itinerated preaching the speedy restoration of the Kuka rule and establishing all the thews and sinews of the Sikh race, but emmissaries were sent to Cashmere, Nepal and Kabul".[81]

Baba Ram Singh had established a systematic organization, right from subas to the village level. At every level be it the district, tahsil on village there were leaders incharge to carry on the movement. "He established a Suba in every district, two Jathedars in every tahsil and one Granthi in every village."[82] However, according to Fauja Singh there were Naib Subas, Jathedars and local *Sangats.* Naib Subas and Jathedars were given smaller areas to operate in and were required to organise and supervise the missionary work of their respective places. The local *Sangat* constituted the base of the Kukas at the lowest level—the village. Every village had a dharamsala (temple) of its own. There was a Granthi (scripture reciter) to look after it and to teach Gurumukhi letters and Gurbani (Sikh scripture) to the members of the *Sangat.*[83] Subas were considered to be pure and clean hearted people and besides their usual duties they were expected to recite (read) one hundred pages of *Adi Grunth* every day.

Baba Ram Singh wanted to create a self-dependent and ideal society where at the first instance there should be less quarrels and bickerings. But in case there were any, the same could be solved at the local level without going to the courts. It seems Ram Singh wanted to restore the traditional *Panchayti* Judicial system. In every village the Namdhari *Sangat* used to meet at the *Gurudwara* or the *Dharmsala.* At the lowest level, clashes among Nàmdharis were tried to be sorted out there itself. Above this there were judicial panchayats at *Patri* level which were under the control of the *Jathedar.* Then there used to be Panchayats of Tapas where justice was done by naib-Subas. There above were the courts of the Subas. Justice was performed according to the appellate system. Not satisfied by the judgement of lower courts *Kukas* could appeal to the next higher courts. Final or Supreme justice was done by Baba Ram Singh himself. Besides Baba Ram Singh there were other members of the central judiciary namely: (1) Suba Jawahar Singh (2) Suba Khan Singh (3) Suba Sahib Singh (4) Suba Sudh Singh and (5) Suba Lakha Singh.[84]

A contemporary native newspaper *Kohinoor* recorded about the judicial system of Namdharis and the role of Baba Ram Singh in that setup. "In the afternoon he comes into his Diwan-e-Khas and holds Ijlas (session) and cases of Kukas were brought. The cases of these people are never taken into courts but if ever a case should go into the Sarkare-e-Adalat' (the brother) is much displeased."[85]

During those days means of communication were primitive and people used to move on foot, horses and camels. Baba Ram Singh developed an independent postal system by which he could remain in constant touch with his followers and *Sangat*. Here it may be mentioned that Baba Ram Singh had been in the army of Ranjit Singh which might have enabled him to know the details of the secret dak system.

Suba Sahib Singh a most trusted lieutenant of Baba Ram Singh was incharge of this department. Honorary messengers were appointed in every village. Most of the messages were sent orally and for secret subjects/matters perhaps a code language was used. Contemporary official and non-official sources both have referred to the *Kuka* dak system. "The Kukas have a private dak of their own about letters and messages. The dak-wallah is entrusted either with a letter or a verbal message, this man goes in great haste to a certain stage where he is relieved by another who takes from him either the letter or a verbal message. Their strict order is not to exchange a syllable with any individual while conveying news. We ought to be very careful nowadays."[86]

The dak system of Baba Ram Singh has also been described in the *Tarikh-e-wakri*: "Whenever Guru wants to issue some new instruction or orders he writes it and gives to one kuka. He runs with the maximum speed and when unable to run he gives it to another fellow. Like this they keep on shifting the messages till it reaches to all the kukas."[87]

Another official source recording in 1872, says, "The secret postal arrangements were so perfect that the orders of the Guru reached with astonishing rapidity the remotest corner of the province and beyond it to wherever kukas to be found in our army or in foreign states and Ram Singh knows that those orders would be obeyed."[88]

J.P. Warburton District Superintendent of Police Ludhiana while writing to H.N. Col. Miller Inspector General of Police Punjab had showed his anxiety and concern over the utmost perfect system of the Kukas that no information can be had from them. He says, "Their system of disseminating news or instructions rapidly amongst the sect is perfect. For example four kukas are dispatched to the nearest kuka villages in different directions from each of which fresh parties according to the urgency of the matter start off and this is continued quietly without attracting attention until the news has reached every village in which there is Kuka. Their communication as a rule are verbal and they avoid taking any one into their confidence unless he is known personally to be a staunch Kuka. This is to guard against secret police agents disguised as Kukas. Our only chance of now getting reliable information is through real Kukas if we can buy them over".[89]

At times Kukas used to avoid the main routes while travelling for passing the information.[90] It is further recorded about their dak system that "The Kukas or as they are called the sant Khalsa have a private postal of their own which appears to be admirably organized. Confidential orders are circulated much in the scottish bygone days important communications are sent verbally and are not committed to writing."[91] The Kukas avoided the use of highways for their suspected interception and arrests.[92]

It seems that the Kuka postal system was not open for their whole community, rather it was with some special purpose and restricted among the selected Kukas. "It was not merely a separate postal system meant for the Kukas as it was not open to use by the ordinary Kukas. In fact it was secret line of communication used for transmitting secret information generally in oral tradition among the members of the volunteer force especially earmarked for keeping the line working."[93]

Referring to the British views, some of the modern writers have also considered it as an underground movement. "Secret line of communication is a basic prerequisite of any underground movement aimed at an unarmed revolt".[94] However, the mere assertion of the Britishers that this movement was an underground movement because of the 'secret dak system' needs reconsideration.

The Namdharis had organized themselves in an open manner and it would hardly be justified to consider it as an underground movement. While it could not be denied that they aimed at setting up a distinct well organized group, it seems their primary object was restoration of original principles and teachings of the Sikh religion.

REFERENCES

1. There is dispute among the historians about the date on which the Nirankari movement actually began. Ganda Singh puts it some where around 1808 AD which is the date of Baba Dayal's shifting to Rawalpindi. (a) While John C.B. Webster relying on the information of Morrison puts it between 1843 to 1845 AD (b) He does not agree with Orbisan who puts it between 1811 and 1821. The reason why 1808 seems to be more probable for the initiative of this movement has been discussed in greater detail in this chapter at a later stage.
   (a) *Sikhism and the Nirankari Movement,* p. 15.
   (b) *The Nirankari Sikhs,* p. 9.
2. *Census of India,* 1891 Vol. XIX, Part I, 1892, p. 156.
3. *The Twentieth annual report of the Ludhiana mission* including stations at Lodiana, Saharanpur, Sabathu, Jullunder, Ambala, Lahore Dehra for the year ending Sept. 30th 1854, pp. 22-23.
   "आतम चीन भये निरंकारी" आसा महला।
   "दुविधा छोड़ भये निरंकारी" धनासरी आसा महला।
   —Adi Grunth
4. The word Nirankar has been used many times in the Guru Granth Sahib and even in the Jap Ji the most known and widely read composition of Guru Nanak the word 'Nirankar' is used five times. Four times from Pauri 16-19 in the words 'Jo tudth Bhave Nanaka Saee Bhalee Kaar, Too Sada Salamat Nirankar. (O Lord what ever you will is good O Formless God you are eternal). It is used for the 5th time in the 37th Pauri as 'such Khand wasai Nirankar' (The Formless God dwells in the world of the Truth) *Encyclopaedia of the Sikh Literature* Bhai Kahn Singh of Nabha, 1931, Vol. III, pp. 2139.
5. *Affairs at Rawalpindi the Home and Foreign Record* July 1861, pp. 211-12.
6. *Census of India* 1891 Vol. XIX, pp. 156-57.
7. Baisakh Sudi Puranmashi 1840 Bikrami, which corresponds to 17th May 1783. '*Nirankari*' Tract No. 12 page 7 Pehli Kiyari Youngmen Association Rawalpindi (31st January 1932).
   It is further confirmed by the *Encyclopedia of the Sikh Literature* Vol. III, p. 2139 that Baba Dayal was born on 17th May 1783 AD.
   Baba Dayal had a sober personality which is evident from his photograph available at Nirankari Darbar Chandigarh, See plate No. II.
8. Ladiki's grand father Bhai Bhagwan Singh was the cashier of Guru Gobind Singh the 10th Sikh Guru. When Devi Sahai (father of Ram Sahai) once visited Anandpur Sahib both the families met and impressed by each other's

ideas about Sikhism they entered into a matrimonial alliance. Ram Sahai got married with Laddiki and a copy of *Adi Granth* was given in the dowry. Laddiki gave birth to Baba Dayal. Baba Dayal inherited spiritual devotion and lofty Sikh ideals from both paternal and maternal sides.
Nirankari Gurmat Praramkhata, p. 78.

9. Gurbani—These are considered the words of Guru contained in Guru Grunth Sahib or Adi Grunth.
10. *Nirankari Gurmat Praramkhta*, p. 9.
11. *Nirankari Gurmat Praramkhta*, p. 12.
About the shift of Baba Dayal from Peshwar to Rawalpindi Nirankari sources say "At Peshwar Baba Dayal Ji every morning and evening would go to the Gurudwara and do the worship of God. He would give exposition of Grunth Sahib and preach the ways Guru Nanak had shown. He would ask people to give up whims and superstitions and love God and practise God's ways. One day he met Bhai Milkha Singh who adviced him to accompany him to Rawalpindi where he would have a better chance to fulfill his mission".
12. *Anand*—Prayers to be sung in the praise of God Raag Soohi Mahala Teeja (Adi-Grunth).
13. *Ardas*—Etymologically the word ardas has been derived from the word "arzdasht" which means petition. Thus ardas is a petition asking for what one desires from God. *Sant Khalsa*, p. 44.
14. *The Punjab Past and Present*, p. 382 Vol. XII-II, 1978.
Also see for details *Sikhism and the Nirankari Movement*, p. 15 Ganda Singh.
Nirankari Gurmat Praramkhta, pp. 15-16.
After the five years of his marriage Baba Dayal was blessed by a son on Wednesday Samvat 1871 (13th April, 1814). He was named Darbara Singh. After that another son was born on Ist Katak Samvat, 1877. This boy was named Bhangal. Then after ten years another son was born in his family on Chetra Sudi Ekam 1887 Samvat. (25th March 1830 AD) who was named Rattan Chand. All the three sons were born in Gali Ganga Ram Wali of city Rawalpindi in his residential house.
15. Nirankaris believe that once Maharaja Ranjit Singh visited Rawalpindi and after hearing about Baba Dayal he sent a *Mohar* for *parshad* through his orderly at the Dharmsala of Bhai Ram Singh, where Baba Dayal used to have discourses. Baba sent back the offering saying that it would be better if Maharaja comes in person to offer this, Maharaja accepted the suggestion and went to Gurudwara himself where he wanted to give a jagir to Baba Dayal. It is said that on refusing it by Baba Dayal, the Maharaja granted it in the name of the Gurudwara Ram Singh which was being enjoyed by the Gurudwara till the partition of India.
Sikhism and the Nirankari Movement, pp. 15-16 an article by Ganda Singh.
Also see *Nirankari Gurmat Praramkhta*, p. 15.
The author went through the Daftar records of Ranjit Singh but did not come across the offer of any such jagir. However, she visited herself the present Nirankari Centre at Chandigarh and the present Chief Baba Gurbax Singh was kind enough to discuss exhaustively about and history in various other traditions of the Nirankaris. He has specifically mentioned that the said jagir was a source of income to the Gurudwara upto the partition.
16. As was done by Bhai Ram Singh of the Namdharis who was considered twelfth Guru in the line of the ten Sikh Gurus by his followers.

17. *The Nirankari Ekta Sandesh,* p. 91. No story is associated with Guru Nanak as to from whom he got spiritual powers and came to be known as Guru.
18. *Nirankari Chalan Da Chitha* Sri Man Rup Singh 12th Baisakh 1941 Samvat (1857 AD)
    See Appendix 'D'.
19. It is in a manuscript form written by Bhai Roop Singh at the instance of Baba Darbara Singh. Various order details of this source have been discussed later on.
20. *Sikhism and the Nirankari Movement,* p. 15 Ganda Singh.
21. *India Lodiana Mission Journal of a Tour from Lahore to Rawalpindi* by Rav. J.H. Morrison The Home and Foreign Record, Feb., 1854, pp. 52-54.
22. *Affairs at Rawalpindi* 'The Home and Foreign Record, July, 1861, pp. 12-21.
23. Dr. Man Singh has done some research on this and he placed Baba Dayal's mother's death in 1801, his call in 1802, his move to Rawalpindi and the foundation of the cult in 1805, his open preaching from 1815 and Maharaja Ranjit Singh's visit in 1820. *The Nirankaris as Harbinger of Sikh Renaissance* The spokesman weekly XXIV anniversary number 1974, pp. 43-46.
24. The staunchest opposition came from Sardar Nihal Singh Chhachi who was later on knighted by the British Govt. and a Hindu gentleman Tauro-Rai. These people one day called Baba Dayal in a meeting and charged him with certain allegations that he does not accept the superiority of the Brahmins and he washed the feet of the people and condemns Gods and Goddess—therefore these people wanted him to pay penalty by giving them feast. But Baba Dayal said he would not pay any penalty because he has committed no crime.
    "This they said was a short of blasphemy and they imposed upon him a fine on behalf of the Hindu Society. True to his conviction Baba Dayal replied that as a Sikh he was doing what the great gurus had preached and was not liable to pay any fine or to be coerced by Ostracism". *Sikhism and the Nirankari Movement,* p. 16.
    Also see for details *Nirankari Gurmat Prarambhta,* pp. 13-14. Consequently Baba was boycotted by these and other people of the society. Doors of the Gurudwara Baradari were closed for him and his followers.
25. Baba Gurbax Singh present leader of the Nirankaris told the author in an interview with him on 22.6.1979 at Chandigarh that he himself had seen the registry of the plot which was destroyed during partition of India and Pakistan in 1947.
26. "प्यारयो जपो धन निरंकार
    जो देहधारी सब खुमार"
    Nirankari Gurmat Prarambhta, p. 29.
27. God is great, He alone is true in the world, He alone should be worshipped.
28. *Indian Ludiana Mission*—Home and Foreign Record, Feb. 1854, pp. 52-54.
29. (i) Nirankari sources say that Baba Dayal passed away on 18th Magh 1911 BK which corresponds to 30th January 1855 AD when his body was entrusted to the running water of Lei at the place he selected, as the people would not allow his cremation at the public cremation ground.
    (ii) But the official sources like the *Census Report of 1881* (p. 138) say "The Nirankaris are the purist of the Sikh religion and their founder was Bhai Dayal Singh who died only twelve years ago". It comes to 1870 which is the date of the death of his first successor Darbara Singh.

(iii) Even the *Hand Book of Indian Army Sikh* (p. 67) gives the wrong date. Perhaps his source of information was the Census Report of 1881.

30. *Bira*—They were representatives of the Nirankari Guru to carry on his message at other places.
"Bp 1873 we note the existènce of biredar appointed by the leader or Guru as Special deputies to watch over those Nirankaris living in the towns and villages outside Rawalpindi". *The Nirankari Sikhs,* p. 11 Webster.
31. Webster says "The office of the biredar like that of Guru tended to be hereditary in practice although probably not in theory". *The Nirankari Sikhs,* p. 11.
32. Regarding the significance of the different colours of the flag a few opinions deserve our attention.
"Shri Baba Darbara Singh hoisted a red flag revolution (the Nirankari flag) along side the yellow flag (Saffron) of sacrifice of the Khalsa". *Nirankari Gurmat Prarambhta,* p. 2 (edt. Baba Surinder Singh Nirankari Chandigarh). Dr. Man Singh interprets it like this that Nirankari flag has three colours. "Blue and Kesri are Khalsa colours. Kesri is of Sikhs in general while blue is of Nihangs. In between it has got red embroidery with golden thread laces. Interview with Baba Gurbax Singh the present leader of the Nirankaris at Chandigarh on 22.6.79, Nirankaris were trying to prepare a common platform for all people. See Plate No. III.
33. *The Sikhs* by Khushwant Singh, p. 89.
34. Now there are three copies of the *Hukamnama* at Nirankari Darbar Chandigarh which the author has seen and read herself. It was prepared in 1913 Samvat which was originally prepared at Rawalpindi, second is copy is the one which Nirankaris got from the Nirankari Gurudwara Golara and was copied by one Pingldass on 12th Baisakh, 1941 Samvat. The third one has been written in gurmukhi script but words are of urdu and it is dated Samvat 1923. This gives some added information about the widow remarriage, which is not available in the earliest two *Hakumnamas.*
35. *The Nirankari Sikhs,* p. 12.
36. *Nirankari Gurmat Prarambhta,* p. 103. Edt. Baba Surinder Singh Nirankari.
37. Parwana of Sahib Ratta Ji Appendix 'F'.
38. Some of these things have been seen by the author on 20.6.79 and Baba Gurbax Singh told her how with great difficulty they managed to bring them in India during the partition crisis of India and Pakistan.
For details see the WILL of Sahib Ratta Ji Appendix 'F'.
39. *Sahjdari*: one who adopts to the Sikh ways slowly. Incidentally even Baba Dayal did not keep long hairs. As Khushwant Singh in *The Sikhs.* p. 88, says "It is interesting to note that although Dayal Dass spent his entire life in preaching against Hindu encroachments on the Sikh way of life he himself was never baptized in the traditional way and did not grow his hair long. Apparently what he intended to revive was the Sikhism of the earlier Gurus and not that of Guru Gobind Singh."
40. *The Nirankaris Sikhs,* pp. 14-15.
41. *Ibid.*
42. For its proper location in Punjab see Appendix 'A'.
43. *Foreign Dept. Pol. A,* March 1867, pp. 111-112 From: JH. Thorton, Secretary to Government of Punjab.
Jaggiasee—one who tries to search truth while living in this world.
Habiasee—one who exercises the name of God.

43. (a) *Gazatteer of the Rawalpindi District,* p. 73, 1893-94 Punjab Government Lahore. However, death of Baba Balak Singh has been recorded by Mufti Ghulam Sarvar Qureshi on Maghar Sudhi Puranmashi 1919 BK which falls on December 6th, 1862 AD *Tarikh-i-Makhzan, I Punjab,* 1877, p. 566.
44. *Census Reports Punjab and its feudateries* 1861, Lahore Govt. of Punjab p. 168.
45. He was a devotee of God and popularly known as Sai When Bhagat Jawahar Mal was going from Rawalpindi to Hazro he had many followers with him who were practising *nam* and the group was known as *Jagiasees and Habiasees.* It is believed that Baba Balak Singh was one of his important disciples.
    See for details—*Kukian Di Vithya,* Ganda Singh.
    Kuka Lahar, Ganda Singh.
    Bhai Jodh Singh—Abhinandan Grunth.
46. Official sources record his name as Dal Singh.
47. (i) One should remember all the twenty-four hours the name of God even while sitting, standing or sleeping.
    (ii) Bath should be taken at least thrice daily.
    (iii) No use of leather bucket for drinking water.
    (iv) Marriages to be performed according to Anand rites and no expensive shows to be made.
    (v) Every month *prasad* of one rupee and four annas to be made in the name of God.
    (vi) Not to eat food cooked by any body other than his co-religionists.
    (vii) No dowry to be given in the marriages.
    (viii) No selling of the girls.
    (ix) Meat, tobacco and wine etc., prohibited.
    (x) To earn one's livelihood by his own efforts and hard work.
    (xi) Not to tell lie and not to indulge in indecent things.
    (xii) To keep one small sword in the Pugri.
    (xiii) To love one's co-religionists and to help them in every way.
    Tarikh-I Makhzan Punjab, pp. 567-68, Mufti Ghulam Sarwar Qureshi, Lahore, 1877.
48. *Foreign Department Political*-A, No. 112, March 1867.
49. He was born on the day of Basant Panchami. He came of a poor carpenter's family of village Bhaini Arain of the Ludhiana District. It was a small community of Sikh Jat Cultivators where his father was catering to the general needs of the village.—*Kooka Movement,* p. 4.
50. *Panth Parkash,* p. 1045, Giyani Gyan Singh.
    "जिला लुधियाने गाम भेणी नाम जाने आम मानत तमाम तिने
    हिन्दु तुरक खालसा जात तरखान पिता जसा माता सदाबाई"
51. *Kooka Movement,* p. 4.
52. *Sat Jag Basant Ank,* 22 Magh 1986, p. 25.
53. His personality could be appreciated from the following lines:
    "He is a spare man 5 ft. 10 inches fairish complexion, pitted with small pox, hazel eyes, long nose and face, grizzled beard and moustache, by caste a Carpenter Sikh, reads and writes Gurmukhi and has worked on occasion as a mason". *Gooroo Ram Singh and the Kuka Sikhs,* Document No. 1, p. 2.
54. *Ibid*—Document No. IV, p. 13.
55. *Ibid*—Document No. VII, p. 143.

56. *Kooka Movement*, p. 4.
57. (i) Among Sikhs *Bhai* is a word used for those who are true Sikhs who by their devotion and Bhakti had reached a higher place.
    (ii) "It is literally known as brother but figuratively one completely soaked in religiousness" *Kooka Movement*, p. 5.
58. Regarding his occupation after leaving the army it has been said:
    "on the taking of Lahore in 1846 Ram Singh quitted the Maharajas army and resumed at Bainie his occupation of carpenter. For the last ten years he has kept a kind of *Banea* shop in which miscellaneous stores and iron are sold". *Foreign Department Political A*—March 1867 No. 112.
59. *Census Report Punjab and its fendateries*, p. 169. Also see *Rawalpindi District Gazetteer*, 1893-94.
60. *The Sikhs*, p. 41.
61. *Jug Paltaco Satguru*, p. 41.
62. *Krantikari Satguru*, p. 31.
63. *A brief account of the Freedom Movement in the Punjab*, p. 7. However, there is difference of opinion about the exact date of the initiation of the movement an almost contemporary sources puts it in 1847 AD.
    While Kooka records place it on the Deepmala day of 1862 AD but Professor Ganda Singh, Dr. Fauja Singh and other eminent scholars accept it as Baishakhi of 1857 AD.
64. For flag see Plate No. V.
65. According to Dr. Fauja Singh the baptism ceremony performed on the occasion was the same as that prescribed by Guru Govind Singh and was Christened Khande da Amrit (Nector of the Sword).
    Kooka Movement, p. 19.
    But when one goes through the official as well as non-official records it appears that Baba Ram Singh's practice of administering *Pahul* was different as he was questioned by the priests of Anandpur. Details are given in the Chapter on Religious Practices.
66. *Foreign Political A, March 1867*, No. 111-112.
    "पहला मरण कबूल कर जीवन दी छड़ आस
    होए के सब की रेन का तो आओ हमारे पास"
    —*Adi Grunth*
67. Nanded—It is a place where Guru Gobind Singh breathed his last popularly known as Hazur Sahib, now it is in the Maharashtra State.
68. *Satguru Biias*, p. 26.
69. Hazur Sahib is still a major pilgrimage centre for the Sikhs but author has observed that despite of Singh Sabha movement, Akali Movement and the reforms brought about by SGPC (Shiromani Gurudwara Prabandhak Committee) there are certain traditions followed at this shrine which do not co-incide with the Sikh practices like ringing of bells, offering of *tilak* of *kesar* and sandal etc.
70. "कहियो जाऊ सी अबचल नगरी दशमेश्वर की रीति सगरी कुछ कु रोज रह कर तै भाई लिख लियाओ रीति सगुराई सिंघन रीति नित्यप्रति जैसी लिख कर लियाओ देखो जै तेती तुम को जै कों भेंट चड़ाऐ अहां की अहां देयो जाये कोड़ी एक लबो तुम नाहिं शादी भी करवाओ नाही"
71. *Mantras*—literally mean Vedic and Puranic hymns. The practice of *Guru-Mantar*

and the emphasis on it by the Namdharis is in fact contrary to the general principles of Sikhism.

Foreign Political A, No. 111-112, March 1867.

72. *Kooka Movement*, p. 21.
73. *Baba Ram Singh Namdhari*, p. 17.
74. *Kirtan*—Singing hymns in the prayer of God.

74a. "घर घर अंदर धरमसाल होवे कीर्तन सदा बसाओ"
Adi Grunth.

75. *Ragi*—one who sings hymns from *Ad iGrunth*.
76. *Dhadi*—are like birds who generally sing the songs and lyrices of bravery in the typical style.
77. *Baba Ram Singh Namdhari*, p. 17.
78. Here it may be recorded that Guru Amar Dass had much earlier established twenty-two *manjis* for the consolidation and expansion of Sikhism. Perhaps Ram Singh was following the same pattern-since even on earlier occasion he had particularly choosen the day of Baisakhi for initiating people into the movement with first initiating the five Sikhs as was done by Guru Gobind Singh at the time of the formation of Khalsa. This leads us to believe that the Namdhari Movement was essentially revivalist in character.
79. List of the Subas is given in appendix 'G'.
80. *Shri Guru Singh Itiaas* was written by Bhanu Dutt in 1883, p. 132.
81. *Home Department, Judicial* A, July 1872, No. 208-211.
82. *The Gurudwara Reform Movement and the Sikh Awakening*, p. 36.
83. *Kooka Movement*, p. 34.
84. *Baba Ram Singh Namdhari*, p. 45.
85. *Kohinoor*, Lahore Urdu, 28th Sept. 1867.
86. *Foreign Political Department*, A No. 383-385 Sept. 1868.
87. *Tarikh-i-wakri*, p. 370.
88. *Home Department, Judicial* A, July 1872, No. 208-211.
89. *Home Department*, Judicial B, October 1881, No. 188-195.
90. *Foreign Department*, Political A, March 1867, No. 111-112.
91. *Ibid*, March 1867.
92. Some modern writers on the subject have asserted that the Kukas avoided the main route for circulating their messages as those roads were constructed by the Britishers. They obviously referred to the main highways. In this connection it may be pointed out that the messengers on foot always take the shorter route than the long and main routes. To imagine that such an instruction was given to avoid the roads made by Britishers is not based on reason. See for details *Baba Singh Namdhari, Namdhari Itihas Krantikari Satguru.*
93. *Sant Khalsa*, p. 50.
94. *Ibid.*

3

Religious Practices

Nineteenth century was the time when Sikhism had lost much of its original principles for which it was created. Sikhs were reverting to workship of idols, *smadhi*[1] and *maris*[2], etc. Such a situation seems to have led to the need of revitalising the basic principles of Sikhism. As a result, two important movements emerged under the leadership of Baba Dayal and Bhai Ram Singh, i.e., the Nirankari and the Namdhari respectively. The basic aim of these movements was to reform the Sikh religion and society.

Nirankari Practices

"The Nirankari was a Sikh puritan movement started with the object of stemming the tide into Hinduism."[3] They emphasized that *Guru Grunth Sahib* or *Adi Grunth* is their only Guru. For all practical and theoretical purposes Adi *Grunth* was their only guide. They had so much faith in *Adi Grunth* that even "the Gurus are to be reverenced as high priests of one single and invisible God".[4] They believed that Grunth and not the idols or pictures of Gurus were to be worshipped. But how far in practice they could follow it remained a disputed point especially in the light of a contemporary account which records: "They adopt the Grunth or Bible of Nanak and while they profess to abandon and abominate, all idolatory they do in fact worship the Grunth just as much in the same way as other Sikhs do. They wave over it the *Chauri*[5] bow down to it with the forehead touching the ground and present their offerings before it just as the other Sikhs do. When taxed with idolatory in this way they say they do not worship the book, but the word it contains."[6]

Nirankari sources emphasize the importance of the practice of remembering God's name. *Nirankari Chalan da Chitha* says, "The Brahmans have in the past misled everyone on to the path of hell. You go and direct them in the way of the name. Thus, having his orders from the divine court he returned to the world of mortals".[8] J.H. Orbison visited Nirankaris in 1861. He records "on further intercourse and inquiry I found that they consider themselves to be the true followers of Nanak and the Grunth. The Nirankari Gurus insists on complete and explict reliance on the one formless God (Nirankar) whom they regard as the creater, Maintaineer and the Destroyer. They insist only on His worship and appeasement. They regard Guru Nanak as incarnation of God who did immense good to humanity and who alone can fulfil all the desires of a man".[9]

According to Nirankari belief salvation is to be attained through meditation. Disgruntled by the rituals performed by Hindus, Nirankaris were trying to separate themselves from such influences which would mar their basic religious principles. They did try to simplify, review, and revitalize it and put it again on the rails. It was with a view to save it from the Hindu influences. This was a time when attempts were also made by the Christian missionaries to propagate their religion. Finding a striking similarity between their religion and that of the Nirankaris the Christians were tempted to come closer to this newly emerging movement and influence it by their own religious principles and bring it within their fold. It was this possibility which led to the visit of two Christian priests Morrisan and Orbison (1854-1861 AD) to the Nirankari Gurus. They had a long discussion with the Nirankaris on the matter of Salvation and record, "the fundamental principle of their religion is the salvation to be attained by meditation".[10] Nirankaris emphasised that salvation is to be attained through meditation and contemplation. Another means to salvation could be remembering God's name constantly. But the Christian priests wanted to know as to who was their saviour and who was going to lead them to salvation. One priest further said, "That meditation could never satisfy the justice of God and, therefore, could be no ground for the pardon of sin nor was it alone sufficient to change the heart and sanctify our natures".[11]

Perhaps on this point the priest had at the back of his mind the role of Christ in the Christantity. It is true that so far the Nirankaris did not refer to Nanak as a saviour, but in their principles emphasized the significance of meditation as the only means of salvation. In course of their discussion they not only disputed means and methods of salvation, as suggested by the Nirankaris. But this had not satisfied the priest who repeatedly asked to name some spiritual preceptor. The Nirankaris replied that they accepted Nanak as their saviour and a person leading to the path of salvation. Incidentally even this could not satisfy the missionaries and they finally broke off with the question that how could Nanak have granted them salvation when he himself was not an immortal. However the Nirankaris stuck to their belief that Nanak was their saviour.[12]

The exchange of views and arguments between the Nirankaris and the Christian priest do reflect, firstly, the principles of the Nirankaris had some similarity with that of the Christianity and as such the Christian priest tried to win them over through reason and arguments. Secondly the incident also helps to measure the keenness of the Christian priest in propagating Christianity in India. Finally and most importantly the Christian priest must have thought that in case they could succeed in their argument, they would have a large number of Nirankaris converted in one stroke. They must have viewed this possibility with greater hope as the Nirankaris were already against Hinduism and were trying to establish themselves as a separate religious identity.

Place of Worship

Contemporary accounts record observations about the Nirankari mode of worship. It gives a vivid discription of the main room where worship was performed. "Dharamshala that is religious house or place of worship is open in front showing a long room the floor of which is covered with coarse cloth.[13] At one end there are several monster books on low wooden stands some of which lie open while others are shut wrapped in embroidered silk covers.[14] In front of that seemed the principal book was a brass lamp burning and over all a square coloured cloth suspended from the roof perhaps to keep particles of dirt from falling on the sacred books of Grunths as they are called. Behind some of the open Grunths were seated Gurus religious leaders and teachers who read for their own benefit or that of their followers[15]. Some of them had *chowries* or fly brushes made of the long white hair of the Yak's tail in their hands and kept waving them to and fro over the books to signify reverence and keep off unholy flies."[16]

Nirankaris used to assemble for their prayers in the morning and evening at a place known as dharamshala. Contemporary sources record that "first they assemble every morning for worship which consists of bowing the head to the ground before the Grunth making offering and in hearing the Grunth read by one of their members and explained also if their leader be present.[17] Nirankaris used to assemble and recite *Gurbani* every morning with their leader and do *Kirtan,* etc. Teachers used to give sermons on *Gurbani* followed by the detailed explanation of the scriptures of the Sikhs.[18]

J.H. Orbison, a Christian missionary posted at the mission station at Rawalpindi sent a detailed report on the city and its people to New York. In 1861 he wrote in detail about the evening prayers of the Nirankariş in the following words, "They arranged themselves all around the room sitting on the floor and following the Guru who began to chant their hyms in which the names of *Nirankar* and Nanak occur very frequently. For a while they sang swinging back and forward and bowing every now and then to the Grunth and kissing the floor fervently while the men were thus engaged several women came one after the other bearing lighted lamps from which they poured each a little oil into the large lamp which stood burning before the Grunth. Then bowing kissed the ground and repeating the name *Nirankar* went away. This is only part the women seem to take in the worship."[19]

Nirankaris usually assembled twice a day for the prayers. The census report of 1881, however records that they associate their special monthly gatherings quite in consistence with the system of Sankranti. The report mentions "The first day of each month to be kept holy by attendance of the temple, reading the Grunths lamentation for sin and giving contributions for religious purposes".[20]

Pilgrimage

One of the major impact of the Brahmanical religion on Sikhism was the rise and institutionalization of their various places of religious importance. In due course places like Amritsar, Anandpur Sahib, Sirhind and Nanded (Hazur Sahid), etc., became important religious centres of the Sikhs. They visited them in large numbers occasionally and on festivals. They gradually became the places of pilgrimage. At these places the mode of worship was deviating and tilting more on the lines of the Brahmanical practices. Thus, they were overpowered in matters of rituals and their fundamentals seemed to have begun merging into Hinduism.

The basic object of the Nirankari movement seems to have been restoring the basic belief in or devotion to one God and His Universality. They emphasized that in Sikh religion at no time was any special significance attached to a particular place or taught to make any special place of unusual religious significance or to perpetuate and commemorate any monument in the memory of the gurus.[21] The purpose behind such a warning was to stop the Sikhs from accepting or establishing specific places with special religious importance. This was a check against the future possibility of creating places of pilgrimage by its followers.

In view of the teachings of their Gurus, the Nirankaris did not attach any importance to pilgrimage which they "regarded as useless", to them "neither Brahmin nor cows are to be revered".[22] For them the expression of religious beliefs were more of internal nature than external. They were emhasizing more on meditation. They condemned the pilgrimage which was more akin to Brahmanical influence.

Hukumnama of the Nirankaris says that there is no use of residing on the banks of the river Ganges and there is no use of drinking its pure water because salvation cannot be attained without meditation.[23] They laid more stress on their own centre which was near Lei River around Rawalpindi. Here annual functions were held on *Maghi*.[24] Census Report of 1891, records that they called "Lei stream as their Amritsar. They burn their dead near that pool and have an annual meeting there." *Nirankari Chalan da Chitha* mentioned that there is no end to places of pilgrimage and Gods to worship, but salvation is possible only by His service.[25] Likewise when Baba Ratta brother of Darbara Singh asked for permission to celebrate *Baisakhi* at Amritsar, Nirankari *Guru* replied "Amritsar is within you" and reading and study of *Gurbani* and to adopt it in life, is like visiting Amritsar.[26] Nirankari used to quote from *Gurbani.* "Go bathe at the place of pilgrimage, the place of pilgrimage, is the name, the place of pilgrimage is where we meditate on the word (*shabd*) and obtain enlightenment".[27] Gradually Nirankaris developed their own religious centre.[28] The Nirankaris, who strictly believed in the authority of *Adi Grunth* opposed Brahminical practies. It is in this light that the spirit behind the Nirankari movement, could be appreciated.[29]

Brahmins Versus Nirankaris

As the Nirankari movement was getting momentum, people were awakened against the evils of Brahmanical practices. The Nirankaris were deadly against the supremacy of Brahmins and the dogmatic and ritualistic religious beliefs.

In the contemporary society the position of the Brahmins was quite dominating. They were considered important at all occasions like birth, death, marriage or when constructing a house, conducting a new business or when going out on tour, etc. *Nirankari Chalan da Chitha* says that one should not consult Brahmins for auspicious occasions or *Mahurat* as it leads to spreading superstitions[30]. For Brahmins it was a matter of financial loss as they used to earn a lot by performing these rituals. Nirankaris were not calling them to their houses rather opposing them. The Brahmins approached the prominent people of the city for help.[31] On their appeal the religious leaders of the Sikhs who themselves were under Brahminical influence called Baba Darbara Singh to visit the Gurdwara of Baradari at Rawalpindi.

Baba Darbara Singh went to Baradari Gurudwara with Bhai Sham Singh, Jassa Singh and Bhai Greeb Singh. On the way he told Bhai Jassa Singh to purchase some grass.[32] The elderly people and the Brahmins told him that if he agrees to accept the position of the Brahmins they will stop opposing him.[33] They also tried to win Baba Darbara Singh in favour of the Brahmins. They said that the Brahmins are his cows and he must agree to feed them. Baba Darbara Singh, then took the grass from Bhai Jassa Singh and placed it before the Brahmins. But when insisted, he however agreed with them to prepare list of fees to be paid to Brahmins on different occasions. Accordingly a list was prepared and he was asked to put his signatures on it. It was agreed that whosoever would call Brahmin to his home should pay rupees five. Darbara Singh left the place saying emphatically, "Only those will pay who will call them, Nirankaris are not going to call them so why should they pay".[34]

Nirankaris were trying to convince the people that Brahmins are acting contrary to their own principles. Brahmins consider taking daughter's money to be a sin, still they take it. Brahmins claim that it is disgraceful even to eat at daughter's house, but they perform marriages of the daughters of their patrons by taking money.[35]

Nirankaris were not only against the Brahmins. They equally opposed those Sikhs who were misleading the Sikh masses. They said that even the preachers of *Gurbani* had forgotten the actual message of *Adi Grunth.* Once in Amritsar, Darbara Singh had an argument with Baba Bikram Singh Bedi, the chief priest of Darbar Sahib Amritsar. One day in the morning Bhai Jassa Singh priest of Darbar Sahib had stomach ache and he died on the cot itself. Then every body was saying that he has died *begatta.*[36] Therefore, for the peace of his soul all Brahminical rituals like *pind-dan*"[37] should be performed. This disturbed Darbara Singh, he thought how could this man be without a salvation if every day he was reciting thy pure name and as well taking bath in the pool of Amritsar. Moreover *Gurbani* itself says, "Those who take bath in the pool of Ramdass are free from the all sins.[38] He approached Baba Bikram Singh to clear his all doubts about the incident, Bikram Singh could not contest the point as Darbara Singh was quoting from the *Gurbani.* He had the only explanation that the wordly people should follow all the rituals prevalent in the existing society. Darbara Singh was enraged and said "why have you then become the Gurus and guides of the Sikhs when you cannot show them the right path".[39] He emphatically told him that neither he nor his men were going to accept the superior position and leadership of those who themselves did not know what was to be done according to *Gurmat.*[40]

Baba Khem Singh Bedi was another great saint of Sikhs who preached *Gurbani* and converted men to Sikh faith. Some of his followers impressed by the teachings of Nirankaris, asked for his permission to adopt Nirankari ceremonies and rites.[41] He replied that he could not subscribe to the Nirankari views as they eliminated the Brahmins totally.[42] He instructed his followers to stick to the old Brahmanic and Vedic rites and not to follow the Nirankaris as they were inexpedient and created conflict.[43] The principles and teachings of the Nirankaris were very appealing and it attracted even the general Sikhs. But the Brahmanical practices and beliefs were so deep-rooted that it was not possible even for the Sikh leaders to permit the masses to join the Nirankaris.

Cow Worship

Through centuries the cow had a special place in the Hindu religion and mythology. Cow worship was not permitted among the Nirankaris. Official sources of the Nirankaris speak that pilgrimages and offerings were useless and Brahmins and cows were not to be scrupulously respected and use of flesh as food abandoned.[44] The census of 1891, also records Nirankaris as worshipping God as a spirit only.[45] Annual report of Ludhiana mission of 1853, alleges that: "The Hindus complain that they give abuse to the cow. This climax of impiety could not be endured. It was followed by some street disturbances which brought the parties into the civil court."[46]

The said report of 1853, gives an impression that the Nirankaris disregarded the cows to the extent of abusing which even led to a litigation. Here it seems that the missionaries have tried to generalise a particular incident. Resorting to abusing had never been permitted in any civilized society, much less in Indian culture. Considering their religious learnings, the Nirankaris could hardly be imagined as using abusive language. Relating any isolated incident with the general views of the Nirankaris was hardly justified. Moreover they had specifically forbidden the use of animal meat which itself demonstrates their regard for animals in general.

System of Charnamrit

Nirankari Chalan da Chitha says "by the blessing of *Nirankar* they wash the feet of the whole congregation in Darbar Sahib."[47] They quote from *Gurbani* that this practice is coming down right from Guru Nanak's time, that after performing evenings prayers (rehrass) and washing the feet of the *sangat,* that water was given to the Sikhs to drink as a nector.[48] Again quoting from the Gurbani of the fifth *Guru* Arjan Dev said "one should wash the feet of the beloved of God and drink it by completely surrendering one's self to him".[49] The *Chitha* orders the Nirankaris that since the Gurus had followed this they were also to follow that practice. According to this ceremony the *Guru* and the members of the whole congregation dipped their big toes into the water and then water was drunk like *prasad* or *Charnamrit.*[50]

Baba Dayal tried to make an important modification regarding the *charnamrit.* Perhaps it escapes attention when one looks at this system as a whole. Baba Dayal was against idol workship and washing the feet and taking that water (*charnamrit*), was not less than idol worship. In this respect the significant modification made by him was washing the feet of the whole "*Sangat*" (congregation) and not of an individual and taking of that water. It seems, the purpose of this modification was an attempt to prevent the possibility of idol worship, which was common in Hinduism. This was by itself an important precaution taken by Baba Dayal against going into the fold of Brahmanism.

Reverence of the Slippers of Baba Dayal

The Nirankaris were opposed to idol worship or worship of any figures form. They strictly believed in the concept of Nirankar. They were against giving any form to their worship—except the total submission to the *Adi Grunth.* Their original principles seems to have changed after the death of Baba Dayal when people started worshipping his slippers. Here it seems that after him the Nirankari unconsciously drifted towards the Brahmanical practice to which this sect was fundamentally opposed.

Census Report of 1891, records "there is also in Rawalpindi a meeting place (*Darbar*) and a shrine of the *Adi Grunth* where are kept the slippers (now covered with velvet) which once adorned the feet of Bhai Dayal. The Nirankaris have degenerated sufficiently to revere these relics and prostrate themselves on their foreheads before them."[51] The Will of Sahib Ratta written in 1903 AD also records about worship of Master's slippers. It says that there was one room for the slippers (where Baba Dayal had expired) two beds for the slippers one Chandowa for the slippers a big cloth hanging from the roof four gold *tikkas* of the slippers which were weighing five tolas. Now they are preserved with the Chief of the Nirankaris and are only displayed at the time of annual gathering[51a].

The beginning of the nineteenth century in Punjab had seen the growth of the Nirankari movement and its expansion in the Frontier region. However, the mid-nineteenth century witnessed yet another movement in Punjab that was Namdhari. This movement developed in a different region, i.e., eastern Punjab in 1857. Both movements had greatly stirred the socio-religious life of Punjab. In order to appreciate properly the principles, practices, similarities dis-similarities of both the movements, an attempt has been made to examine them in some details.

In this connection the religious practices and teachings of the Nirankaris have already been seen in the preceeding pages. In the forthcoming section an attempt will be made to bring out the salient features of the religious activities of the Namdharis and thus, bring out a comparative study of some of their contributions to the religious life of the Sikhs.

The Namdharis

Another important movement of the nineteenth century which had a considerable impact on the religious life of Punjab was the Namdhari Movement. Its founder Baba Ram Singh felt equally concerned about the religious and social problems which faced the Sikh society.

"Baba Ram Singh's work in the religious and social field was of fundamental character. He wished to create a new individual having a strong character, deep and steady in faith, firm in conviction and fearless in action, a model human being an embodiment of love, truth, valour and self sacrifice."[52] The official sources also write about his noble motives. "From the reports now submitted by many officers it appears that Ram Singh is endeavouring to effect a reform in the Sikh religion and some of his doctrines and precepts are not only harmless, but also beneficial".[53]

Baba Ram Singh's firm belief was that such a man can be created only by the reading of the *Grunth* constantly and remembering the words of the *Guru* by heart. In his letters which were intercepted by the British government when he was imprisoned at Burma and Mergui, he constantly emphasizes the importance of the *Gurbani.* He said, "In short '*Nam and Bani*' are a priceless treasure[54]. It is not possible to estimate their value. O' Khalsa the Guru Sahib has been graciously pleased to confer upon you this Nam and Bani day and night. Whether moving or working always strive to step forward and never backward. The present is the time for your amendments, as here after, you will not receive the present birth (i.e. the human form) excepting the human race, no species of Creation enjoys the privileges of *Nam, Dan* (charity) and *Ashnan* (ablution). All who recite the *Nam* of God will inherit explanation, joy, perpetual happiness and prosperity. The praise of the *Nam* is endless".[55]

Satguru Bilas (a biography of Baba Ram Singh) gives a graphic account of his routine. It says "All had a common mass. The Holy Book was always kept open and recitations from there were continuous. There were both morning and evening services. *Asa di war* was a regular morning feature which was attended by all. In the evening there was a community hymn singing programme conducted to the accompaniment of musical instruments, Guru Ram Singh had his bath in the ambrosial hours of the morning . . ., himself recited *Asa di war* . . . receited *Rahiras* in the evening, sang the *Arti Sohela* and then offered *Ardas* to God and then he would go to bed".[56]

Ram Singh said that there was no age bar for remembering His name, men and women, old and young, all should commit the *Bani* to memory. In one of his letters he said "Communicate my orders of *Bhajan Bani* to all".[57] Ram Singh links *Bani* with *Guru Mantar* (the word power of the Guru) without which man is like an animal.[58] By Bani, Baba Ram Singh meant the words written in *Guru Grunth* Sahib. "Telling the importance of the name of God (literally meaning *Gurubani)* Baba Ram Singh says first he became the disciple of *Udasi* then followed the *Nirmalas,* but could not find any respite, but after initiated by Baba Balak Singh, I have received the comforts of all types of health, wealth and heart, etc. Even in imprisonment the name of God gives the happiness".[69] Mr. Kinchant reporting in 1867, about the Kukas said "Gobind Singh's Grunth was the only true one written by inspiration and is the only sacred writing. Gobind Singh is the real Guru. Any person irrespective of caste or religion can be admitted a convert. Sodees, Bedees, Mohunts, Brahmins and such like are imposters as none are Gurus, except Gobind Singh. The coverts are allowed to read Gobind Singh's Grunth and no other book."[60] At another place an official source records. "The Grunth is their only accepted inspired volume. The brotherhood may be known by the tie of their *Puggrees 'Seedha Pug'* by a watch word and by a necklace of knots made in a white woollen cord to represent beads and which are worn by all the community".[61]

There was a striking similarity among the Nirankaris and Namdharis as both emphasized the significance of His name and the source of their teaching—*Adi Grunth or Gurbani.*

In one of his intercepted letters, Baba Ram Singh wrote "O brother of the *Khalsa* read the *Grunth Sahib* yourselves as often as you possibly can and get others to read it. If one individual can not read fully and completely the *Grunth Sahib,* then have it completed by two or four Sikhs".[62] Baba Ram Singh told his people about the elaborate ceremony with which they should perform the path.[63] It is important to note that no such specific instruction was given to the Nirankaris as regards the ceremonial recitation of the *Adi Grunth.* To the Nirankaris His name was more a matter of personal reverence than a visual expression. They emphasized the adoption of the spirit of Gurbani in practice and not on superficial ceremonies.

In order to appreciate the religious outlook of the Namdharis, it would be necessary to have some idea about the nature of the ceremonies prescribed by Baba Ram Singh to his followers. First of all the place was to be washed with the mud and not cow dung."[64] All clothes or carpets and the covering of the stool be washed. All coloured clothes to be removed and the cloth cover stitched to the binding of the Grunth washed like-wise. The readers were also supposed to wash and clean their clothes after which they had to abstain from touching others. Even after passing urine they were supposed to be purified with water. After passing urine they must wash their hands and feet and gargle their mouth three or four times.[65] The place purified for the reading of the *Grunth* must not be entered by any outsider. If they enter they must sit perfectly silent.[66]

This seems to be an attempt to establish the exalted position of the *Grunth* revered by the Namdharis. Inspite of the best efforts of Baba Ram Singh to avoid the prevalent Brahmanical religious practices if seems he could not totally escape the influence of Brahmanism. In Baba Ram Singh's personality one could see the combination of adoption and rejection of the prevalent social and religious practices. However he could not stop the practices like *Havan, jot, jyoti* which were mainly from traditional Hinduism. A lamp of *ghi* was to be kept burning all through the *Akhand Path* and concluding with the *Hom* (incense offering). The person performing the *Hom* must not speak, but should remain reciting the *jap ji* (the first book of the *Adi Grunth*) dropping the *akhand ahuti* (incense) on to the fire at the end of each verse. Every time he dropped the incence, the person had to recite the words *Sri Wah-Guru.* At night two lamps of oil and one of *ghee* should be used.[67]

After attending to the call of the nature entire body including the hair of the head should be bathed and cotton clothes should be washed. Four readers, four incense burners and four others should be present as attendants throughout the *path.* The reading of the *Grunth Sahib* in this manner was considered most beneficial. After the *Bhog,* the *Ardas* (Prayers for special blessings) should be offered in all humility for personal safety and protection. The *Akhand path* should invariably be performed in the manner described above. It could not be performed to perfection without the help of twelve persons.[68] Here it may be pointed out that while at one place Baba Ram Singh was arguing for making the religious and social ceremonies inexpensive, on the other place, a very simple ceremony of reading or reciting the *Grunth* was made so complicated. Sikh religion in general has no place for *Havans*, etc. But why Baba Ram Singh could not do away with it certainly poses a question. Perhaps it was too difficult for the Brahmanical influenced society to do away with *havans.* As Baba Ram Singh was making a moderate attempt to have more following from among the non-Sikhs he perhaps accepted the practice of *havan.* Moreover although we do not come across any instance of *haven* and *hom* during the Sikh Gurus period up to Guru Teg Bahadur. But the *Dusam Grunth* which is supposed to be written by Guru Gobind Singh there are clear references of *Hom* or *Havan*. When he gives the description of *Kalyug* he mentions such pure and pious practices would be obandoned.[69] Again he relates how sacrifice or offerings to fire is like an act of bravery which could destroy the enemies.[70] Perhaps this practice was followed at Nanded where Baba Ram Singh sent a special messenger to get full information about the practices followed there when Guru Gobind Singh breathed his last. At the same time it can not be denied that the whole ceremony was made quite expensive an affair.[71]

Kuka's elaborate *Havan* ceremony has even been depicted in the records which mention "Their assembly generally lasts for two or three days and the following ceremonies are observed : First two or three maunds of wood are collected and set fire to, then *ghee*, *halwa*, fruits, etc., are thrown in to make the wood burn more slowly. The assembled Kukas sit round whilst one reads the Grunth and others repeat *shalocks*. After this has been going on for a time, some of the fraternity become so excited that they endeavour to throw themselves into the fire".[72] This particular excitement has been referred to in the letters of Baba Ram Singh and is described as state of ecstasy or *sootra*.[73]

Sootra was a state of ecstasy in which Kukas used to dance around the *Havan* shaking and waving their head to and fro. This practice was not prevalent among the Sikhs, perhaps it was adopted from the *sufis* a state known *wajd*. But Baba Ram Singh forbade people to pretend this stage. He said that such a man would suffer a bad name in both the worlds.[74] Baba Ram Singh told his *Sangat* that if somebody wanted to throw himself in the fire of *havan-kund* let him do so because when one is prevented to do so many more would come, but when fire would burn then they would get aside themselves.[73]

T.H. Thorton Secretary to Government of Punjab while writing to S. Willie, Officiating Secretary to the Government of India said that the Kookas were accustomed to meet together and read the *Grunth* and *Chundee Path*.[76] *Chundee Path* was a prevalent prayer in the honour of Goddess Durga. In the present context M.M. Ahluwalia has interpreted the *Chundee Path* in a different way. He says "devotees must fight against demons.[77] According to Kuka belief *Chandi Path* practice was started by Guru Gobind Singh to prepare the Sikhs for struggle against the oppressors to instill war-like temper.[78] In the official records *Chundee Path* performed by the Kukas is described as "one of the many Hindu religious books were written in praise of Chundee Devi. Hindus select their shalocks from it but it appears strange that a book encouraging idolatry and which is usually read with flowers in the hands of reader to be placed after each verse on the idol should be held in esteem by the Kukas."[79]

However, the Namdharis continued to denounce idolatory and worship at graves and tombs. They believed "Brahmins and such like are imposters and none are Gurus except Govind Singh. *Devee dwaras, shibdwaras* and *mandirs* are a means of extortion to be held in contempt and never visited. Idols and idol worship are insulting to God and will not be forgiven. Kukas used to sing popularly as given below:

(1)	Murhee Mussetan dhake Kardeo maidan	Throw down tombs and mosques and make all level
(2)	Pahle Mare Pir Bunnoe Phir Maro Sooltana	First annihilate (or throw down Pir Bunnoe after do the same for sooltana.
(3)	Oomut Subhe Mohemdee Khap jai maidan	All the followers of the prophet will disappear at once.
(4)	Soonat ki na kar sukka kumbun turkana	Trembling turks will not in future be able to circumcise.
(5)	Bhainee Satguru Jagaes aur jhut jahana.	The true guru has arisen in Bhainee the rest of theworld is full of lie.[80]

Satguru Bilas records: "There was a grave and people used to worship it, but guru Ram Singh disobeyed the place and said people are worshipping the earth,"[81] because "the worship of one and only one God was strictly enjoined upon the members of the Kuka brotherhood. In no case were they allowed to worship or pay homage to any god or goddess or any idols, etc."[82] The view that "idols and idol worship are insulting to God and will not be forgiven" created a different problem.[83] Instead of denouncing it inspired the Kukas to attack the tombs and graves. Reports of the demolition of the tombs and graves of notable *pirs* (Saint) or ordinary graves thus, came under the Kuka attacks.

Reports were received from different districts of Punjab that they were engaged in the destruction of tombs and graves. This was with special reference to Firozpur, Ludhina, Sialkot and Goojranwala.[84] "However, this radical method of dealing with the problem was as quickly abandoned as it was adopted. The main reason for this was its strong disapprobation by Baba Ram Singh as has been mentioned by Colonel Mc Andrew".[85]

Kukas had great respect for the tenets of the sect and were keen to restore the Sikh religion to its original purity. They were opposed to consulting the Brahmins to know about the auspicious dates for marriages, etc., or for various occasions from birth to death.[86] This was bound to adversely effect the position enjoyed by the Brahmins and above all, their source of income. It was natural to aggravate the feelings of this class against the Namdharis. This is established from the account given in the official sources of the period which says "The *pujaris*, Brahmins and other spiritual persons who live by the votive offerings they receive from orthodox Hindus are naturally the bitterest enemies of the new sects as the spread of its tenets would derive them of their marriage fees and other gains and exactions".[87] Namdharis and Nirankaris seem to be identical on the point of rejecting the Brahmanical authority and liberating the Sikhs from their influence.

Propagation and Consolidation

Baba Ram Singh took extensive tours of the neighbouring districts to strengthen his mission and to spread the principles of his faith. He went to Hardwar to attend the *Ardh Kumbh Mela* in April 1861. On the way he stopped at Khanna, Ambala and Saharanpur. After coming back from Hardwar Baba Ram Singh went to other places. "In Samvat 1918 he went to Muthda and then to Puhaad, Dhuleta etc. in Doaba Siyarh in Ludhiana, Raipur in the Tapas of Grewal, Khote in the Tapa of Jungle. By this he was not only attracting people to his faith but these villages themselves were becoming his agencies for missionary work".[88]

While Nirankari Gurus used to have their tours with all pomp and show, Baba Ram Singh believed in simplicity. He wore a white dress, carried white flag and rode on a white horse called Chini.[89] The Nirankaris used to carry the *Adi-Grunth* in a polanquin with their procession, but Baba Ram Singh used to visit a village where *Sangat* had recited the whole *Adi Grunth.* He went only to complete it which was known as *Bhog.* Otherwise wherever Baba Ram Singh would go, he would first enquire about a *dharmsala* or a *gurudwara* where the *Adi-Grunth* could be available. When found it would be opened with due respect and people were preached.[90]

The followers loved him so much that they wanted him to visit their village for which they were ready to perform *Akhand Path.* This in itself was helping in the expansion and propagation of his faith. This process helped in increasing the number of the Kukas. More and more people were baptized when he visited their villages. Official and non-official contemporary sources speak about the fast increase in the number of the Kukas.[91]

Conversions to the Kuka faith were largely from the rural areas. Anybody irrespective of caste, creed, colour and background could be admitted to the Kuka faith and fraternity. Mr Kinchant reported in 1867, that "any person irrespective of caste or religion can be admitted a convert".[92] In Ambala captain Harris District Superintendent of Police noticed that prior to 1866, there were few Kukas in the district "but the tenets of the new faith have largely gained credence of the late in the pergunnahs of Umbala and Ladowa where now might be found some fifteen villages composed almost of believers in Ram Singh's creed. The population of these villages be estimated consisting principally of the lower castes such as Ramdasia, Tirkhan, Lohar and Jats".[95] Different sources refer to the fact that the Kukas were mostly from the lower strata of the rural society.[94] The reason why the followers of Ram Singh were mainly from the lower caste may be traced from the social oppression which they were undergoing within their own social set-up. Here it may be pointed out that even the Muslims were coming to the fold of Kukas and people as far as Kabul were sending Missions to learn about the Kukas. This was a matter of concern for the Britishers and they were quite apprehensive of Kuka activities. The conversion to Kuka faith by several Mohammdans and the mission by Abdul Razzak of his two sons to Bhaini were also incidents that deserve notice.[95]

How Baba Ram Singh was growing popular among the masses could be known by the observation of Mac-Andrew Inspector General of Police of Lahore who said, "when he became the chief of Dera after becoming the disciple of Guru Balak Singh of the Hazro he was a Mahant then he was called guru Ram Singh then he was known as Satguru and now he is known as Sacha Padshah".[96]

According to the letters of Baba Ram Singh written from exile it appears that he was reluctant out of humility to be called a guru and said "I am like auto a Mazkuri (Peon) . . . I have not the virtues of a Guru in me not so much as the thickness of a hair and brother to me you are like life and body. I am even glad to meet a sweeper of the Punjab. It is most difficult for me to get sight of a Punjabi.[97]

Humility and greatness were the twin qualities of Baba Ram Singh. In one of his letters he writes "I of my oneself can write nothing, before commencing my letter I with folded hands beseach the guru to inspire me to write whatsoever is pleasing to him".[98]

Dr. Ganda Singh interprets this statement differently. He says it appears that Baba Ram Singh in the beginning did not disapprove disciples calling him *Sri, Guru, Satguru, Sacha Padshah.* Perhaps in the beginning he was rather impressed by it. But when he was in exile and studying *Gurubani* he had a change of heart and in his letters he termed himself as the postman or reporter of God. Perhaps he also thought that if he would forbid his people to place him on the high pedestal of Guru, they might again turn to the *bedees* and *sodhee.* An ordinary Sikh normally looked to an alive *guru.*[99] On this point Kapoor Singh says "Babaji was undoubtedly forbidding people from calling him Guru but in the thousand years of Indian History, there was not a single person except Guru Gobind Singh whose ideals were so high. Baba Ram Singh wanted to take his people to the height of achievement in every field of life social, cultural, religious and political. So it was quite natural that very soon people thought him to be the true Guru."[100]

Ram Singh, who was often invited by his followers, visited village Khote in Firozpur District. Somehow the fast growing popularity of Baba Ram Singh and increasing number of his followers created some political apprehension. His religious tours were seen by the authorities, as being seditious activities instead of a purely religious matter. This led to Baba Ram Singh's confinement surveillence in this home Bhaini and his religious tours were suspended.[101] However the missionary work was carried out by his lieutenants. He remained confined to Bhaini upto 1867, when on the basis of his good conduct and lack of evidence to prove charges of sedition levied against him, he was granted permission to attend the Holi festival at Anandpur on his request. The British were quite alert about the activities of Baba Ram Singh who was under close watch.[102]

Baba Ram Singh's visit to Anandpur had attracted huge gatherings of Kukas. Describing this visit of Ram Singh to Anandpur *Siri Satguru Bilas* says "Ram Singh was riding his pet Chini (horse) while other Subas including Jota Singh were on other horses. In this procession there were about fifty horses. Many others were adorning the procession on foot. Suba Sudh Singh was incharge of this procession. There were colours and the beating of drums echoed in all the directions".[103] However, the *Nihungs, Akalees, Bedees* and *Sodhees* were unhappy over Ram Singh's visit to Anandpur Gurudwara for worship. But when persuaded by the British officials the *Mahants* of the *Garudwara* agreed to allow Ram Singh to visit it with certain conditions imposed on him. Fazal Hussain Inspector of Police, Hoshyarpur reported on 20th March 1867, that *Pujaris* of these Gurudwaras had put some conditions on the *Kukas* at the time of Ram Singh's visit. According to the report the *Kukas* would, not take off their turbans, not open the hair and not to shout at the time of the visit.

Ram Singh accepted the said conditions and he alongwith his followers, visited the Kesgarh and Teg Bahadur Gurudwaras on 20th March, to worship. He gave an offering of Rs. 25 at each place. But he was offended, when the *Pujaris* of the *Kesgarh Gurudwara* refused to pray for him. However Baba Ram Singh was happy with the conduct of the *Pujaris* of the *Teg Bahadur Gurudwara* and paid them an extra rupee as they prayed for him.[104]

The unfavourable response of the *Pujaris* towards Ram Singh's visit indicate their reaction against his reforms. In fact, Ram Singh's teachings against the superstitions and blind faith in them had shaken their authority. His teachings had also put them under financial loss. After his return to Bhaini Ram Singh wrote a letter to the *Mahants* of *Gurudwara Kesgarh* enquiring from them as to why they did not consider him a *Gurusikh*. Ram Singh further said that a true guru of the Sikh was one who was not proud. Not satisfied with these queries, the Pujaris posed some counter charges against him. Their allegations were (i) that he sets himself as a god, (ii) that when making a convert he does not give him *Amrit* as is the custom but whispers a *muntra* in his car, (iii) that when he makes a convert says to him to repeat *Junum gooroo Huzro ur Bashi Guru Nundpore,* (iv) that whereas the Sikhs entering a place of worship do not untie their hair or remove their turbans, *kukas* do (v) that Kukas in exciting themselves to such a degree as to be at times insensible act like some sufis and so they can not be Guru Sikhs".[105]

These questions of the *Pujaris* naturally call for some explanation from Ram Singh. To explain the queries of the *pujaris* was felt necessary by Baba Ram Singh in order to set aside any doubt about him and his teachings. In this connection he pointed out the shortcomings of the *Pujaris.* He replied that "if they really acted upto the Sikh religion they would appreciate his doctrine. That they all quite contrary to the 'Grunth' by eating meat, drinking, lying, licentiousness, female infanticide and, therefore Kukas do not consider them Sikhs".[106]

However, Baba Ram Singh said "Do prayer and *Ardas* for me whatsoever punishment you give I would accept but do not create rifts in the sect or *panth* itself. I am the servant of God and I have not said anything new. I have just re-established the *maryada* (disciplined code of conduct) of the tenth Guru. I have just moved people towards the reading of the Gurbani".[107]

However, the immediate reaction of this incident was the closure of the door of the Gurudwaras for the Namdharis[108].

But this did not change Baba Ram Singh's approach and he advised his followers to "Read and believe in the *Grunth* which is greatest of the Gurudwaras. Do not go where you are ill treated. If the Guru is resolved to take us to the Gurudwaras we will go but if not we must submit to the will of the *Guru.* They (the orthodox Sikh priests) are cursed by the *Guru* and consequently can not help abusing us. They are blind and deaf and they will meet the same fate as a dog which is shut up in a glass room and which barks in vain till he dies".[109]

It may, however, be pointed out that the significance of Amritsar continued in the mind of Baba Ram Singh as he visited it on the occasion of Diwali in 1867. "When Baba Ram Singh visited the sacred shrine he gave some *alms* and received in recognition of his religious character" from the *mahunts* of the Darbar Sabib, a *dushalla*[110] and a *Purgree*[111], from Jhunda Bunga a *deputta*[112] and *Pugree."*[113] Namdhari sources also confirm his visit of these Gurudwaras at Amritsar and receiving Siropa (Robe of honour). But at Akal Takhat Pujaris refused even to perform an Ardas for him and the plea was that they can only pray for the one who is a Gursikh according to the principles laid down by Guru Gobind Singh. Here it may be pointed out that an incident of a similar nature happened with Baba Darbara Singh of the Nirankaris when he visited *Akal Takhat.*

But Baba Ram Singh was welcomed by several people of the city. From a native account it appears that "a large number of the native gentry and trades people of Amritsar visited Ram Singh and presented him with offerings amounting to the value of rupees 700. He also received 12 *thans* (pieces) of the cloth.[114]

Had there been some understanding among the *Pujaris* and followers of Baba Ram Singh as regards to the basic teachings and practices prevalent among both of them, there could have been greater possibility of a better socio-religious life of the Sikhs society as a whole. Baba Ram Singh was apprehensive that the small points of differences might lead to conflicts rendering his followers in the form of a mere sect. Incidentally the apprehension of Baba Ram Singh came true as the Namdhari movement could hardly become very popular after a certain time. But it did pave the way for socio-religious awakening among the Sikhs and can be considered as the emergence of the Singh Sabha movement which developed in the late nineteenth century.

Among the matters of differences in the religious customs of the Nirankaris and the Namdharis mention may be made of the practice of *charnamrit*[115] and *sitprasad*[116] while the Nirankaris emphasized the significance of *charnamrit* and insisted on its taking, the Namdharis rejected it and disuaded their followers from taking *sitprasad.* Regarding this Baba Ram Singh said "In regard to your request for *sit-prasad* I say that the words of the *guru* are the real *sit-prasad.* He who hearing the Guru's words gives them a corner in his heart will reap a great reward. Refuse food is not a *sit prasad.* Tell all to refrain from giving or partaking of refuse food. *Bhajan* and *Bani* are fruitful, good and the only means of blessing".[117]

The socio-religious reforms by the Nirankaris and the Namdharis originally aimed to restore the Sikh faith on basic principles of Guru Nanak. Nirankaris looked as guide towards *Adi Grunth* and the teachings of the ten Sikh gurus. These movements were a protest against the growing Brahmanic influence and Brahmanism with its rituals and practices on Sikhism. However, it is interesting to note that while the Namdharis essentially wanted to oppose the Brahmanical practices they could not escape the same in their own rites and rituals. They could not leave the practice of *havan, jot, chandipath* and *gurumantar* etc. Thus, the Namdharis in spite of their best efforts could not remain absolutely immune to the Brahmanical influence.

With the process of the institutionalization of the socio-religious practices of these movements, vested interest among their leaders became more prominent.

Surprisingly enough, these movements ultimately concentrated their major efforts to retain their separate identity. In the process of doing so, they forgot the basic objectives of the movement, i.e., to reform the Sikh society in the light of its original religious principles.

In fact they initially wanted to discharge their functions, while considering themselves as an integral part of the Sikh society. It was an effort within the Sikh society and what was expected from these movements was to retain this particular goal before them. But incidentally their growing insistence on retaining their separate religious identity led to exclusiveness. Thus, it seems that instead of uniting the religious fiber of the Sikh society their attitude gave a separatist trend to these movements. It was, indeed the very negation of their original conviction.

REFERENCES

1. *Samadhi*—A monument erected at the cremation place of some notable Hindu or Sikh Saint.
2. *Mari*—is a place where Muslim Saints are burried.
3. *Report on the Census of the Punjab,* 1881, p. 138, Vol. I. Cal.
4. *The Sikhs,* p. 88.
5. *Chauri*—Fly whisk.
6. *The Home and Foreign Record,* Feb. 1854, No. 52. 54.
7. It refers to Baba Dayal.
8. *Nirankari chalan da chita* Shri Man Bhai Roop Singh 1857, *Baisakh* 12 *Samvat* 1941, Wednesday. There are three such *hukumnamas* now available at Nirankari Darbar Chandigarh with slight variations in the end and with different dates of their issue *Samvat* 1913 (2) *Baisakh* 12 *Samvat* 1941 (3) *Magh Samvat* 1923. See Appendix 'D'.
9. (i) *Affairs at Rawalpindi. The Home and Foreign Record,* July 1861, pp. 211-12. (ii) They used to quote from Sukhmani Sahib written by Guru Arjun Dev., the Vth Guru of the Sikh.

   * "जन लागा हर ऐके नायं ताकी आस ना बिरथी जाये"

   'One who is attached with the name of the one God shall not find his hope going in vain.'

   Sukhmani Sahib is part of *Adi Grunth* and has been widely quoted by the Nirankaris in their *Hukamnama.*
10. *The Twentieth Annual Report of the Ludhiana Mission,* 30th Sept. 1854, pp. 22-23.
11. *The Twentieth Annual Report of the Ludhiana Mission,* Sept. 30th, 1854, pp. 22-23.
12. 'That God does and causes everything to be done.' This was recorded by H.H. Morrison when he had a long discussion with Nirankari on the point of salvation on behalf of India Ludhiana Mission. *The Home and Foreign Record.* Feb. 1854, pp. 52-54
13. A central shirnine was developed at Rawalpindi which was described in 1861 by Orbison as a long low building open in front with a long room inside at one end of which were several copies of Adi Grunth set upon wooden stands. According to Webster "Orbisons description fits both the older, temporary darbar at Chandigarh as well as the large new one just next to it. This would suggest that the Nirankaris developed their own distinctive architectural style. Whether this differences is a matter of Historical accident or a deliberate intentions is not clear'.

    The Nirankari Sikhs, pp.11-12. Author has seen the photograph of Rawalpindi Darbar and both the buildings at Chandigarh and it appears to her that perhaps same design was taken up because of emotional and sentimental reasons and to revive their memories of the original place of Nirankaris'. See plate No. VI.
14. Whereas Namdharis used to have plain white piece of cloth to cover the Adi Grunths Nirankari used to adorns the grunth with colourful embroidered costly

cloth. *See Plate No. VIII.*

15. It refers to Canopy which is popularly called Chandowa or Chandani. Its purpose is not merely to keep the dust from falling on the Grunth but it adds to the honour and regality of place because in India kings used to have such clothes hanging from the roof on the throne.
16. *Affairs of Rawalpindi. The Home and Foreign Record,* July 1861, pp. 211-12.
17. *Census of the Punjab,* 1881, Vol. I, Calcutta 1883, p. 138.
18. *Nirankari Gurumat Prarmbhta,* p. 19.
19. *Affairs at Rawalpindi. The Home and Foreign Record,* July 1861, pp. 211-12. This practice of pouring oil by different devotees in the community lamp placed at the place of worship has been discontinued, in the course of time. Author had occasion to discuss this aspect with Baba Gurbax Singh Chief of the Nirankari Darbar at Chandigarh who explained that the reason behind this practice seems to provide light at the place of worship to which every devotee had his contribution.
20. *Census of Punjab,* 1881, p. 138.
21. Religious places of historical importance are there and are much reverenced even today but it was never encouraged by the Gurus themselves. According to a common belief, it was to the extent that once Guru Gobind Singh had specifically warned that if any attempt was ever made to commemorate his memory the person who does attempt shall be completely ruined.
22. *A glossary of the tribes and castes of the Punjab and North West Frontier Province,* p. 171.
23. कबीर गंगा तीर जो घर करे पीवह निरमल नीर
    बिन हर भगति न मुक्ति होये एऊ कहि रमें कबीर
    Adi Grunth
    Nirankari Chalan da Chitha.
24. *Maghi* on 18th Magh (31st Jan. 1855 A.D.) Baba Dayal had died. It was on the death anniversary of Baba Dayal and the practice is still prevalent when *kirtan* and scripture reading is held for three days continously for day and night.
25. नावन को तीरथ घने मन बऊरा रे पूजन को बहुदेव,
    कहु कबीर छूटन नही मन बऊरा रे छुटन दृरि को सेब
    Adi Grunth
    Nirankari Chalan da Chitha, Bhai Roop Singh.
26. *Nirankari Tract No. 14,* p. 35, Jan. 1932.
27. *Nirankari Chalan da Chitha.*
28. "After his (Dayal) death the sect established an Amritsar of its own at the Ley river near Rawalpindi". *Nirankaris* p. 21, Balwant Singh Gargi, *The Illustrated Weekly of India,* Vol. X CII 43 Sunday 24, 1971.
29 "Some Nirankaris were away from the active centres of Sikh religion. They established their own Amritsar tarantaran and Darbar Sahib. It is likely that this might have mitigated the influence of Sikh places of pilgrimages insisting and taking auspicious bath at these places but as a result of this the importance of their worship places gradually increased and historicity and miracles are attached to these places". *Banumule Itihasik Lekh,* p. 33, *Sikh Sudharak Lehran* by Hira Singh Dard.
30. *Mohurut*—An auspicious day to start or inaugurate some new thing calculated on the basis of astrology.
31. Important being Baba Khem Singh. Nihal Singh Chachi and Sardar Nand Singh. *Nirankari Gurmat Prarmbhta,* p. 69.

32. *Ibid.*
33. On the appeal of the Brahmins on earlier occasions important people of the city had passed resolutions against him and had boycotted him. Now they give him assurance that if he accepts the position of Brahmins all the resolutions passed against him would be turn-off and he would be again taken back into the society. *Nirankari Gurmat Sandesh*, p. 13.
34. *Nirankari Gurmat Sandesh*, 13. Also see *Nirankari Gurmat Prambhata*, p. 70.
35. ससे सजंम गएओ मूडे एक दान तुष कुथाएलपा
    साई पुत्री जजमान की सा तेरी एत धन खादे तेरा जनम गया
    "Patrons daughter is like your own daughter still you have broken the rule by taking an improper gift". *Nirankari Chalan da Chitha.*
36. *Be Gatta*—Among the Sanatan Hindu, one who dies on the bed is begatta or one who can not attain to salvation. That is why they put the dying man on the earth.
37. *Pind daan*—Offering of some prescribed things in the name of the dead to the Brahmins.
38. "राम दास सरोवर नाते सब उतरे पाप कमाते"
    Adi Grunth.
39. "कबीर माऐ मुंडआी तै गुरु की जाते भरम न जाई
    आप डुबे चहूं वेद में चेले दिये बहाए"
    Adi Grunth
40. *Gurmat:* Practices followed according to the ways prescribed by the gurus.
41. *The Nirankari Tract No. 12* Dooji Kiyari Sri Satguru Darbara Singh arte us samen de sikh, p. 51, 1926.
42. *See Appendix* 'C'.
43. *Nirankari Tract No. 14*, p. 83, 30 Jan. 1932.
44. *Report of the Census of the Punjab* taken on the 17th Feb., 1881, Vol. I (Calcutta 1883), p. 138.
45. *Report of the Census of India*, 1891, Vol. XIX, pp. 156-7.
46. *Annual Report of the Ludhiana Mission*, 1853, pp. 22-23.
47. *Nirankari Chalan da Chitha* (1857 A.D.)
48. चरणा धोए रहरास कर चरनामृत सिखा पिलाया
    कल तारन गुरु नानक आया
    Ibid.
49. "चरणा साध के धोयें धोय पीओ
    आरप साध को अपना जीओ"
    Ibid.
    Adi Grunth.
50. *Charnamrit*—Generally this practice was among the Hindus who used to take *Charnamrit* from the priest which was made of the water with which diety was given bath and then it was sweetened. May be Hindu practice perhaps it was adopted by Baba Dayal to emphasise that Nirankar resides in every heart and every soul. So whole Sangats (congregation) feet were considered pious and that was the real amrit prepared by the touch of living gods (men) but the author was told by Baba Gurbax Singh that it went out of practice during Baba Gurdit Singh's time.

51. *The report of the Census Part I,* The Punjab and its Feudateries, 1891, Vol. XIX, pp. 56-57.
51a. *Tikka:* It has been mentioned in the Will of Sahib Ratta Ji for other details see Appendix 'F'.
52. *Kuka Movement*, p. 22.
53. *Guru Ram Singh and the Kuka Sikhs,* Document No. 11, p. 10.
54. *Nam*—has been mentioned in the translation of these letters as mystical emblem of the Kukas.
55. *Home Deptt. Judicial B,* Oct. 1881, No. 188-195.
56. *Namdhari Itihas,* Part I, p. 109.
(a) Asa di war (b) Rahiras (c) Arti (d) Sohila have been discussed later on. These were the prayers to be performed by the Sikhs on almost everyday.
57. *Home Judicial B,* September 1880, No. 232-36.
58. *Home Department Judicial B,* October 1881, No. 188-195.
59. *Kookiyan di Vithya,* pp. 259-261.
60. *Home Judicial Proceedings,* August 1872, No. 273-284.
(ii) According to Dr. Fauja Singh (Kuka Movement, p. 23) this refers to the Sikh scripture The *Adi Grunth.* But M.M. Ahluwalia (Kukas, p. 47) considers the Grunth of Guru Gobind Singh to be the *Dasum Grunth* which is given equal importance as Adi Grunth among the Namdharis.
61. *Foreign Department Political A.* March 1867, No. 111-112.
62. *Home Department Judicial B,* No. 188-195.
63. By this he means Akhand path which is reciting the Grunth constantly without interruption and break till it finishes. It is still prevalent among the Sikhs.
64. This practice seems to have been encouraged with a purpose, it is well known that the Brahmins consider cow-dung as purifying thing the cleaning by it the place of worship becomes purer and cleaner. The Namdharis were specifically instructed to avoid the cow-dung and use mud for cleaning the place of worship. The significance of this does not lie in clearning the place of worship by cow-dung or mud but it lies behind the spirit with which the Brahmins used the cow-dung for purifying the place and the attempt of the Namdharis seems to be the changing of this practice and thus by creating a distinction in one of the processes of worship.
65. Too much emphasis was stressed by Baba Ram Singh on the personal sanitation and cleanliness of his followers perhaps in order to show that the Namdharis were much purer in their performance of their religious practices then the Brahmins and again the idea seems to be of creating a sense of distinction and not falling in line with the prevalent practices of Hindus in this connection.
66. *Home Department Judicial B,* October 1881, No. 188-195.
67. Certain letters of Baba Ram Singh which Ganda Singh saw with Namdharis in Punjab also speak of the detailed method for performing the Akhand Path, Havan, Hom etc. *Kookiyan Di Vithya*, pp. 245-250. For details see Appendix-H.
68. *Home Department Judicial B,* October 1881, pp. 188-195.
69. "कहूं ना होमं कहूं न दानन
कहूं ना संजम कहूं न इसानं
कहूं ना तसबी कहूं ना माला
कहूं ना होमम कहूं ना ज्वाला"
Dasam Granth, p. 563.

70. इक होम दान जु बीरा
अरि करि जासु अधीरा *Dasam Granth,* p. 683.

71. Method to make insence.
1. Badam 2. Coconut 3. Chuhahre 4. Raisins 5. Ilaichi Chotti 6. Illachi Bari 7. Long 8. Vermillion 9. Mushak Kapoor 10. Kapoor Kala 11. Lal Chandan 12. White Chandan 13. Kesar 14. Kasturi 15. Char 16. Mutha Kali 17. Indu Jaun 18. Desi Jaun 19. Til 20. Goal 21. Bhoj Patra 22. Sugar 23. Ghee.
Sri Mukhwak Padhshahi Barah
Ath Akhand Path ki Riti
Kookiyam di Vithya, p. 332. See Appendix X.
For various details see Appendix, *Ibid.*

72. *Foreign Department Political A,* February 1867, No. 154-157.

73. *Kookiyan di Vithya,* Letter No. 45, pp. 306-307.

74. *Ibid.*

75. *Ibid.*

76. *Foreign Department Political A,* Feb. 1867 No. 154-157

77. Here it seems that M.M. Ahluwalia (Kookas, p. 48) has over simplified the issue and created an impression that this Chundee path was essentially and fundamentally different from the traditional Chundee path prevalent among the Hindus. However, if it was so why the word 'Chundee' was not deliberately avoided to remove any such misunderstanding of its association with the Hindu Goddess, secondly the emphasis on Jyoti again leads one to believe that 'Chundee' of Namdharis was hardly different from the Chundee of the Hindus and Jyoti the symbol of the Goddess remained important among the Namdharis.

78. *Kookas,* p. 48.

79. *Foreign Department Political A,* March 1867, No. 111-112.

80. Second stanza of the above couplet : has the name of sultan who was a sufi saint popularly known as Sakhi Sarwar in Punjab.
Sakhi Sarvar : No one knows exactly when sultan lived. Mr. Ibbestin places him in the 12th century and Major Temple in the 13th while there are accounts in the sakhis of the Sikhs which represent sultan as contemporary of Guru Nanak and as having presented a water melon to him.
Census Report 1891, p. 132, Lahore.
Foreign Deptt. Political A, March 1867, No. 111-112.

81. *Satguru Bilas,* p. 132.

82. *Home Department Judicial Proceedings,* August 1872, No. 273-284.

83. Likewise a total ban was placed to the visit of such places of popular resort as *marhi* (cremation mark), *Khanquah* (Muslim monosteries), *Mazars* (graves of saints). These places were generally visited by ignorant and superstitious people who begged the granting of their wishes and often made offerings to them.

84. *Foreign Department Political* A, February 1867, No. 154-157.

85. *Kuka Movement,* p. 24. For Reference about MC-Andrew See *Foreign Department Political* A, Feb. 1868, No. 202-203.

86. *Foreign Department Political A,* Feb. 1868, No. 202-203.

87. *Namdhari Itihas Part I,* p. 64.

88. *Ibid.*

89. Baba Ram Singh was popularly known by the name of his horse also. As it says Ram Singh "himself rode a favourite mare and was addressed as 'Chiniwala Padshah' Lord of the Chini Horse". In the contemporary painting also he is seen riding on a horse. See plate No. VIII.

90. *Namdhari Itihas Part I,* p. 141.
91. Author of Tarikh-e-Wakri (p. 146) Maulvi Ghulam Bhikh Jullundri had visited Bhaini Sahib himself. He records that this sect increased very fast and within no time whole village and mauzas had adopted the Kuka faith. Official sources also speak of this. See for details *Foreign Department Political A,* 2nd February, 1868, No. 202-203.
92. *Foreign Department Political A,* March 1867, No. 111-112.
93. *Foreign Department Political A,* 2nd Feb. 1868, No. 202-203.
94. (i) Major Perkis District Superintendent of Ludhiana writes that conversion were generally made from "Jats, Tirkhan, Chamar and Muzbees. Very few are obtained from amongst Khuttrees, Brahmins and Bunneas".
(ii) It was reported from Gurdaspur "that the most Kuka disciples are viz. Tirkhan, Lohar, Libanee, Saynee, Bhatee, Kulal etc.".
Foreign Department Political A, 2nd February, No. 154-157 see Appendix 'I'.
95. Report of Mac-Andrew 20th Nov., 1871 *Kuka Papers* No. 356, 1872.
96. *Home Judicial 'B' Proceedings,* Aug. 1879, No. 257-259.
97. *Ibid.*
98. *Home Department Judicial B Proceedings,* October 1881, No. 188-195. Translation of correspondence between Ram Singh and some of his followers. Demi-official letters from J.P. Warburton S.P. Ludhiana H.N. Miller I. General of Police Punjab dated 31st August, 1878, Ludhiana.
99. *Kookiyan di Vithya,* p. 35.
100. *Sapt Sring,* pp. 14-15.
101. *Chowkidar* of village Khote on 4th June, 1863, reported at Police Station 'Bagha Purana' District Firozpur that for "two or three days Ram Singh with four or five hundred followers had assembled at his village and were behaving in a very extraordinary manner. They talked sedition, said the country would soon be theirs and they would speedily be one lakh and twenty five thousand armed men to back them, that they would only take a fifth of the land's produce from the cultivators and were altogether comporting themselves in a very extraordinary manner".
Document No. I *Guru Ram Singh and the Kuka Sikh,* p. 23.
102. Colonel Mac-Andrew Deputy Inspector General of Police Lahore were appointed to take care of the Mela at Anandpur. Mac-Andrew made good preparation to watch the mela and take action if something happen, "I informed the Commissioner of Jullunder and consulted with him at that station on the 12th. I also sent orders to Hoshiarpur to collect as many police as could be spared from other duties. On the 13th I arrived at Hoshiarpur and consulted Mr. Perkins Deputy Commissioner as to the arrangements to be made taking with me an Inspector, Deputy Inspector and 50 men of the Hoshiarpur Police and and a Deputy Inspector and 10 men from Jullunder. All were picked all men were old soldiers, Mohammedans and Rajputs".
Document No. XVII
Copy of the letter from T.H. Tharton Esq. Secretary to Government of Punjab to T.D. Forsyth Esq.
C.B. Commissioner and Supdt. Jullender Division No. 279 dated 27th March 1867.
Guru Ram Singh and the Kuka Sikhs, p. 51.
103. *Sri Satgura Bilas,* p. 173.
104. *Foreign Department Political A,* February 1868, No. 202-203.

105. *Ibid.*
This record describes some words as follows:
(a) *Amrut :* is holy water given to all Sikhs converts. It is simply *sherbut* of sugar and water.
(b) *Munter*—means a charm incantation, secret consultation, private advice.
(c) Translated this would be "God was born at Huzro, but lives at Bhainee".
(d) This means "God was born at Patna, but lives at Nundpore.

106. *Ibid.*
Incidentally Baba Ram Singh had given no satisfactory explanation to the allegations levelled against him by the Pujaris. The counter allegation is hardly an explanation for the questions posed by the Pujaris.

107. *Basant Ank of Satjug Samvat 1986,* p. 43, Column I.
108. *The Gurudwaras Reforms Movement and the Sikh Awakening,* p. 37.
109. *Home Department Judicial B,* October 1881, 188-195.
110. *Dushalla*—A cloth to cover the body used as an upper garment.
111. *Pagree*—Turban
112. *Doputta*—A cloth to cover the head generally used by the ladies. In this context it means a robe of honour.
113. *Foreign Department Political A,* Feb. 1868, No. 202-203.
114. *Sri Satguru Bilas,* p. 88.
Says at Darbar Sahib he got one *Dashala* and one *Dastar* and *Siropa* from Jhunda Boonga he received one doputta and a *dastar.* At Baba Atal he received one kinari Dupatta and a dastar.
115. *Charanamrit*—Discussed at length earlier.
116. *Sitprasad*—Food left by a spiritual guide.
117. *Home Department Judicial B Proceedings,* October, 1881, No. 188-195.

4

Reactions to Social Problems

Both the Nirankari and Namdhari movements were basically religious reform movements. They wanted to bring changes in the Sikh religion and society. Sustained efforts were made by them to revive Sikhism in the light of the teachings of the Sikh Gurus. For any religious reform it was essential to change the Sikh society also. Religion and society are so inter-linked that change or reform in one is bound to have an impact on the other. Both these movements aimed at creating a Sikh society which was based on the principle of equality without the class and caste distinction, was free from evils like cheating, superstitions, and where one could build his or her character without fear. These movements pictured a society which could be free from the dominance of the Brahmins, and superficial rites and rituals. A society where everybody could earn honestly to meet his both ends.

Thus, both these movements were conscious to various socio-religious superstitions and ceremonies that had crept into the Sikh society. It was with this end in view that they tried to generate social awareness against the superstitions, dogmas, rituals and other social taboos. To appreciate it properly one needs to study the contemprary social life and the view-points of both the movements towards them. Thus, a separate and comparative study of the social reforms undertaken by these movements is imperative.

Nirankaris

As far as the Nirankaris were concerned they either challenged or reformed various social ceremonies and practices performed at the time of the birth, marriage and death, conrning polygamy, prostitution, widow remarriage, caste system and untouchability. Nirankari *Guru* taught the Sikhs and others to have full faith in the *Adi-Grunth*. Only the rites and ceremonies consistent with the teachings of the *Adi-Grunth* were to be performed at different occasions. *Nirankari Chalan da Chitha* records in detail the methods or rites to be performed at the time of birth. It says when a child is born whether a girl or a boy one should read God's words and 'Karah Parsad'[1] should be offered in the Gurudwara. There is no *Sootak*[2] at all, because birth and death occur according to the will of God. Forty days after the birth of the child, mother and child be taken to *Durbar Sahib* and again *Karah Parsad* be offered and the child be named according to the first word of the *shabad* (couplet) which comes in *Adi Grunth* after opening it.[3,4] It was indeed a very simple ceremony considering the then prevalent system, among the Hindu and Sikh society which placed much emphasis on the functions which were held the 13th, 21st and the 40th days after the child birth. On these occasions not only were the relatives invited and big feasts were offered, but Brahmins were also given large sums of money for performing various ceremonies.

After 'attaining a certion age he or she was engaged and even at that time *Karah-Parshad* was offered and words in the praise of God were to be sung and later the marriage was performed as prescribed in the *Adi Grunth*.[5] Prior to the Nirankaris despite the system of *Anand Viyah* or *Anand Karaj* as recorded in *Adi Grunth* it was performed according to the Hindu, Brahmanical and Vedic rites. *Prem Sumrag Grunth* an important source speaks about the ways and means of Sikh living, that boy and girl should sit on their own respective couches. Fire should be burnt with *ghee* and wood and they should seek the blessings of god of fire, goddess and other duties. After giving the details of their names name of the parents, grandparents and their caste, they should put *ghee* in the fire seven times.[6]

During Ranjit Singh's time marriages in the royal family were performed according to Brahmanical practice. In this direction the Nirankaris had a major contribution in simplifying the marriage ceremony which they called 'Anand marriage'. Baba Dayal was strictly against the dominant role of Brahmins in religious and social matters. He, therefore, could not tolerate that his marriage be performed by the Brahmins. Moreover, his vast study of the *Adi Grunth* had taught him that the book contains instenctions pertaining to all social functions and ceremonies. Baba Dayal's marriage itself was a big milestone on the way to Anand Marriage.[7]

The Anand Marriage was performed in the local Gurdwara with the recitation of *Lavan Anand*[8] and other hymns from the *Adi Grunth* "This marriage is very significant in history for its simplicity, freedom from Brahmanical rites and devotion to the words of Gurus. It also added to the reputation of Bhai Dayal as a practical reformer".[9] Baba Dayal used to say "follow not the custom that maketh thee forsake the lord blessed is the love sayeth Nanak that maintaineth thy honour with the loard.[10]

Even after the performance of the marriages of Baba Dayal and his children without the help of a Brahmin, such marriages could not be made popular. As these marriages were not considered to be in accordance with the Hindu Dharamshastra. As was recorded by the Census report, "The bride and the bridegrooms instead of circumambulating the sacred fire, walk round the *Adi Grunth.* The ceremony is conducted not by a Brahmin, but by a *granthee* and the finance or bride sits in public with her face uncovered".[11] This is a description of the Anand Marriage performed by the Nirankaris[12]. Credit for popularizing the *Anand Viyah* goes to Baba Darbara Singh.

Historic Anand Marriage

On Chet 1, 1911 BS (13th March 1855 AD) Baba Darbara Singh called a conference of the members and admirers of the Nirankari faith.[13] In this conference he made special reference to the then prevalent marriages where priest used to recite some verses in Sanskrit which nobody could follow. He considered it quite irrelevant and meaningless. Baba Darbara Singh wanted to give a practical shape to Anand marriages, therefore, he called out for a boy and girl who could offer themselves for this type of marriage. Because month of Chitra was considered inauspicious for marriages nobody was ready to take the curse on him. But Nihal Singh stood up with his only son Bhola Singh. Hari Singh[14] offered his daughter Nihali to be married with Bhola Singh according to *Gurmat.*[15] The couple was married in the presence of *Guru Grunth Sahib* with the recitation of *lavan*. The couple walked around the holy scripture four times accompanied recitation of the four hymns, or *lavan* and then bowed down before the Guru Grunth Sahib, thus symbolizing a complete submission to its teachings. This simple marriage was performed in the morning without the assistance of *Pundits* and *Brahmins.*[16] One of the *Hukumnanas says,* "If Adi Grunth was not available those lavan could be written on a paper kept on a couch and the couple could circumscribe that" Indeed the marriage ceremony was made very simple by the Nirankaris.[17]

After the successful performance of the Anand marriage several such marriages were performed in the areas of Pothohar.[17a] Baba Darbara Singh himself used to go wherever such marriages were to be performed. It was always done against heavy opposition and protest by other sections in the village like Brahmins, barbers and the leaders of village. At Fateh Jung, Kala Gujran and Jubbie prominent marriages were performed in his presence.[18] However, during the initial stage it was never performed without strong protest.

Anand Karj at Amritsar

Amritsar was great centre of Sikhism. Consequently, Baba Darbara Singh wanted to perform at least one Anand marriage there to practically demonstrate the extent to which he had simplified this ceremony which so far had been dominated upon by ritualistic practices under the Brahmin leadership. Because *Darbar Sahib* Amritsar was a common platform for the Sikhs any order coming from there had the religious sanctity of the *Gurus.* Had this marriage been performed there it would have created greater impact on the Sikhs in general. But the Jathedar of *Akal Takht* and head *grunthee* of *Darbar Sahib* did not allow him because they themselves were sunk deep in the Brahmanical practices. Darbara Singh was keen to perform it at Amritsar only, so he chose the *Dharmsala* of Mahant Dayal Dass. While performing this marriage at Amritsar in 1861 Baba Darbara Singh prophecied, "Today people do not allow them to perform this marriage according to *Gurmat* at *Akal Takht* but a time will come when all Sikh marriages would be performed in this way".[19] Long and sustained efforts of the Nirankaris paved the way for the enactment of the Anand Marriage Act.[20].

Position of Women

Polygamy was quite common in the Indian society since long and the Sikhs were no exception to it. This customs had underrated the importance of women mostly making their lives miserable. Some sort of attempt was needed to improve the position of women in the Sikh society. Polygamy needed to be discouraged. In this direction, the Nirankaris made a pioneering effort when they opposed it among their followers. The Glossary of Tribes and Castes, refers "polygamy is prohibited among the Nirankari".[21]

Widowhood has been a perpetual curse for women in Indian society. They were considered inauspicious and at times were debarred from holding property. But the Nirankaris took great initiative in taking up the cause of the widows and arranging their marriages. It is recorded that "some fifty such marriages have taken place among them during the last ten years".[22] In one copy of the *Nirankari Chalan da Chitha* preserved at Nirankari Darbar, Chandigarh it is said "Baba Dayal has ordered one thing more that when the husband of some lady dies and she becomes a widow, she can be married to the brother of the deceased husband and in case that lady does not agree to marry her brother-in-law, she can be married into some other family. The point is to avoid the widowhood of the lady".[23] It was essentially to check her deteriorating position in the society and at the same time prevent her from adopting an immoral path because of her neglected position.

Prostitution was yet another social disease which was widely prevalent in Punjab like any other part of India and the problem needed some remedy. The Nirankaris were against the institution of prostitution. Nirankari sources mention that during Baba Dayal's time one prostitute used to take some ingredients from the shop of Baba Dayal. Once, she forgot to bring money. She told the Baba to send his son with her, who could bring money and then take the things. When other shopkeepers asked Baba Dayal that when he knew the lady and she was his regular customer, then why he did not send his son with her. Baba Ji replied that one should not have the company of such people because even that can bring a bad name to the person and the family.[24]

Against Caste System

The Nirankaris did not believe in any caste or class distinctions within their fold. Maclagan records "The sect recruits all classes".[25] However, on becoming a Nirankari the caste or social status of one who accepted it was not affected, in any way. Conversion to the Nirankari sect was thus going to change their religious outlook and not their social status.[26] A Nirankari could be taken into the ranks of the British army without any fuss and they were not debarred from any service simply by vietue of being Nirankaris.[27] On the contrary Kukas were earlier serving in the British and native states' armies but after their clash with the butchers British government became apprehensive and services were debarred for them. However, some modern historians are of the opinion that it was an order of Baba Ram Singh which made the Kukas leave the services of the British Government. On seeing the British attitude towards the Kukas, the native states of Kuka regions like Patiala, Nabha, Jeend, etc., also prohibited Kuka enlistment in their army and other services. "No Kuka was to be taken into the services."[28] For the Nirankaris, anybody who was not drinking and smoking could be a Nirankari. An old magazine of Punjab *Phulwar* says "*Sahajdhari* and *Kesadhari* both can be Sikhs because Nirankaris were not much bothered about the outer appearance of a man". But Hindus had to disassociate themselves from the sale and use of tobacco."[29] But H.A. Rose says that smoking was prohibited for the Hindus, but they could deal in its materials. "The sect is recruited from all castes and number some 38,000 Sikhs".[30]

Rites of the Dead

Death is generally a matter of grief and sorrow but the Nirankaris had a different view about it. According to them, "Death is the eternal truth of the world and one who comes into this world has to retire and go back. It should be a matter of rejoicing and happiness".[31] The *Hukumnama* of the Nirankaris says that one should only lament the death of others if he himself is going to live for ever.[32] Wailing is futile, Kabir says, "Why weep at the death of a saint who is in fact returning to his own home. One should cry only for the wordly people who are living a futile life."[33]

A Missionary report of 1854 says, "They do not bury their dead because the Musalmans and Christians do so, they will not burn them because that would assimilate them too much to the Hindus. They, therefore, throw them into water".[34] According to the Nirankari sources it was done for Baba Dayal and that too to avoid clash and conflict. They were boycotted by the Hindus and Sikhs under the influence of the dominated society. Public places of water worship and cremation were forbidden for them. Thus, when, "Baba Ji passed away in 1855 AD at the ripe old age of seventy two, his body was entrusted to the running waters of the Leyee River at the place he selected as the people would not allow his cremation at the public cremation ground. That place hereafter came to be called as Dayalsar".[35] The *Hukumnama* of the Nirankaris says, "And when by the grace of the Formless one, a Sikh has completed his life and call comes and the Sikh departs then, we cover the body with a white cloth and singing hymns carry for cremation or for releasing it into a flowing stream".[36] All other after death rituals which the Brahmins prescribed were not allowed. "Similarly, at funerals they dispense with the Brahmins and the Hindu ceremonial generally, instead of weeping and mourning they sing hymns".[37] They only recite *Gurbani*, put on white clothes and go to their shops or business. They do not mourn for many days. Neither do they attach any impurity to the house of the dead. *Sootak*[28] and superstitions etc. were not followed.

Sootak

The Nirankaris were not only condemning the superstitions, but were breaking them. They were defying the hitherto strong rituals and dogmas. After the death of a person in some homes, people used to think that there was *sootak* in that particular home so they would not take food there. To the extent that even saintly and godly people were not free from it. Once Bhai Diwan Singh a saint of village Mangwal was on a visit to Rawalpindi. He had a large following of his own and was much respected. He was explaining the Sikh scriptures and holding long discourses on them. Two brothers who were followers of Baba Dayal asked for his permission to invite Bhai Diwan Singh at dinner, the invitation was extended and accepted, but a tragedy took place and one of the brothers died and cremational preparations had to be done alongside the dinner. Bhai Diwal Singh came to know of it and said, "How can I take such dinner when some one dead is there. Ordinarily the food in such cases is polluted for thirteen days, but for a saint it is polluted for 21 days".[39] Dinner was refused by the saint and his other followers. When Baba Dayal came to know about the incident, he brought the food to his own congregation and asked his followers to eat it if they really believe in Nirankari principles and teachings. Baba Dayal said "Birth and death is the will of God and eatables are pure. Those who really know God do not fear from superstitions".[40]

Saradh Ritual

Among the Hindus, after the death of a person his *Saradh*[41] is observed annually. In a particular month it is done and *pandits* tell the date of the *saradh* of a person. On this day a big feast is prepared and offered to relatives, Brahmins and birds, etc. Nirankaris had forbidden their followers to observe death anniversaries or *saradhs.* The *Hukumnama* directed the Nirankaris that no *saradh* should be observed because Brahmans declare that the ancestors of the Khatris and other castes have become crows, dogs, snakes, cows and frogs. They demand the feast for themselves. "Fathers are not obeyed when they are alive but when they die offerings are made to them. Unfortunate ancestors can not receive that because crows and dogs had already eaten that".[42] Nirankaris wanted to bring up the youngsters among their followers with certain convictions and respect for the elders. This would have helped them to achieve their goal. They were given a code of conduct as to what should be the behaviour of the children towards their parents. "They must serve them because parents were the ones who brought them into this world. The Mother took care of the child and protected by keeping him in her womb for ten (nine) months. Then during childhood his bringing up and care was done by the parents".[43] The *Hukumnama* especially ordered that at no stage should a child forget his duties towards his parents.

The Nirankaris enjoined upon their followers by the order of the *guru* to abstain from drinking and eating meat or falling in other vices. They were made to understand by quoting Kabir : "All those who eat meat, consume opium or drink wine would lose all the charities or pilgrimages they had done".[44]

The Nirankaris who were always inspired by the teachings of Nanak in their basic principles had attempted to institutionalize the element of charity as one of the inherent elements of the Sikh society. They propagated the idea that the benefit of one's earning should flow from the 'haves' to the 'have nots' and to give a religious sanctity to this idea, they used Nanaks' saying 'kirt karo'[45] and 'wand ke Chhako'.[46] This naturally aimed at establishing a practice in which fulfilling the needs of the poor may be looked upon as a matter of duty and not as mere charity. It seems that through this way the Nirankaris looked to the productive capacity and the consuming need of their followers in totality. If this principle was to be followed in work and spirit, it was bound to solve the problem of the 'have nots' to a great extent.

The majority of the Nirankaris came from the urban regions of Rawalpindi, Pothohar, Dhanni, Peshawar and other places in North West Frontier. Most of the followers came from the business communities who were Khatris and Aroras, many of whom were shopkeepers and traders. They were preached another tenet in the words: *Sach Bolo Poora Tolo* which means speak the truth and weigh accurately.

The Nirankari *Gurus* wanted to take out their followers from the gulf of debt and loans. They were against the money lenders who had adopted usury as a profession.[47] The followers were also asked not to take loan for the purposes of *dowries,* etc. and infact prohibited their followers from making a show through *dowry*. Although they could not restrict the expenses on marriage like the Namdharis, still there was a check on the extravagance and mere show which had come to characterize marriages within the Sikh society.

It seems that this movement being essentially urban based had a relatively greater impact on the people living in cities and towns than in the villages. Therefore, it would not be far from truth to call it a movement which aimed at reforming the social life of the people of a class which could roughly be termed as the 'middle class'. The reformers of this movement took special note of various social evils prevailing in the Sikh society as a result of the influence of Brahmins.

The Nirankaris instead of reacting mildly against it or adopting a middle path for achieving their objective, insisted on radical changes. It seems that they purposely avoided any change within the prevailing framework of Brahmanical practices. They felt that it was likely to be merged in Hinduism in due course of time. They, therefore, through their teachings tried to retain a separate identity and taught social values to their followers with a specific purpose. Their attempt in the direction of social reforms indeed arrested the drifting of Sikh society towards the fold of Brahmanical religion.

For most of their teachings they relied on the *Adi Grunth* and considered it as the basic source of religious, social and moral authority for the Sikhs.

Namdharis

In the preceding pages an attempt has been made to see the various social reforms undertaken by the Nirankaris. It has also been pointed out as to how they had protested against such social customs and traditions which were essentially based on Brahmanical practices. These reforms, though confired relatively, to the middle class, gradually created a social awareness in the Sikh society. By the mid-nineteenth century another movement, i.e., the Namdhari emerged with its relatively greater impact on the peasants and the common class of people in a different region of Punjab. However it seems that the receptive capacity of the Sikh society in general had largely increased because of the efforts of Nirankaris. Perhaps both the desire and the need for social reform was increasingly felt.

As far as the Namdharis were concerned their social reform could be broadly divided into two sections, first reforming individuals' personal life and action and secondly protesting against the prevalent social taboos. It may be pointed out that their dislike of Brahmanical practices was milder and in many of their practices the prevalent belief in the Hindu customs could be noticed. However, the fact remains that Punjab witnessed another social reform movement in the 19th century which took special note of the prevailing social customs and superstitions in the rural society.

Baba Ram Singh considered that no social reform was possible with weak health of the people and therefore to him the sound health and body was the prerequisite for any reform. Therefore, he wanted to deal with it before conceiving or undertaking any programme of social reform. He thus, emphasized much upon the personal health and hygiene.

He paid much attention even to matters like brushing of the teeth everyday, cleaning the hair or taking bath. They were very minor things, but to his rural following it became a more significant part of life when stressed by their religious *guru*. Official sources record "the converts are ordered to bath the entire body and wash the hair of their heads every morning at three o' clock. After bathing they are to pray, read aloud or repeat shalocksor selected verses of the Grunth."[48] He was stressing this even when he was in exile. In one of his intercepted letters he writes "I can, but repeatedly write to the brethren that they should bathe early every morning. For it is the Guru Sahib's order that all who rise in the third watch of the night and after bathing themselves (including the hair of the head) will receive a reward equal to that of giving strings of pearls in charity"[49] (Sic).

Individuals constitute the society. Preaching of moral and social values collectively is hardly possible without making the individuals subscribe to those principles. Therefore in the teachings of Namdharis, individual conduct received a significant position. Major Parkins wrote in 1866: that "On initiation all vices are supposed to be fore-swrong such as lying, stealing, drinking adultery etc. are strictly forbidden."[50] Baba Ram Singh emphasized greatly on developing the capacity of self-control. He instructed his people, "No one should take or steal anything belonging to another. Whosoever disregards these instructions will suffer eternal hunger and nudity".[51] In order to lead a pure and simple life, wine and meat were prohibited to the fraternity.[52] Here the Namdharis resembled the Nirankaris who also put restriction on eating meat, drinking wine and smoking.

Baba Ram Singh used to give more weight to the moral values. He said that only the virtues of man could improve the society. He especially emphasised the virtue of Charity. In one of his letters written to his *sangat*, he said "Give food, drink and clothing as much as you can to the poor and hungry."[53]

Whereas the Nirankaris emphasized on the correct weighing and truthfulness, Baba Ram Singh also did not believe in taking too much profits or false weighing. *Satguru Bilas* records that Baba Ram Singh was giving to *seers* more than the general rate.[54] He adviced his brother in a letter from exile, "The profits of the shop will increase considerably if you avoid demanding too much gain and if you look to unreasonable gain your profits will diminish."[55]

Emphasis on Equality and Opposition to Caste System

A sense of equality among the members of the fraternity was established through the practice of touching the feet of one Namdhari by the other, after the prayers. It was done irrespective of age and status in the society. This reminds one of the practice of *charnamrit* among the Nirankaris, aimed at perhaps the same object. While the Nirankaris had done away with the practice of *charnamrit,* among Namdharis the practice of touching feet remained prevalent.

Like the Nirankaris the Namdhari also did not subscribe at least in principle to the caste distinction. As early as 1863, official sources were reporting, "The leading features of the doctrine, Ram Singh preaches are, he abolishes all distinction of castes among Sikhs."[57] According to Dr. Fauja Singh, "Rigours of the caste system were an anathema to Baba Ram Singh. He refuses to have any regard for the artificial caste barriers. His mission was for all castes and all religions."[58] Although Ram Singh's fraternity accepted followers from all castes and classes, but it is doubtful to say that they had made any substantial achievement in that direction in the light of the practices prevalent among them. Quite contrary to the Nirankaris, the Namdharis were forbidden to dine with anybody except the Kukas. They did not eat food cooked by others. They had no social or matrimonial alliances with any one other than Kukas.[59] In their effort to retain separate identity of Namdharis, Baba Ram Singh unconsciously made it a small group based on close and sectarian grounds.

Marenco Elsiep Ethne Kaplan has tried to look at this movement from a different angle. He is of the opinion that the spread of the movement remained in a particular caste Ramgharia. Sikhs because Baba Ram Singh offered them an upward mobility.[60,61] There is no doubt that the very desire for an upward social mobility created a larger following among the lower caste of the society. However this must have provided less incentive to the people of higher class in joining the Namdharis.

Attitude Towards Social Ceremonies and the Allied Issues

In the matter of general social practices Baba Ram Singh tried to enlighten people through his teachings. He advised his followers not to cry and weep at the death of their relatives or friends because it happens according to the will of the God. He wrote "O, Khalsa if a relative dies you should not mourn or grieve after him but in keeping with your means perform in the name of your departed relative, an act of charity, *bhog*, *path* and feeding and clothing of the Brahmin should be done. Mourning and grieving is rebellion against God and a trouble of the body without any recompense."[62](Sic) Baba Ram Singh said mourning and crying not only harms the living beings but it troubles the departed soul also "I have also heard that the person mourned for is occasioned for grief, the droppings from the eyes and noses of the mourners fall upon the soul of the departed and make him cry out "Oh! God some of the mourners may die it will be well in order that I may rest at peace."[63]

Nirankaris did not believe in the elaborate ceremonies to be performed after the death of a person. In their socio-religious practices, there was no place for Brahmins. But one can infer from the letters of Baba Ram Singh that he could not completely break off with the influence of Brahmins so far rites of the dead were concerned. He writes in detail about the ceremonies to be performed after his death if he died in exile. He said "In case I die here get *Akhand Paths* done after me, give clothings to *Sadhus* and Brahmins, get five (*Akhand Paths*) to be done at Muktsar and spend one hundred fifty rupees for that."[64]

The major contribution of the Namdharis in the field of social reforms relates to the matter of education, marriage ceremony and the social neglect of the women. No reform is possible without social awareness, which is always linked with education. Therefore, Baba Ram Singh emphasized the importance of education. He writes, "As soon as children grow to an undestendable age make them learn the letters."[65] In another letter he emphasizes that education should be imparted to both boys and girls. It is important to note that he not only wanted his people to read and write, but he also strongly recommended that as soon as they come to understand they should be given education and taught properly.[66]

These instructions were not only for boys but for girls also. He advocated education for women: "Educate your sisters, women, daughters and sons and they will easily learn the *bani* (prayers) without education prayers can not be properly learnt."[67] To the agriculturist class Baba Ram Singh definitely gave a new message of enlightenment. Once a Sikh told Baba Ram Singh that he cannot read letters. Baba Ram Singh replied, "You keep on throwing one stone here everyday and within few days there will be a heap of stones. If by throwing one stone everyday there is such a big heap then if you keep on learning one letter everyday, you can read and write."[68] Baba Ram Singh was trying to impart education to his rural followers through simple and practical examples. In the teachings of the Nirankaris there was no special reference to education because such a need was not felt by them as perhaps most of their urban followers were educated. According to Dr. Fauja Singh, M.M. Ahluwalia and Jaswant Singh Jas, he prohibited his followers from learning English or attending the schools or colleges run by the Government. However Ganda Singh has contested this view.[69]

The marriage ceremonies which were dominated by the Brahmins, was another important issue which drew Baba Ram Singh's attention. "Guru Ram Singh was conscious of the prevailing poverty in the land. He also knew how the Brahminic influence had increased immensely since the days of Ranjit Singh. He decided to save his meek and simple disciples from costly marriage ceremonies and other expensive rituals. This was to save them from avoidable indebtedness as well as the over-powering sway of the *Pundits*."[70]

He initiated Anand marriage system in 1863 at village Khote in district Firozpur.[71] On this occasion the daughter of a carpenter was married in the family of the Aroras. Regarding this aspect Dr. Fauja Singh remarks "Inter caste marriage was considered an essential factor in the emotional integration of the society."[72]

Some details about the marriages performed according to Namdhari practice deserves mention. According to it on the day of the marriage early in the morning after *kirtan* of *Asa-de-war*[73] *Havan* was started in a *Vedi* and five Singhs used to recite the bani of *Jopji Sahib*,[74] *Jasp Sahib*,[75] *Chaupai Sahib*,[76] *Chandi charitar*[77] and *Akal ustat*[78]. Then *lavan* was recited from the *Adi Grunth* and the couple used to circumscribe the *Havan*. Bride used to sit without covering the face. It meant denouncing the *parda* system. The only new thing in this marriage was his doing away with the Brahmins. But it must be noted that he could not do away with the *Vedi* or fire. In matter of details of the practices at the time of marriage the Namdharis differed from the Nirankaris who claim to have initiated Anand marriage as early as in 1855. Though, Namdharis also take the credit of being the pioneers in this field, but historically and chronologically it was performed first by the Nirankaris. However, the Namdharis emphasized more on making the marriages inexpensive. Generally, the expenditure on their each marriage used to be in current terms, Rs. 1.25 as fee for baptizing, Rs. 1.25 paise for tying the knot of the cloth of bride and groom and Rs. 2.50 paise for *karah parshad*. Such marriages were performed in big gatherings. According to Dr. Fauja Singh, "A simple and inexpensive form of marriage was substituted for the old one which was so notorious for complexity and extravagance ... this reform was not merely a social necessity to save the girl's, parents from tentalizing life-long mental agony and to stamp out the root cause of all female degradation, but also an economic urgency to prevent the unfortunate among the people from falling precipitably into the iron-clutches of the money lenders."[79] Bhai Jodh Singh was also of the opinion that Namdharis contributed much in reducing the expenditure and show at their marriages. It was made a very simple affair, but it is felt that the Namdharis could not stop the use of *vedi* even though fire had no significance among the *Sikhs*.[80]

This programme of making marriages simple and inexpensive must have attracted more and more people into the fraternity of *Kukas*. It is confirmed by the official record which says "It is stated that the attractions the sect presents which induce men to come forward and join it are the moderate expenditure at marriage ceremonies and immunity from Brahmanical oppression and exaction which the Namdhari followers enjoyed."[81]

Position of Women

One of the most striking and significant contributions of the Namdharis was their attempt to undertake various reform measure to improve the condition of women.

Since long women enjoyed a respectable position in the

Indian society and mere even linked with different goddesses in the mythology, yet it seems to be a paradox that they have never been able to get an equal position as compared to men for all practical purposes. The difference in their status in theory and practice had kept their position unstable. The very fact that women were looked down upon in the society had further degenerated their position. This had often got expression in form of such social evil practices like selling of girls, widowhood, *Sati* and prostitution.

In a society where the birth of a girl was considered an ill omen, she was very often killed at the very time of birth because a son was considered as the real maintainer of the race. The Hindu mythology enjoined upon the people that without a male issue salvation can not be attained. Though the custom of infanticide had neither the sanction of religion nor was it recognised by society, yet, it was like a threat on the part of the 'custodian' of both religion and society

The kind of belief was common even among the *Sikhs, Khatrees, Bedis* and *Sodhees.* At one place Baba Ram Singh said, "If in future some body will kill a girl or sell a girl he will be punished. Because there are great qualities in girls. They give comforts of varied nature and I can not explain their qualities. Girl killing is a greater sin in my eyes than cow killing."[83] At another place he said, whosoever makes money by the marriage of his daughter is a rascal who commits infanticide or exchanges his daughter is equally so."[84]

Those girls who escaped the fate of infanticide were usually married at an early age, often between five and ten years. This left no opportunity them with for the improvement of their mental or physical faculties. Baba Ram Singh had forbidden his followers to marry their children at young age. He wrote, "This is my order and should be told to everyone that none except a girl of eighteen and a boy of twenty should be married."[85]

The position of women had degraded so much in certain sections of the society that at times parents of relatives sold or bartered them away. "Women were the virtual cattle who could like other cattle be sold or bartered away, for the practices of bartar or exchange, marriage and the sale of brides were fairly common among the people."[86] To sell young girls for money to some mentally retarded or an old man was prohibited by the Sikh

Rahtnamas also.[87] Baba Ram Singh strongly opposed such marriages and he said, "Whosoever makes money by the marriage of his daughter cannot be forgiven by God."[88] In case somebody was marrying girls in exchange or taking money for the marriage of the girl 'he was to be boycotted by the society.'[89] In fact, it had such an impact on the *Kukas* that they used to sing popular songs against the selling of girls.[99]

Widowhood was yet another curse for the women and girls in the Indian society. It was equally common in Punjab. Widows were considered inauspicious and they were put to tortures and sufferings. Baba Ram Singh had advocated the remarriage of widows, as a contemporary source records: "If a widow wants she can be married again among the *Kukas*".[91]

Sati was a long established practice in Punjab. As early as 4th century B.C. Alexander's soldiers found the practice *Sati* in Punjab "It was practised by half the city of Taxila along with other startling customs".[92] By the end of 18th century such practices became common in the Sikh society also. After the death of Maharaja Kharag Singh his all queens except the chief queen were forced to be burnt alive on his pyre by *wazir* Dhiyan Singh.[93] But Baba Ram Singh protested against this inhuman practice and insisted on the remarriage of the widows for starting a new life. The result of his teaching was that even widows of considerable age got married and could get a respectable life.[94]

Baba Ram Singh not only taught the women to fight against the superstitions, taboos and the imposed stigmas, but also tried to offer them a happy life and higher status in the society. In order to give them complete equality, Baba Ram Singh started to give them *amrit* (Baptism). In 1858 he baptized one lady Khemo of village Siyahar in the district of Ludhiana.[95] Hitherto women were not baptized at the major centres of Sikh religion. Baba Ram Singh even appointed women as *Subas* to carry on his missionary work. Bibi Hukmi of village Variyah in district Amritsar was appointed as a *Suba*.

Baba Ram Singh's contribution to the upliftment of women is notable "After the Sikh Gurus, Nanak and Gobind Singh, he was a great reformer and thinker, who worked for a complete equality of the sexes in the society and achieved notable success in his efforts. Even if his other great achievements are left out of consideration, this preaching of his alone, that man and woman are entitled to equal rights in the society will rank him with the leading most reformers of the world".[97]

The Namdhari movement was essentially a religious movement which mainly aimed at the revival of Sikh religion on fundamental principles. There was a strong feeling that Sikh religion was fast declining. But the Namdharis took equal interest in social problems of the Sikhs also. They wanted to revive the religion with a view to improving the Sikh society as a whole.

Thus, they tried to create social consciousness through religious principles which was likely to be more effective. In the contemporary society they had visualised a certain political threat to their basic social values. It was perhaps because of this reason that they could not afford to ignore the political developments. Broadly speaking this movement could be characterized as a socio-religious movement with partial political leanings.

REFERENCES

1. *Karah Parshad*—Sweet offering for God made of ghee, sugar and flour.
2. *Sootak*—A superstitions according to which some people do not visit where a child is born for certain days.
3. *Darbar Sahib*—Gurudwara of the Nirankaris was known as Darbar Sahib. See Plate No. V.
4. *Nirankari Chalan da Chitha*, 1857 A.D.
5. "साध सत एकतर बालक करो मंगेवा लाधे से जन कुड़म भले वडो अमृत मेव।"
   All the noble and saintly people have gathered here for the engagement of the child. Distribute sweets and dry fruits because we have found good in-laws. *Nirankari Chalan da Chitha*.
6. *Prem Sumarag Grunth*—Part two, Chapter IV, p. 34.
7. *Anand Marriage*—Once he visited Bhera in 1809 where Bai Charan Dass was so much impressed by his religious devotion that he offered the hand of his only daughter Mool Devi in marriage to him. This was the month of *Chaitra* which is considered inauspicious for marriages by Brahmins who would not agree to perform the ceremony during *Nahs* for ill-omened days. But Baba Dayal had no belief in the sinister aspects of the stars and looked upon it as a superstition.
8. It is believed that first such marriage was performed by Guru Ram Dass IV Guru of the Sikhs and the Lavan (Couplet in whose recitation marriage was to be performed) were first recited by him later on it was incorporated in the Adi Grunth.
9. *Sikhism and the Nirankari Movement*, p. 15.
10. "जालऊ ऐसी रीत में प्यारा वीसरे
    नानक साई भली प्रीत जित साहिब सेतीचित रहें"
    Vadhans Var I—*Adi Grunth*.
    Also see *Nirankari Gurmat Prarmbhta*, p. 47.
11. *Census Report* 1891, Vol. XIX, pp. 156-157.

12. See Plate No. IX.
13. *Nirankari Gurmat Prarmbhta,* p. 46.
14. Ganda Singh refers the name of the father of the girl Nihali as Hari Singh while *Nirankari Gurmat Prarmbhta,* p. 47 records, it as Bhai Waiguru Singh and explains that since fellow was constantly remembering the name of God or *Waiguru* he was known as *Waiguru* Singh. *Sikhism and the Nirankari Movement,* p. 19.
15. *Gurmat* Rites in consistence with Sikh practices.
16. *Nirankari Tract No. 12,* Dooji Kiyari Sri Satguru Darbara Singh, pp. 44-45.
17. See appendix IX. This Hukumnama is dated 12th Baisak 1941 Samvat and the writer is Pingal Dass.

17a. *Pothohar*—A region now part of Pakistan.

18. For details see *Nirankari Gurmal Prarmbhta.*
19. *Anand Viyah di Itihastic Kranti,* p. 12.
20. These types of marriages continued among the Nirankaris. In 1906 Maharaj Kumar Ripudaman Singh of Nabha visited Sahib Ratta Ji at Rawalpindi with his father in 1906. Impressed by the performance of an *Anand Marriage* he proposed the Anand Marriage Bill when he was member of the Imperial Legislative Council. Consequently with the efforts of Nirankaris and others on 22nd October 1909 Anand Marriage Act was passed by which even Anand Marriages got the sanction of law and were proved valid in the court, etc.
    Legislative Department Act 7 of 1909 V. Vol.
    For the telegrams which Nirankaris sent to the Government See Appendix 'J'. Also see Appendix 'K' as to how these marriages were made valid according to law.
21. A Glossary of Tribes and Castes Punjab & North West Frontier Province, Vol. III, p. 171.
22. *Census Report of India,* 1891.
    The Punjab and its Feudateries, Vol. XIX, pp. 156-57.
23. Hukumnama (Chalan-da-chitha) 25 Magh Samvad 1923 Language of this manuscript is urdu but script is Gurmukhi. See Appendix 'D'.
24. "साकत संग न कीजिये दूरों जाईये भाग,
    बासन कारो परसीये तऊ कुछ लागे दाग"
    Adi Grunth
    Nirankari Sanehra, p. 18.
    Author had a detailed discussion with the present chief of the Nirankaris, Baba Gurbax Singh at Chandigarh who explained that *Sakat* is a word used for sect who believe in consuming all types of intoxicants and it is used for prostitutes also. Interview held on 20.6.79 at Chandigarh.
25. *A Glossary of Tribes and Castes of the Punjab and N. West Frontier Province* p. 171.
26. *Ibid.*
27. *Ibid.*
28. *Foreign Department, Patiala,* No. 1-86 of 1923.
29. *Phulwari Ank Musik Patar Itihasik Number,* July, 1928.
30. *Hand Book for the Indian Army* "Sikh", Capt. A.H. Bingley, p. 67.
31. *Census of India* 1891, Vol. XIX, p. 156.
32. "अबर मूऐ क्या सोग करीजे
    तऊ कीजै जो आपन जीजै"
    Adi Grunth

"Why one laments on the death of other it should be done only if one is going to live for ever".
Nirankari Chalan da Chitha.

33. "कबीर संत मूऐ क्या रोईये जो अपने ग्रह जाये
रोवहू साकत बापुरै जो हाटो हाट बिकाये"
Adi Grunth.
34. *The Home and Foreign Record,* Feb. 1854, pp. 52-54.
35. *Nirankari Gurmat Prarambhta,* p.19.
For a better view and location of Dayalsar See Plate No. 10.
36. *Nirankari Chalan da Chitha,* 1855 A.D.
37. *Census of India* 1891, p. 156.
38. *Sootak* is defilment of food on account of death and visit to these houses is prohibited for certain days.
39. *Nirankari Gurmat Prarambhta.*
40. "जमन मरना हुक्म है भाने आवे जाये
खाना पीना पवित्र है दितोन रिजक सबाय
नानक जिना गुरमुख बुझिया तिना सूतक नाहिं"
Adi Grunth
Nirankari Chalan da Chitha.
41. *Saradh*—is an offering in the memory of the dead once in a year by his near and dear. According to Hindu system, the whole year is divided into fortnightly divisions known as *Pakhwara* one of these divisions is known as *Pitrpaksh* (ancestor fortnight) period. Any person dyeing in any date within that fortnight division is remembered and charity and offerings are given in his name on that particular date, corresponding in the fortnight known as *Saradh.*
42. "जीवत पितर न माने कोऊ मुऐ सराध कराई
पितर भी बपुरे कहु क्यों पावै कऊआ कूकर खाहिं"
Nirankari Chalan da Chitha. Adi Grunth.
43. *Ibid.*
44. "भागं माछली सुरापान जी जो प्राणी खाहि
तीरथ वरत और नेम किये ने सभे रसातल जाये"
Kabir—*Adi Granth.*
Also quoted in the *Nirankari Chalan da Chitha.*
45. *Kirt Karo*—to earn ones livelihood by doing labour with his hands.
46. *Wand ke Chhako*—To use the earned money collectively.
47. Baba Dayal's father used to deal in the exchange of coins and it appears that he used to give loans also. The customers of his father would come to settle accounts with him. One day Baba Dayal took out the accounts books of his father and asked his indebtors to accompany him to a suitable place for settlement of accounts. Baba Dayal took them to a stream and then opened his fathers account book, removed the pages tore it up into pieces and threw them into the running water saying "Satguru himself manages to clear your debts".
48. *Foreign Department Political A,* March 1867, No. 111-112.
49. *Home Department Judicial B Proceedings,* October 1881, No. 188-195.
50. *Foreign Department Political A,* March 1867, No. 111-112.
51. *Home Department Judicial B Proceedings.*
March 1867, No. 111-112.

52. *Kukiyan di vithya*, p. 333.
53. *Home Department Judicial Proceedings.* August 1879, No. 257-259.
54. *Satguru Bilas*, p. 86.
55. *Home Department Judicial Proceedings,* August 1879, No. 257-259.
56. Author met with Kuka Guru Jagjit Singh on 16th March 1981 and not only herself saw this practice but also held a discussion with the Kuka chief on this point.
57. *Foreign Department Political A,* March 1867, No. 111-112. Also see for details *Foreign Department Political* A, February 1858, No. 202-203.
    This aspect has been discussed at length in the chapter on Religious Practices.
58. *Kuka Movement*, p. 30.
59. There were popular sayings at that time that Kukas are very selfish they even do not share their mugs for bath.
    कूके बड़े कसूते गड़वा ना दिंदे नावन नूं
    (i) *Baba Ram Singh Namdhari,* p. 151.
    (ii) *Kuka,* p. 100
    Bhai Jodh Singh Abhinandan Grunth.
60. *Ramgharia*—The Ramgharia is a subcaste of the Tarkhan Sikh carpenter caste. *Caste and Class among the Sikh of North West India,* p. 66.
61. Marenco Elsie in his thesis says "one may note here that there is a relation between the membership of religious sects to particular caste groups when some caste members are persuaded to join particular sect offering certain advantages usually in the term of upward mobility others of the same caste may also follow.
    Ibid, p. 49.
    At another place he says "An interesting point about the Namdhari movement or sect of Sikhism is that religious beliefs of the Namdharis were accepted by some sections of Ramgharia sub-caste to which the leader Ram Singh belonged and by some others. The mechanism of corporate caste efforts for upward mobility of the Namdharis was the same as those of an ordinary castes striving towards upwards mobility.
    Ibid p. 66.
    Official records do show Namdharis coming from the castes other Ramgharias but their number was quite negligible. Occupation wise Kukas were generally from the lower classes of the Society.
    See Appendix I.
62. *Home Department Judicial B Proceedings.* October 1881 No. 188-195.
63. *Ibid.*
64. *Home Department Judicial B Proceedings,* Oct. 1881 No. 188-195.
65. *Kookyan di vithya*, 318.
66. *Ibid,* p. 329.
67. *Home Department Judicial Proceeding 'B'* August 1879 No. 257-259.
68. *Kookyan di Vithya*, p. 224.
69. Ganda Singh is of the opinion that when Baba Ram Singh started preaching there were hardly any English schools in the rural area. In the districts alone such schools could be found. In villages primary education was through Persian.

Upto December 1862 from whole of Punjab including Frontier provinces, Sindh Baluchistan, Jammu & Kashmir and other native states only 8 people had passed Matric or enterance examination. Punjab University was established only in 1882 i.e. about eleven years after Baba Ram Singh left Punjab. There were hardly any Hindu or Sikh private schools, *Kukas* did not try to open schools and if they were forbiden to join any Government schools then where else could the children go for studies. He further said that it looks astonishing that saintly, simple purehearted social reformer could tell his followers to remain illiterate or order them to abstain from education.

For details see *Kuka Lahr*, p. 116 by Ganda Singh in *Bhai Jodh Singh Abhinandan Grunth.*

70. *Kukas the freedom fighters*, p. 49.
71. Such reformed marriages henceforth called Anand were first performed at village Khote when Brahmins and barbers were completely eliminated from the scene. They were deprived of the fees they usually got on such occasions. On this issue Brahmins threatened to put themselves into the burning Pyre if the new system of marriage was not stopped. Baba Ram Singh refused to yield. It was reported to the government that Ram Singh talks of sedition and rebellion against the British Government and was put in surveillance at his home Baini. This has been discussed in detail in Sat Jug (Hola Ank 2012 Chetra) p. 23.
72. *Kuka Movement*, p. 31.
73. *Asa-di-war* by Guru Nanak it forms a part of Adi Grunth and is supposed to be recited, early in the morning.
74. *Jap* is known as Jup Ji written by Guru Nanak and Sikhs are supposed to read it everyday.
75. *Jaap*—A composition of tenth Guru Gobind Singh supposed to be read everyday.
76. *Chaupai*—Written by tenth Guru.
77. *Chandi Charitar*—written by Guru Gobind Singh to invite spirit of chivalry.
78. *Akal ustat*—written by Guru Gobind Singh in praise of God.
79. *Kuka Movement*, p. 29-30.
80. The author had a long discussion on this issue with eminent and learned scholar of Sikh religion and history who was also an ex-vice-Chancellor of Patiala University. Despite of his weakness and old age Bhai Jodh Singh gave his precious time and views. Meeting was held on 22.6.79 at his residence Model Town Ludhiana.
81. *Foreign Department Political A Proceedings* Feb. 1868 No. 202-203.
82. There were different way to kill the infant baby *District Gazattear of Houshiyarour* records in 1883-84 that in Punjab girls were burried under the ground with the sugar to eat and cotton to spin.

    गुड़ खाई पुनी कती,
    आप ना आईयों भाईया घली

    "Eat gurt spin your cotton,
    Don't come send brothers instead"
83. *Kookiyan di Vithya*, p. 305.
84. *Foreign Department Political A Proceedings*, March 1867 No. 111-112.
85. *Kukiyan Di Vithya* p. 280-293.
86. *Kuka Movement*, p. 73.
87. *Rahtnama* is a code of conduct to be followed by the Sikhs. Bhai Nand Lal says in one of the *Rahtnamas*

"धी बहन का पैसा खाये गोबिन्द सिंह धक्के यम लाये"

"One who takes the money of the girls or for the girls goes straight to hell and gets kicks from the dharamraj".
Gurumat Nirnay p-16 Bhai Jodh Singh.

88. *Foreign Department Political A Proceedings.* March 1867 No. 111-112.
89. *Kukiyan di vithya* p. 293.
90. There was a popular folk song.

"न बेच कुमारी वे बाबला लालचीया
गल गऊ कटारी वे बाबला लालचीया
तेरी गई मत मारी वे बाबला लालचीया
न बनी व्यापारी वे बाबला लालीचया।

"It said oh my selfish father do not sell a virgin it is like the slaughtering of cow why have you lost wisdom to become a trader by selling me."
Baba Ram Singh Namdhari p. 153.

91. *Sri Guru Singh Itihas* p. 314.
92. *Oxford History of Indi*, p. 665.
93. See for details.
    (i) *Dogra Gardi de Gujhe Bhet* Prof. Ganda Singh
    (ii) *Phulwari Da Sikh Itihasik* Number 1930 p. 228.
    (iii) *Birdhan de* Byan Karam Singh historian Phulwari da Sikh Itihasik Number 1930 p. 277.
    (iv) *History of the Punjab Sayyad* Muhammad Latife p. 594.
94. *Baba Ram Singh Namdhari*, p. 85.
95. *Ibid.* p. 82.
96. *Sapt Sring*, p. 11.
97. *Ibid.*

5
Kine Killing and Kuka Religiosity

The cow has always been held pious by the Hindus since ancient times. Any disrespect to it could have led to political disturbance. The sentiments of the Hindus on this matter had been appreciated even by rulers of medieval India. Akbar had prohibited cow slaughter and himself avoided beef. With a view to appreciate the religious sentiments of the Hindus, the rulers of Punjab had also shown due respect to the cow.

When Sikh rule was established in Punjab under Maharaja Ranjit Singh, the killing of cows was prohibited. This practice continued during the regency of Maharaja Duleep Singh. By the orders of the Governor General, kine killing was prohibited in the holy city of Amritsar and a declaration to the effect was engraved on a copper plate which was hung on the main gates of *Darbar Sahib.*[1] It mentioned "The priest of Amritsar having complained of annoyances, this is to make known to all concerned that by order of the Governor General British subjects are forbidden to enter the temple called Darbar at Amritsar or its precinets with their shoes on, kine are not to be killed in Amritsar nor are Sikhs to be molested, or in any way to be interfered with. Shoes are to be taken off at the Bunga at the corner of the tank and no person is to walk round the tank with his shoes on".[2]

But once the rule of the Sikhs was over and Punjab passed on into the hands of the Britishers, things changed completely. On 25th April, 1849, Board of Administrators modified the orders on the plea that this concession was given to them on Punjab being a Sikh sovereign state at that time. The new declaration said "No one should be allowed to interfere with the practice by, his neighbour, of customs which that neighbour's religion permits".[3] According to M.M. Ahluwalia this order was a confirmation of their policy of 'Divide and Rule'. This was to create rift between the Hindus and the Muslims.[4] In every large town a spot for shambles and butchers' shop should be fixed, but particular care should be taken to see that those places were not to be in the neighbourhood of Hindus religious buildings and beef should not be allowed to be exposed for sale like other commodities in the city or town. All those who wanted to have it could go out of the city to butcher shops. But even that was to be brought into the city properly covered in a piece of cloth. Butchers had given an undertaking to abide by the laws and regulations.[5] Any violation to these rules could be sued in the court for fine and punishment.

This was a negation of the earlier practice of prohibiting cow killing. The story of change from prohibition to permission is a journey which tells its own tale. It had led to many socio-religious tensions which later on became one of the important factors in accelerating the socio-religious movement in the region. Butchers were often violating the rules, fringment was done as beef was openly paraded in the thickly populated non-Muslim areas of the city. Hawkers were openly selling it in the Hindu and Sikh localities as well.

Officiating Commissioner Major W.G. Davies writing to Officiating Secretary to the Government of Punjab attributed some causes to the increase of the sale of beef which in turn led to the general discontent among the Hindus and the Sikhs of Amritsar, thus, leading to the murder of the butchers.[6]

Butchers were careless about the laws and procedures, prescribed earlier for the sale of beef. This had led to resentment among various sections of Hindus and Sikhs. In this connection a British Officer observes, "The knowledge that they held the Government monopoly has emboldened them and rendered them careless of the manner in which the flesh was brought into the town and thus prejudices of Hindus have often been offended".[7] There were occasions even prior to the murder of the butchers, when complaints were made against them.[8]

Hatred among Hindus, Sikhs and Muslims was increasing for quite some time especially when a man named Dewa

Singh took a beef bone into the temple and placed it before the *Adi Grunth.* Dewa Singh was imprisoned and sentenced to three years rigorous imprisonment. This incident agitated the mind of the Hindus and Sikhs. However with the efforts of the local authorities normalcy was restored,[9] and trade and commerce was resumed.

But, "the inocent, illiterate and religious minded people of Punjab found a new picture of ugliness and injury in the holy city of Amritsar which completely differed from the picture of those days when Maharaja Ranjit Singh and his successor ruled at Lahore".[11] *Kukas* were also aware of this situation. Whenever they used to visit Hari Mandir Sahib they were enraged by such a condition. When some *Kukas* saw a few butchers taking cows for slaughter, while they were passing through the city, the *Kukas* decided to save the cows and at the same time to teach a lesson to the butchers.

On 14th June, 1871, a team of ten Namdharis under the leadership of Sardar Beehla Singh Narli attacked the butchers. In this sudden attack four butchers, Peera, Jeevan, Shadi and Imami were killed on the spot, while Kheeva, Ilahi Baksh and Karam Deen were seriously wounded.[12] While going back, the *Kukas* had thrown a disc and a blue turban. The incident is referred in the sources as follows: "The only trace of the city assassins found were a blue turban and a steel disc such as worn by the sect of the fanatics known as Nihangs or Akalis but this only had the effect of misdirecting enquiry".[13] This was perhaps done to create suspicion in the minds of the police that the killing of the butchers was done by them.

The police investigated and arrested many persons whom they suspected to be responsible for the incident.[14] The anxiety of the British government over this issue could be judged by the appointment of a team of officers to investigate into the matter. The government apprehended that such incidents might spread in other parts of Punjab, resulting in serious communal riots and a grave law and order problem. Consequently, the Deputy Commissioner deputed another police officer a known detector, Mr. Christie who announced an award of rupees two thousand to any person giving any clue in the matter.[13]

While the British government was investigating into the

incident of the butcher killing at Amritsar, another incident[16] of the similar nature took place on 15th July, 1871, at Raikot,[17] which further baffled the government.

The description of the location where the butchers lived at Raikot as given by the Home-Judicial papers, clearly indicate the background in which the butchers were expected to live. It had been clarified that they were required to reside in the areas outside the town. The basic purpose behind imposing this condition was to avoid the possibility of any disatisfaction and annoyance to the people of some communities who objected to cow killings. The description of various developments of the last quarter of the 19th century clearly indicate the simmering discontent over the matter among the Sikhs and Hindus alike.

The matter was gradually taking a serious turn. These communities it seems, had decided not to take this issue lying low and the incident of butcher killing at Raikot was the manifestation of that feeling. Whether the dwelling place of the butchers was out of the town or not became a matter of secondary importance.

In this connection, the evidences available show that though the place of incident was out of the township for all practical purposes, yet the very practice of cow killing had produced sufficient irritation to different shades of people. The place of incident was "unfortunately located outside the city near a Gurudwara which was associated with the name of the 10th Guru".[18] The holiness of this place was often spoiled due to the bones and pieces of meat of the slaughtered animals. Fauja Singh remarks, "The Sikhs of Raikot and elsewhere had a special grouse because birds carried the bones and bits from the slaughter houses and perching on the temple walls, would often throw them into the Gurudwara enclosure".[19]

The dirty and unhygienic conditions of the place was mainly due to cow killing. This had made the life of the people living around quite miserable. There were also gross violations of the provision of the municipal laws which required a healthy and hygienic condition to be maintained at such places which had hardly been practised. There is evidence that Buta butcher was fined Rs. 10/ by the Municipal Committee.[20] Deputy Commissioner of Ludhiana, Mr Cowan reported, "It is true that for some time past the Municipal Committee have offered to give the butchers another land to build on as the cattle of the entire town drink the water into which the bones of the slaughtered animals are thrown".[21] On this point complaints and petitions against these butchers were made by both the Hindus as well as the Muslims.[22] Mr Cowan reported, "But the complaint was preferred by Mohammadans and Hindus alike and the site of the present slaughter house at Raikot is decidedly objectionable".[23]

The Kukas who were always full of religious fervour and used to pass through Raikot often visited the Raiket Gurudwara to offer their reverence and respect. They had observed how the bones and the pieces of hide and flesh had spread all over the area leading to unhygienic conditions. It had also made the life of the local inhabitants miserable. They came to know about several attempts that were made to remove the butchers from these localities which had failed. They were told that even the imposition of the fine had not improved their behaviour. But what was most agitating to them was the sacrilege to which the Gurudwara was subjected because of these butchers. Perhaps they were convinced that unless the butchers were shifted from the area, the sanctity of the atmosphere of the holy shrine was likely to remain polluted. It seems that this was the basic reason behind the incident of the butchers' murder on 15th July 1871 at Raikot.[24] Incidentally, the butchers escaped and their guests were killed. Buta and Ranjha the permanent residents of Raikot escaped miraculously.[25]

The wounded persons failed to provide proper description or the religious background of the murderers. Even the police could not get any clue. Some footprints were followed which led to the Patiala territory around the village Cheeniwala "After a few days of hectic investigation, the slayers of the butchers were tracked down with the aid of the trackers Bhupa and Bhanga".[26] Assistance of the Maharaja of Patiala was sought, which he rendered very promptly. Besides, a reward of Rs. 250 was also announced by the Maharaja of Patiala anyone who gave any information regarding the culprits. Mr Cowan wrote to the Commissioner of Ambala that the general belief was that crime has been committed by the same gang who had committed murders in Amritsar".[27]

Conspiracy un-earthed and Confessions

The mystery of the murders of Amritsar had not yet been solved and a number of innocent people including some Nihangs and traders of Amritsar were still in judicial custody. However, it did not take much time to locate the killers of Raikot. Deputy Inspector General of Police Col. Bailly himself went to make enquiries and took stern measures against the suspected people at Cheeniwala. During the course of interrogation they named a few. Subsequently three, *kukas of* Pithoki and Dal Singh of Cheeniwala were apprehended. Dal Singh gave the clues about Gulab Singh Choohar-chak. Mr Cowan Deputy Commissioner of Ludhiana sent a report about the matter to the Secretary of Punjab Government Mr Griffin as follows, "Four of the seven *kukas* arrested are undoubtedly the murderers. Their swords have been found, four of them with blood hair and skin on them. One of them, Dal Singh has turned approver on an offer of Pardon".[28] The murderers were apprehended tried and sentenced to death. Gulab Singh offered to give the names of all those involved in the Amritsar case, provided he was pardoned. Gulab Singh admitted that he was a party to the killing and mentioned the names of his other accomplices who were Fateh Singh, Beehla Singh, Hakim Singh and Lehna Singh Tarkhan, all from Amritsar, besides Lehna Singh Jut of Lopoke. Jhunda Singh of Thutti, Mehar Singh of Lopoke, Lachman Singh and Bhagwan Singh of Mehran—they were all *kukas.*[29]

When Gulab Singh was brought to Amritsar things were further clarified as indicated by Major Davies, the officiating Superintendent Police Amritsar division, who reported, "It was further discovered that Lehna Singh a wealthy contractor of Amritsar and one of the Subas of Ram Singh and Lal Singh a Police constable had actually abetted the commission of the crime, the former by allowing a burnt sacrifice (*Hom*) for the success of the enterprise to be offered up in his own house, himself presiding at it and the latter by providing weapons on one occasion for the use of the murderers.[30]

Whereas Beehla Singh, Fateh Singh, Hakim Singh and Lehna Singhs were given capital punishment, constable Lal Singh and Lehna Singh were given life imprisonment, Gulab Singh saved himself as he had turned approver.

In the Raikot case Mastan Singh, Mangal Singh and Gurmukh Singh of village Pithoke, were given death sentence, while Dall Singh Cheeniwala was pardoned because he had also turned approver.

British Attitude

Those who were directly involved in that case were punished. However, the British Government was determined to punish all those whom they suspected of creating trouble in future. After three months and eleven days on 26th October, 1871, two more people were hanged in connection with the same case. They were Gyani Rattan Singh of Mandiwala and Rattan Singh of Naiwala.[31] Whereas the other Subas were also called for evidence at Bussian near Rajkot, the Government wanted to be ensured as to whether this butchers killing at Amritsar and Raikot were done at the instance of Baba Ram Singh. Deputy Inspector General of Police while preparing this report on the Raikot murders recorded evidences which showed that Ram Singh had instigated the *Kukas* "There is 1st story of Lehna Singh planning that a *kuka grunthee* told him that Ram Singh had preached the murder of the butchers and that his followers had promised to obey him. The *Grunthee* (Dull Singh denies it and the story is a lame one)".[32]

The second evidence was of Harnam Dass who said that he himself had heard Ram Singh in the *Durbar* instigating his followers to kill the Amritsar butchers. He was assuring them that for each butcher killed they would receive a reward of hundred cows. But an important point in this connection which deserves mention is the fact that Harnam Singh had made this statement while he-himself was under a trial for the murder of a Chowkidar in Ambala district.[33] This could explain to some extent as to how far he could be under police influence for getting his statement recorded.

A memorandum of Mr Cowan, Deputy Commissioner of Ludhiana dated 24th July, 1871 says, "The approver and the witness by whom many of his statements are corroborated, state that when Ram Singh was at Raisur a few weeks before the Amritsar business mention was made to him that one *kuka* had murdered another in the Ferozpur District whereupon Ram Singh in a speech or sermon upraided the followers for killing the butchers and asked them if they knew of no enemies of their religion whom they could kill and then he went on to allude to the defilment of the holy places at Amritsar by the presence (there) of the slaughter of cows. Several of his followers cried out "If you order it we will kill the butchers" Ram Singh replied "Do not do any thing in hurry the time has not yet come".[34]

However, according to the version of Sant Nidhan Singh Alam, Guru Ram Singh had told the *kukas* "If you can stay your hand for a year more, I would achieve without the help of weapons the object for which you are drawing out your swords".[35] Although Baba Ram Singh had made it quite clear that he had not advised or instigated the *kukas* to take up arms or to kill the butchers yet British government could not be satisfied by this statement. They wanted to implicate him on some ground or the other. The Punjab government asked Commissioner Mancabb and Dy. Inspector General of Police Mr. Macandrew to prepare a detailed report about the activities of Baba Ram Singh and the Namdharis.

The defiant attitude of the *kukas* did not end with the killing of the butchers, but it was later on manifested in other ways also. In this connection attacks were made on Malodh and Malerkotla.[36] Tracing the genesis of the attack on Malodh and Malerkotla, M.M. Ahluwalia says "The native Muslim States had offered the same provocation which the authorities in British India had offered to *kukas.* Secondly the *Kukas* were greatly agitated due to the execution of their colleagues at Ludhiana and Amritsar. Thirdly, they had been greatly inspired by the glorious way in which the martyrs of Raikot and Amritsar had gone to gallows.[36a] However, while explaining the background of the attacks on Malodh and Malerkotla Mr Macnabb's report mentions, "Prophesies of the overthrow of the English and the restoration of the Khalsa rule have been circulated among the *kukas*...formed the plan of sending a body of hundred men to seize the capital of Malerkotla State where arms and horses would be found and distributed to the rest who should join".[37] Since it was a "notoriously weak and misgoverned state".[38]

The *Maghi* fair of Bhaini Sahib took place on 11th-12th January 1872. The atmosphere was extremely tense and some *kukas* were in a very agitated mood. At the end of the fair a band of hundred *mastanas* (persons in a state of trance) determined to make an attack on Malerkotla.[39] According to Dr. Fauja Singh, "There was complete agreement between the Baba and his followers on the basic issue. His opposition was not to the cause but the selection of the time for attack'.[40] However, according to Namdhari traditions when Baba Ram Singh learnt about the plan, he tried to dissuade them from taking up arms or for creating any disturbance.[41] This fact was supported by Deputy Inspector of Police Sarfraz Khan who was present at that time and who also reported the same thing to the authorities.[42] Some details in this connection deserve to be mentioned to understand the real situation.

The team under the leadership of Hira Singh and Lehna Singh of Sakrowdi started for the attack on Malerkotla. They halted for the night at village Rubbo, they had hardly any arms with them except a few swords and choppers. They decided first to go to Malodh for getting some arms, amunition and horses etc. When the Sardar of Malodh came to know about the proposed use of the arms, he refused to oblige them. This led to a struggle in which two *kukas* were killed and four other were wounded. They could get only three swords, one double barelled gun, two horses and one mare.[43]

This attack on Malodh created a stir among the officers of the British government. Immediately telegrams were sent to the Punjab Government and the native states for seeking their assistance.[44]

On the 15th January, 1872, the *Kukas* attacked the palace of Malerkotla. Meanwhile the army and the police, which was much larger than *kukas* came to seize them. After this, some severe fighting took place between the two parties in which several casualties were suffered by both sides.[45]

Being unsuccessful in getting more arms, money or horses the *Kukas* decided to leave Kotla. During the of the chase, a few bloody skismishes were fought in which they invariably had an upper hand. By 11.00 A.M. the *Kukas* succeeded in reaching the village Rur.[46]

While the *Kukas* were taking care of their wounded fellows and relaxing at Rur they were arrested by Naiz Ali and *Naib Nazim* of Amargarh in Patiala State.[47] However, the papers of the native state of Jind have a different story to tell. These recorded that it was not because the bravery of Niaz Ali that they were caught but because of the treachery of the local people of Rur who first scattered them in different houses in the village and then got them overpowered by the police.[48] Sixty eight badly wounded and injured *kukas* were handed over to Mr Cowan, Deputy Commissioner, Ludhiana. Cowan did not want to miss this opportunity to curb the *kukas* and teach them a lesson. On 17th January, 1872 forty-nine *kukas* were blown away by guns and one was cut to pieces when he tried to attack the Deputy Commissioner.[49]

Next day on the 19th January, 1872, sixteen more *kukas* were shot dead with guns. Mr Cowan and Mr Forsyth Commissioner Ambala division were directly responsible for this operation against the *Kukas*. Mr Cowan had firm conviction that the attack on Malerkotla was the beginning of the *Kuka* rebellion. Writing to Forsyth on 17th January, 1872, he said, "A rebellion which might have attained large dimension was nipped in the bud".[50] Mr. Forsyth informing the Punjab government on the incident and the position of Mr Cowan said, "I regret exceedingly this hasty action on Mr Cowan's part, His reason (for such) is that he felt it necessary to stamp out the incipient rebellion by a swift and terrible punishment. That his prompt and vigorous action had this effect is, I think undoubted while laminating the hasty and irregular action of Mr Cowan, I am bound to express my conviction that the very prompt and terrible measures taken by him crushed in its birth a very serious outbreak".[51]

Lt. Governor congratulated Forsyth on his performance.[52] He even supported the actions of Cowan and Forsyth on the ground that their decisions were "taken in good faith". Lt. Governor went to the extent of recording "blowing from a gun is an impressive and merciful manner of execution well calculated to strike terror into by-standers".[53]

However, shooting people dead with guns in the civilized age of 19th century was not liked and appreciated by the British government as well as the press. Questions regarding this matter where raised in the parliament and severe criticism was done in the newspapers.[54] The Home Department was of the opinion that the trial would have meant a delay of only a day or so which was not a difficult matter. However, the Maharaja of

Patiala wrote a letter to the Secretary of the Punjab Government, justifying the actions of Forsyth and Cowan.[55]

The Government of India held both Cowan and Forsyth guilty of this crime, "The prisoners were absolutely helpless. A large proportion of them were badly wounded and under these circumstances their illegal and indiscriminate executions was a measure for which there was no execuse".[56] The Government charged Cowan with an allegation for deviation from the legal path. His Excellency in council was compelled to direct that Mr Cowan be removed from service. Likewise, Mr Forsyth was censured and transferred from Punjab to Rajasthan and he was debarred by the Government of India from holding any important administrative assignment in future.[57]

Baba Ram Singh and his Subas, being leaders of the movement still remained to be punished. Lt. Governor of Punjab sent a telegram to the Governor General, informing him of the incidents, "Following an antecedent these outrages show incorrigible conspiracy in leaders of the sect. The country is not safe while leaders are at large. I have therefore authorised Forsyth to effect the capture of Ram Singh and the principal subas, report by post."[58] Reply came by return telegram which read "Your action entirely approved. He shall be anxious to hear further particular."[59]

Forsyth was entrusted for the arrest of Baba Ram Singh and his subas. Lt. Col. Bailley was deputed to bring Baba Ram Singh to Ludhiana. Baba Ram Singh reached Ludhiana on the night of 17-18 January, 1872 accompanied by two attendants and two *Subas* Sahib Singh and Jawahar Singh. The Baba was interrogated and the replies could not satisfy the Commissioner. Baba Ram Singh said he was ignorant of the British laws and thought that he had no obligation to report the matter to the Government. Considering the man to be most dangerous if left at liberty,[60] orders for his detention were issued under Regulation III of 1818.[61]

Besides Baba Ram Singh his prominent and influential *subas* were also arrested and detained in the Allahabad Fort.[62] They were Suba Sahib Singh, Rur Singh, Lakha Singh, Kanh Singh, Man Singh, Hukma Singh, Pahara Singh, Jawahar Singh, Maluk Singh, Brahma Singh and Sardar Mangal Singh of Raipur. All the Subas and Baba Ram Singh were never brought before open trial in any court of law and the original detention under Regulation III of 1818 was made permanent.

Government was still afraid of the *Kukas.* Thorough search of *Bhaini,* the *kuka* centre was made by the police but no arms were recovered. The place was dug at several points but nothing came out. Still Bhaini was put under strict surveillence with several other restrictions, "All those of influence remain under surveillance and their movements are carefully watched. The headmen of rural circles (*Zaildars*) and the headman of the villages have been enjoined to report under penalty of deprivation of office or other punishments, the movement of all *kukas* within their villages or circles. The assembly of more than five *kukas* has been forbidden throughout the province. The carrying in public places of axes, iron-bound sticks and other weapons which is not coming under the arms act are still formidable in the event of riot has been strictly prohibited."[63]

These restrictions on the *kukas,* exile of Baba Ram Singh and other prominent *subas* and a police post at Bhaini had definitely given a setback to the *Kuka* movement for the time being. But in 1876 it was announced that a book of prophecies was discovered from the *Pahlad Sagar* or *Bad Tirath* tank at Hazirpur in Sirsa.[64] This book had revived the hopes of the *kukas* which is evident from the official sources. On 17th March, 1881 around one hundred and fifty *kukas* were seen holding a secret meeting in the Dhak Jungle near village Laton.[65]

In 1885 Baba Ram Singh died at Mergui in exile. It was a great shock for the *kukas* but they refused to accept this because according to a popular *kuka* belief Baba Ram Singh could not die and he must have escaped from detention. It is a *Kuka* belief that Baba Ram Singh is still alive and would live for many many years.[66]

There is a difference of opinion among historians regarding the nature and the political role of the *kuka* movement.[67] Besides Fauja Singh, other modern historians like Jaswant Singh Jas and M.M. Ahluwalia also consider these movements as emphasising on Swadeshi and non-cooperation to the British Government.[68] But Professor Ganda Singh has strongly contested the views of above scholars.[69]

However, the fact remains that with the death of Baba

by the Khatris of the place". But according to British and official records both Hindus and Muslims community had grudges against the behaviour of these butchers.

23. *Home Judicial A* 29th July 1871, No. 45-61A.
24. *Home Judicial A* 29th July 1871, No. 45-61A.
It gives the following details about the incident.
On the night of the attack on butchers, Ranjha was sleeping on the roof. Buta's wife and visiters were sleeping in the open space of the house. Attack was suddenly made by swords and gandasas (wood chopper). After killing and injuring the culprits left through the water. All those killed and wounded were:
    1. Dussundi Goojar, dead.
    2. Bassi Dussundi's wife dead.
    3. A child of Dussundi Ranja two years dying hacked all over.
    4. A child of Dussundi (20 days old) dying left arm cut off.
    5. Musammat Rahuntie daughter of Dussundi (20 years) dying head cut open and three other wounds.
    6. Mussamat Kownie-Buta's wife (kisab) dying.
    7. Musammat Reja daughter of Kownie (8 years) four fingers cut off.
    8. Akka Rajput 13 swords wounds in a dangerous condition.
25. Among the butchers who were attacked by the *kukas* the list does not mention the name of the Buta and Ranjha. It was Buta who was fined Rs. 10/- by the municipality for creating an unhygienic condition. On the fateful night Buta was absent from his home as he had gone to make an appeal against the fine imposed on him and Ranjha was sleeping on the roof top where his presence was never imagined by the *kukas.*
26. *Kuka Mavement,* p. 83.
27. *Home Judicial* 29th July 1871, No. 45-61A.
28. *Home Judicial* 29th July 1871, No. 45-61A.
29. *Home Judicial A* Feb. 1872, No. 57-58.
30. *Ibid.*
31. A few minutes before the execution, Suba Gyani Singh according to the author of *Satguru Bilas* addressed the following brave words to the English Officer on the spot. "Billa (Blue eyed Farangi) Have your face and not back towards me, passing ten month in the womb of some Jat lady I will be again here to avenge myself. Here O Billa your mind is polluted. It is not justice that you have done. Injustice is overcoming you. My end will not be the end of the movement against you... I too will not be out for ever. Some mother will give birth to me. In the new form and getting young I will once again take up the sword and have it out with you". *Kuka Movement,* p. 84.
Also see pp. 346-347 *Namdhari Itihas.*
See Appendix 'S'.
Papers of Sangin Munshikhana File No. 741.
32. *Home Judicial* 29th July 1871, No. 45-61A
33. *Ibid.*
34. *Home Judicial* 29th July 1871, No. 45-61A.
Dr. Fauja Singh's interpretation is "now why did he want time and only for killing the butchers of Amritsar, who were so few and could be finished in no time? Obviously he wanted thorough preparation to be made before any step was taken. The Amritsar butchers were not the only one to be decimated. There were butchers scattered all over the Punjab who would have to be

destroyed...under the circumstances an attack on the butchers would, in reality be an attack on British Government."
Kuka Movement, p. 78.

35. *Kuka the Freedom Fighters*, p. 83.
36. See Appendix 'R' and 'S'.
36a. *Kukas the Freedom Fighters*, p. 83.
Kukas were provocated by the insult of one Gurmukh Singh in whose presence an Ox was slaughtered. For detailed also see *Namdhari Itihas*, pp. 377-78.
37. For details of Sau-Sakhis or prophecies of Kukas. See M.M. Ahluwalia *Kukas*, pp. 182-89.
38. *Home Judicial Proceeding* June 1872, No. 112-113.
39. *Ibid.*
40. However one would find difficult with the views of Fauja Singh that Ram Singh was in agreement with the team who were going to attack Malerkotla and according to him disagreement was to "the time and not on the cause", but the subsequent development and the way Baba Ram Singh took the precaution to avert an ugly situation by informing Deputy Commissioner Ludhiana indicates that Ram Singh was neither in agreement of time nor cause.
41. For details See *Satguru Bilas*, p. 406.
42. *Parliamentary Papers*, on Kukas, No. 356-1872.
43. For details see *Baba Ram Singh Namdhari*, pp. 108-109.
44. See appendix 'N'.
45. Although Baba Ram Singh had sent Suba Lukha Singh to Ludhiana to inform the British authorities about the forthcoming attack on Malerkotla and Deputy Inspector of Police Sarfraz Khan had also reported to the Authorities yet the Government did not try to check the attack. They allowed it to take place so that on some grounds Kukas could be implicated especially their leader Baba Ram Singh. Even earlier to these attacks the authorities were anxious to find out a way to prosecute Baba Ram Singh. In a confidential letter dated 9th Sept. 1871 Secretary of the Punjab Government wrote to the Government of India that Lt. Governor of Punjab considers that it will be difficult and may be impossible to obtain, any such evidence as would warrant his prosecution in a criminal court.
Recorded in Home Judicial Proceedings, 13th Jan. 1872, No. 52-53.
This shows that Government was looking for an opportunity to rope in Baba Ram Singh.
46. *Kuka Movement*, p. 92.
47. See Appendix 'T' H-9-R Office Foreign Ministry, Patiala.
48. *Jind State Records* Sangin Munshikhana, File No. 741 of 1872.
49. For more details see *Satguru Bilas*, p. 419.
Also see *Kukas*, pp. 82-89 for greater details on the incidents of Malodh and Malerkotla.
Following verses became current in those days.
लदन से मलेछ चढ़ आये,
इन्हां ने घर घर बुचड़ खाने पाये
गुरां दे इन्हां घात कराये
सानूं हुन सिर देने आये।
(The unclean have come from London and have established slaughter houses in every place. They have killed our Gusrs. And we must now sacrifice ourselves.

K.S. Talwar Early phase of the Sikh Renaissance and struggle for freedom Punjab past and present October 1970, pp. 291-92.

50. *Parliamentary Papers,* No. 356 1872, p. 16.
51. *Ibid.*
52. *Home Judicial A July 1872 Proceedings,* No. 208-211.
53. *Ibid.*
54. Native Opinion N.W. Frontier Pioner Nov. 13, 1871, 1871-72-73 A/C No. 94 to Feb. 5, 1872 A/C No. 1455.
55. *Home Judicial Proceedings,* June 1872, 107-111 For details see *Kukas* pp. 98-100.
56. *Home Judicial Proceedings,* June 1872, No. 112-132.
57. *Ibid.*
58. *Home Judicial,* 20 January, 1872 Proceedings, 55-71.
59. *Ibid.*
60. *Parliamentary Papers,* No. 356 of 1872.
61. Dr Fauja Singh points out that warrants were issued on 22nd January while all the arrests had been made before that date is a strange thing. *Kuka Movements,* p. 114.
62. *Ibid.,* p. 117 see for details, pp. 116-119.
63. *Home Department Judicial Proceedings,* June 1872, No. 11.
64. For details of Sau-Sakhi and prophecies of kukas see Kukas, pp. 182-89.
65. *Home Judicial Oct.* 1881 Proceedings 185-95.
66. Author had an interview with the Guru of Namdharis Baba Jagjit Singh when various aspects of Namdhari sect were discussed and Kukas still strongly believe that Baba Ram Singh would live up to two hundred and fifty years'.
67. Dr. Fauja Singh is of the opinion that the independent postal and judicial service set up by kukas gave a semblance of a parallel Government. Boycott was extended even to the Government service and Educational institutions and the British manufactured cloth. They were advocating non-cooperation and swadeshi. See *Kuka Movement,* pp. 182-83.
68. According to Jaswant Singh Jas Baba Ram Singh had initiated Swadeshi and cooperation and the instrument he used for its were (i) not to have sort of cooperation with the British Govt. (ii) to save Sikhs from the Western impact (iii) to have a self-sufficient economy (iv) to create passion for the independence (v) to disobey British rule (vi) not to go to schools or accept titles etc, and (vii) to boycot British means of communication.
    Baba Ram Singh Namdhari, pp. 49-53.
69. *Kuka Lahar* by Ganda Singh Bhai Jodh Singh Abhinandhan Grunth, pp. 115-21.

6

Attitutde Towards the Kukas

Kuka movement was the product of such a society which represented people of different stratas, drawn from various segments of socio-economic life. There were chiefs of the native states who had at some time rallied around the British Government for support. It had originated in such an atmosphere, where native states had at some time taken British protection.[1]

Another section of the society was that of the religious people. It consisted of priests of the Gurudwaras, *Bedis, Sodhis* and *Mahants* besides the *Brahmins.* The Raja *Zamindar, Jagirdar,* and the officials of the native states consituted the elite of the society. Moreover the masses constituted another important and perhaps the largest group of people from the lower strata of the society. It included the peasants, masons, traders, shopkeepers, artisans and the landless labourers.

The *Kuka* movement had in its fold, people, drawn from various sections of the society. It is, therefore, necessary to examine the impact of this movement on different sections of the society in Punjab and also the reaction and attitude of these section towards the *Kuka* movement. While we have some evidence of the former it is much less for the latter.

Attitude of the Native States

The region in Punjab where the *Kukas* flourished was called Malwa and it consisted of the states of Nabha, Jeend, Patiala and Malerkotla, all in the neighbourhood of the *Kuka* centre. Among these, Malerkotla was a Muslim state while others were Sikh states. After the annexation the British brought to Punjab a new civilization, which was alien to its people.

The *Kuka* movement initially started as a religious movement, but gradually it rose to prominence and attracted the attention of the British. Particularly, it came to light with the famous Anand Marriage at Khote. Though, the *Kuka* movement had its beginning in 1857 AD any significant references about it are not mentioned till 1866 AD in the records of the native sates. Here it may be added that the activities of the *Kukas* from 1857 to 1866 AD were in a formative stage and perhaps during that period there was nothing so striking in it that could have attracted the attention of these states. However, in 1871 the incidents of the butchers' murder and attacks on Malodh and Malerkotla brought it in the lime light and after these incidents, the records of the native states are full of references about the *Kuka* activities.

From the official records it appears that the *Kukas* were not considered as good people and some sort of rebellion was always apprehended from them. The revolt of 1857, must have added to such a suspicion.[2] Even their religious activities were not seen with favour. The rulers of the native states thought that the hidden motives of the *Kukas* were other than mere religious.[3]

The records clearly indicate the growing apprehension of the native states in view of the increasing number of the *Kukas.* Even a rough estimate indicates that the number of *Kukas* was around eleven to twelve thousands in the districts of Ambala and Ludhiana besides around ten thousands in the districts of Firozpur and Patiala territory. Besides, there were not less then twenty thousand in the armies of Jeend and Nabha states.[4] It was reported that there were some *Kukas* in the forces of Patiala states also. One of the records mentions that the number of *Kukas* was growing according to a pre-planned programme made by Ram Singh and some day they might rebel.[5]

Incidentally the information available gives the version of the native states only and other sources in number which could give an independent assessment of the *Kuka* movement. However, one fact cannot be denied that due to one reason or the other, the native states had great hostility towards the *Kukas.* This fact is amply established by the official records of the Patiala State which provide specific information about the strict measures, adopted to suppress the *Kukas* and curb their activities. The *Kuka* meetings were prohibited even if they were peaceful and meant for religious purposes.[6]

The state of Patiala had already dismissed a number of *Kukas* from service and issued a warning that in future if any person of the state service subscribed to the ideology of the *Kukas,* he would be dismissed.[7]

The state of Patiala had given wide publicity to this decision through posters mentioning that an action, under section 309 Indian Penal Code would be initiated against the *Kukas.*[8]

In order to have some moral and religious justification for their action against the *Kuka* activity the Patiala state made it widely known that their decision against the *Kukas* was mainly because their activity was considered against the principles of the Sikh religion, it was neither possible nor justified on its part to allow the continuance of religious activity of a section of people, who by their teachings had threatened the very principles of the State's religion.

How far the Patiala state was justified in taking action against the *Kukas* in the garb of subscribing to the fundamentals of Sikh principles is a matter which hardly needs an explanation. However keeping in view the size and status of the state it seems that the state was trying to reconfirm its loyalty to the British by taking steps against the *Kukas.* In doing so, in fact, they were rather overdoing in order to appease the British.

Incidentally the attitude of the British towards the *Kuka* activity was relatively milder than those of the native states. It is evident from the fact that Khursheed Muhammad Hussain, *Vakil* of Patiala writing from Kohmari informed, "British Government only wants to keep *Kukas* under control and not to oppress them in any way, they only want to keep them under check—*Kukas* are not be troubled or harassed in any way.'[10]

Perhaps the British thought that the *Kukas* had religious leanings and if they were harassed, the masses might become more sympathetic to them and with a more broad-based support they might create more trouble. Therefore, it seems that the British government only tried to harass them by getting them deprived of their jobs and honour. However, the rulers of the native states tried to exhibit more loyalty to the British government, rather than to their own people. In fact, the rulers where overzealous in taking a much harder action against the *Kukas.* It seems that the rulers tried to be more loyal to the British government than the Britishers themselves.

The native states were also worried and apprehensive because of the fast expanding activities of the *kukas,* who were now resorting to violence. *Kukas'* attack on the butchers of Amritsar and Raikot and their attack on Malodh and Malerkotla gave the native rulers an opportunity to suppress this growing movement. Records of Jeend and Patiala narrate in detail about attacks on Malodh and Malerkotla.[11]

Perhaps the greatest apprehension of the rulers of the states was that the *Kukas,* ultimately might take the power over from them. As is evident from one of the documents, "So they decided that there was no ruler in Kotla. So first, they should take over Kotla and then Sangrur, Nabha, Jeend, Patiala and Ambala—thus, after taking permission from their Guru they started for an attack".[12]

The native states gradually felt that the *Kuka* movement might pose a serious challenge to their political authority. Therefore, they thought that unless some firm action was taken against Ram Singh, this movement could not be stopped. They wanted to deprive the *Kuka* movement, of its spiritual leadership, besides the inspiration that the *Kukas* were getting from Ram Singh. To the *Kukas* Ram Singh was not only a genius, but an incarnation of Guru Nanak. This feeling was so deep-rooted that Ram Singh and the movement had become almost synonymous to the mind of the native chiefs. It is in the light of this fact that they advised the British government to send Ram Singh in exile to a place commonly known as '*Kala Pani*'. The view of the native states on this point was as follow. "This all trouble has been created by Ram Singh, who is the Guru of the *Kukas.* Earlier he was a poor man now he is wealthy and rich. Although he does not come outwardly and remains quite, but from within, he is busy on some conspiracy. He is leader of the *Kukas* and *Kukas* think whatsoever is there in the world they own that and when swords will clash every think will be their's".[13]

After the incidents of Malerkotla, telegrams were hurriedly exchanged between the states and the British Government. States rendered prompt help with arms and ammunition, for which, the British Government and the state of Malerkotla thanked the states of Nabha and Patiala.[14]

The Patiala Government helped in arresting the *Kukas* who after the skirmishes at Malerkotla were taking rest at the outskirts of village Rur. There are, however, two versions about the nature of the *Kuka* submission at village Rur as recorded in Patiala and Jeend states papers. While in the former, there is an indication about the desire of resistance on the part of the *Kukas* before submission, but in the latter there is no indication of the possibility of any resistance by the *Kukas* as they were already divided in small groups in different houses.[15] As fas as the theory of resistance recorded in the Patiala papers are concerned it seems it was more to show the chivalry in arresting the *Kukas.* The mention of violence and resistance by the *Kukas* was likely to yield more credit to the forces which had gone to contain the *Kukas* under Niaz-Ali *Navab Nazim.*[16]

However, the persons, who helped in the arrest of the *Kukas* were richly rewarded in terms of ranks, titles, promotions, cash, jewellery and costly clothes, etc.[17] It may be pointed out that even after 1877, those people who got the *Kukas* arrested were rewarded.[18]

In the records of native states of Punjab there are several statements, whereby *Kukas* had admitted that they had renounced *Kukaism* and in future they would not have any link with the *Kukas* nor would they allow any *Kuka* to come to their house. Here it may be noted that in earlier works written on the Namdharis in Punjabi, Hindi and English no scholar has referred to these statements of the *Kukas.* Perhaps they wanted to project the *Kukas* as great heroes. It might have been considered that such statements would reduce the importance of the *Kuka* movement. Besides, it must have been against their self-respect to give such an undertaking to denounce their faith in *Kukaism.* However, such an ommission on the part of the scholars was either due to oversight or due to their emotional attachment with the *Kukas.*[19] The Fact that such undertakings were given by the *Kukas* could not denied as Basawa Singh had given an undertaking that if found guilty he would undergo three months rigorous imprisonment.[20] Other *Kukas* such as Tahal Singh and Punjab Singh had said that they had taken the *Amrit* of *Kukas,* but after the incident of Raikot they were no more *Kukas.*[21] Yet, by another statement, twenty-five persons collectively denounced the *Kuka* faith. They had also given an undertaking to disassociate themselves from *Kuka* activities in any and every form. They promised that neither they would visit the *Kukas* nor invite them to their homes or villages. Not only that, but in case they would come across any *kuka,* they would inform the Government.[22]

Thus, the *Kuka* movement was under active vigilance of the Government. Nobody could help even an ailing *Kuka* without the consent of the Government.[23]

There were cases, when people were denouncing *Kukaism* even without the pressure of the Government. For example, one Hari Singh Kuka wanted to renounce this faith, he approached Deputy Commissioner Gurudaspur Mr J. Fendall who advised him that mere recantation in his presence would not serve the purpose and he and his sons must recant in the temple at Dera Baba Nanak and be formally readmitted into the Sikh fraternity.[24]

Attitude of Native Chiefs

The attitude of the native chiefs and the elite towards the *Kukas* was quite unfavourable. They had supported the anti-*Kuka* activities of other native chiefs since they were aware of the British attitude towards the *Kukas.* These chiefs through various representations and memoranda had conveyed their appreciation and support to the action of the British taken to suppres the *Kukas.* A few of them are mentioned to explain the point. It reflects the attitude of chiefs and to what extent they could express their sense of appreciation for the measures adopted against the *Kukas.*

It is indeed interesting that these chiefs mobilized public opinion in support of the actions of Cowan and Forsyth. A meeting was held in Jullunder under the chairmanship of Sardar Bikram Singh Bahadur and Ahluwallia. A petition was drafted. The petition said, "To Hon'ble Lieutienant Governor of Punjab, may it please your honour, we the subject of her majesty the Queen most respectfully beg to appeal...against the order recently passed by the Government of India whereby Mr Cowan has been dismissed from the service and Mr Fosyth Commissioner of Ambala has been transferred...It is not a hidden fact to the experienced officers of the Government that the Kuka sect never wished that the British administration should continually enjoy tranquality".[25] It further said that all the Rais of Amritsar were brought under difficulty because of them. Had they not been punished according to the gravity of the crime their property, honour and lives would have been exposed to greater danger. The petition was signed by eminent people of the area besides four hundred and thirty seven other including Jagirdars, Member of Municipal Committees, Zaildars, Sahukars, etc., of different towns and villages.[26]

Another memorandum was sent by the Rais of Kalsia which read 'The rebellious and mutinous conduct of the *Kukas* who pretended to the votaries and worshippers of the Diety was not viewed in its true light as it ought to have been ... It was the beliefs of the natives of Hindustan as well as Punjab, generally that the *Kukas* ever since the sect came into existence for their real object, the acquisition of temporal sovereignty of the country".[27] In this long memorandum they trace each act of the *Kukas* towards violence' insurrection and riots. They even said that if Cowan was dismissed and Forsyth was eliminated from the service it would have adverse effect and *Kukas* would revive again. Another petition of the same kind came from the *Rais* and *Jagirdars* of Karnal district. Petitions of similar nature were also sent by the Rajas of Rajaspuri and Bijwara.

However it is surprising that instead of jointly condemning the act of the brutal killing of their native brethren by the mouth of Canon they were supporting the act of Cowan and Forsyth. The significance of the incident could be judged by the fact that questions were raised in the British Parliament for such an uncivilized act of the British officers. While the *Kukas* were blown up, the people from their own religion applauded the action of the Britishers in their own interest.

Officials

In any society challenge to the established authority is viewed unfavourably. It has never been convenient for the smaller units of authorities to ally with the descending voice. The stream of favour flows from higher to lower authority. In this background of the prevailing system it would hardly be surprising to find the elite and more particularly the officials of Punjab expressing their opposition to the *Kuka* movement. There are several instances in which these officials had supported the activities of the native chiefs. Some of them may be mentioned here.

The states were so anxious about the *Kukas* that the *Patwaris* and *Numberdars* were asked to keep a vigilant eye on their activities. They were expected to submit *muchalkas* that they would inform at the nearest police station, whenever some *Kuka* would enter or leave the village. They were often enquired about the presence of *Kukas* in their village. One such document says[8] "It is admitted that the *Numberdars* belong to the region known as Kalaran and with a view to investigate the real state of things, the Kalaran therefore we confess and write down that there is no person by the name of *Nanna Kuka* in our village. If however, the presence of *Kuka* is established in any manner we would be liable to the proposed punishment. Hence these few words in the form of *muchalka* are being written so that it might be available at the proper time and the proper place".[29]

Orders were passed by the Court for the *Numberdars* and *Patwaris* who were held responsible for the presence of *Kuka* in their areas. At times many *Numberdars* collectively used to file a petition with surety and security that they would report about the arrival of any *Kuka* in the village.[30] No *Kuka* would be allowed to leave the village without the permission of the government. *Numberdar* gave an undertaking, "We confess with Rs. twenty-five as a security and we write down that in case we fail to act up to the order noted above then we would be liable to punishment proposed by the court in the shape of *muchalka* and we will have no pleas against it. Therefore, these few words in the shape of Muchalka have been jotted down to be available at the right moment".[31]

Religious Priests

Another important section of the society was that of the religious heads, priests and mahants of the *Gurudwaras* and Brahmins of temples. *Bedis* and *Sodhees* were annoyed with Ram Singh because he had taken their monopoly of baptizing people into the Sikh faith. Which till then could be done only at major Sikh centres like Amritsar, Anandpur Sahib, Patna Sahib and Hazur Sahib, etc. So much so that when Baba Ram Singh visited

Darbar Sahib at Akal Bunga priests refused to do *Ardas* on his behalf.[32]

At Dera Baba Nanak the religious priests asked several questions as to why Ram Singh did not follow the particular Sikh ways of life. At Khote, Brahmins of the village had managed to report Baba Ram Singh's activities to the Government. These reports at once brought a change in the attitude of Government and it is known that for four years he was put in surveillance. Even when he was exiled almost all the priests of different major Sikh centres had praised the decision of the British Government.

A few incidents mentioned above by way example indicate the reaction of the religious class against Baba Ram Singh, the founder of the Namdhari movement. His teachings and insistence on simplifying the religious rituals were obviously against the interests of the Brahmins who not only considered themselves as the custodians of the religious beliefs and practices but had material gains through those practicles. It seems the religious reforms suggested by Baba Ram Singh were opposed by them not so much on religious ground but as a loss of their personal gains. They therefore, not only opposed the reforms of Baba Ram Singh but also tried to remove him from the scene in their own interest.

Reaction of the Common Men

The Namdhari movement under Ram Singh had a large following and within no time he had made it a mass movement.[33] As common with all popular movements, this movement also had a large impact on different sections of the soceity. The Lieutenant Governor of Punjab, in one of his confidential letters to the Governor General had remarked, "The real danger of that creed, in the form which it has now assumed consists in this that it appeals strongly to the sympathies of a large section of native community out side the circle of the avowed *Kukas.* The denunciation of kine-killing and even active measures taken against the butchers of at Raikot and Amritsar have enlisted to a certain extent the sympathies of even well disposed Hindus. While predictions of a restoration of the Khalsa rule appeal to the sympathies of all Sikhs who have not forgotten the traditions of the past. There is evidence no doubt to show that no general coalition exists at present between the orthodox Sikhs and the *Kukas.*[34] This document further speaks of the moral support of Hindus on the matter of cow slaughter, it says "Those who least give way to his pretensions admit that the hearts of all good Hindus are with him in his holy horror of kine-killing."[35] The Namdhari movement due to its teachings had much influence among the Hindus also.

It seems indeed a paradox that while the reaction of the *Kukas* against kine-killing to the extent of violence made them the champions of cow protection on the one hand, but same violence gave them a setback on the other hand, when they were considered as extremists.

Deputy Commissioner Cowan in a letter dated 24th July 1871 reported, "The murderers have lost sympathies of many, who might have rejoiced at the death of the butchers only. The demeanour of the people is good. Salaams to European Officers are more frequent then before ..."[36]

Resolutions at different places were passed against the *Kukas*. "The Sikhs of all classes in Amritsar beg unanimously to submit that we have (sic) no connection or sympathy with the *Kukas*. We are (sic) happy that the Government have adopted most cooperative and excellent measures for controlling this wicked and misguided sect. They are our mortal enemies. Since by their misconduct and evil designs they injured our honour in the estimation of the Government. We are thankful to the Government for the measures, which have been adopted whereby the desire of our hearts has been fulfilled."[37]

With whatever little material is available an attempt has been made to get some ideas of the response and reaction of the various sections of the society in Punjab towards the *Kukas* and their movement. It may be said that various sections of the society were not favourably inclined towards the *Kukas*. Here an obvious question may arise as to whether they genuinely had the dislike for this movement or the political, social and religious factors had somehow conditioned their vision to appreciate this movement. Every section with some political, religious and social authority felt threatened and insecure because of the activities of the *Kukas*. Government constantly kept on "bestowing favours on the gentry to keep it attached to its interest and use it as as a bulwark against the popular forces. These people spied on the *Kukas,* sent secret reports and mobilized public opinion in favour of the Government."[38]

As far as the people who participated in the *Kuka* movement are concerned a more rational and less emotional analysis is needed. In any movement, people committed to a particular ideology and those whose interests were at periphery could be noticed. Similarly in the *Kuka* movement, it would be incorrect to assume that every *Kuka* had the same intensity of feeling about the faith. Keeping in the reaction of different sections of the society and the activities of the *Kukas,* it may be said that they were emotionally involved in the movement. They never reconciled to the idea of submission. But at the same time some *Kukas* succumbed to the pressures of local people and that of the rulers.

REFERENCES

1. In order to appreciate the attitude of the native states one has to go back to Ranjit Singh's time when he took over the territories of Tara Singh Gheba in 1907. This caused great disturbance among the chiefs of Sutlej States, Khushwant Singh in *A History of the Sikhs,* Vol. I. p. 220 writes "The Malwa chiefs were apprehensive and appealed for the British Protection", After records of Ranjit Singh in *Umdatul-Twarikh II* P. 79 says "we do not have a very long life as both the British and Ranjit Singh means to swallow us up. But where as the British protection will be like consumption which takes long life to kill Ranjit Singh's advent will be like a stroke of paralysis". This indicates the apprehension of the native states that Ranjit Singh would destroy them within no time. To counter the aggressive designs of Ranjit Singh a delegation of the chiefs of native states met the Resident at Delhi and stated that they looked upon the British as the sovereign power and wished to be protected by the British power against Ranjit Singh.
2. The anxiety on the part of the native states about the *kukas* is shown when one Chandidass Vakil of the Patiala sent an application to the Commissioner in Ambala on 6th July 1866. He remarked "they were not good people and as in 1857, back people had revolted, these *kukas* can also take up arms at some time". *Mad No. 1-86 of 1923 Foreign Deptt., Patiala.*
3. Chandidass emphasizes that although *kukas* proclaim that they meet to propagate their religion but he fears that they mean something else than just religious purpose.
4. *Mad No. 1-86 of 1923 Foreign Deptt.,* Patiala.
5. Referring to the programme and plans of Ram Singh this document says "Ram Singh has instructed his people to go on adding the number wherever and whenever it is possible and on some opportune movement a successful rebellion could take *Ibid. place.*
6. Kuka meetings and gathering were prohibited in the native states in accordance with the instructions of Deputy Commissioner Ambala Mr. Barkley who said "Kuka meetings and even religious gatherings were to be dispersed by the police and even if they do not dissolve the meeting under section 339 Indian Penal Code he should be challaned and arrested." *Mad No. 1-86 of 1923 B.K.*
7. A parwana was issued on behalf of the Government of Punjab by the Patiala Government about the dismissal of the *Kukas* "we have understood the situa-

tion that the officer of the Sarkar in regard to the *kukas* have taken the steps of dismissing them from the service of the Government. *Ibid.* See Appendix V(i)

8. "For the future this arrangement has been made that wherever any *kuka* would be found in Government service his name would be struck off from the list. This thing has been notified to the public. Posters have been put up on behalf of the Court." *Ibid.*
9. Further justifying their attitude this document says "this new religion is against the Sikh religion. Therefore who so ever will embrace this religion he will be punished by the Court. Officials also hoped that this arrangement would prove satisfactory in future."
   Mad No. 1-84 B.K. Foreign Ministry, Patiala.
10. *Mad No. 1-86, 1923, B.K.*
    This attitude is future confirmed by the letter of Chandidass which he wrote to Maharaja of Patiala See Appendix V (ii).
11. See Appendix R and S.
12. *FF No. 741 Sangin Munshi Khana Jeend State.*
    It is a point of dispute as to whether *kukas* acted on the advice of Ram Singh and has been discussed earlier in the other Chapter (V).
13. *File No. H-10-R 1938, B.K.* Foreign Ministry, Patiala See Appendix U.
14. *FFIA, F-FIB Mirasla of Malerkotla.*
15. Sangin Munshikhana paper of Jeend State mention about the arrest of *kukas* in this way "Numberdars of the village Rur after careful thought and consideration offered them to take meals. They accepted the offer for food since they had not taken for last three days. To ensure that there is no further conspiracy they were trapped and divided in different houses of the village from two to three. Then two persons were sent for the Nazim that *Kukas* have come there for riots and we have divided them. Assistant administrator come with force and all of them were arrested." *FF No. 741 Sangin Munshikhana Jeend State* See Appendix S.
16. Patiala records gave different versions of the arrest of *kukas,* Niaz Ali in his report said that when he went to arrest them with the help of Amar Singh, Uttam Singh and Mastan Ali, Sixty to seventy *kukas* who wanted to resist their arrest but when Niaz Ali disclosed his identity and of Sardar Punjab Singh Raipuria arrived with his double barrel guns, the *kukas* submitted without any resistance.
    File No. H-9-R Foreign Ministry Patiala.
    File No. H-92 M Foreign Ministry pol. Patiala See Appendix T.
17. For greater and other details see Appendix 'T'.
18. In 1877 some more people were rewarded for helping in the arrest of Kirpal Singh alias Khusal Singh who was absconding, Mehar Singh Sergeant and Ganesha Ram Constable thana Bhadsom Nabha states were rewarded with Rs. Twenty-five and Rs. Five respectively for their services, *FF. 3 A Mirasala Malterkotla.*
19. There are references in state paper about such submission-One of these records "I i.e. Gyani Singh Kuka alias Suba Singh resident of Mandi hereby vouch with a *muchalka* to the effect that hereafter we would not follow the creed kuka nor we would ever meet Ram Singh and will not get out of the Gurudwara of Jeend without Government orders. If we disobey then we would be liable to furt her imprisonment over and above the imprisonment of two years. Therefore, I am tendering this *muchalka* with my blood that I will remain confined within the precincts of Gurudwara Darbar Sahib and I will follow the directions as laid down by the head priests of Darba Sahib and if some persons were to make allega-

tions from Jeend that I have departed a hair breadth from matters noted above then whatever punishment is laid down would be binding on me."
Mutfarka Munshikhana 1365 Jeend State, See Appendix O.
Similarly in another statement it is mentioned as follows. Harnam Singh says "I am chela of Ram Singh residing in the village Mehdikalan but I assure there is no kuka here and nobody is visiting me, even I am myself so much terrified that I am not going out."
Ibid.

20. *Mutfarka Munshikahana 1362 Jeend State,* p. 33.
21. *Ibid.,* p. 37.
22. *Ibid.,* p. 197.
23. Ganga Singh and Basawa Singh who were zemindar of mauza Kakarpur gave an undertaking and surety that they want to take Deva Singh Kuka who was seriously sick with them since he was imprisoned. They undertook that when ever called by the Government he would honour the orders.
Ibid., p. 249.
24. When Hari Singh went to the temples on the advice of the Deputy Commissioner he was accompanied by many othr kukas for the same purpose. With him were Kartar Singh Bedi (an important suba of Ram Singh), Amar Singh, Gunda Singh, Partap Singh and Jagir Singh. They were enquired by the priests as to why had they left Sikhism on this they replied "They had been deceived and cajoled by Ram Singh ... was an imposter ... and out caste and no better than a sweeper than they bowed down to the Grunth. Hari Singh was fined fifty-five rupees while others had to pay only customary one rupee and four annas. After this they were blessed by the priest and re-admitted into the Sikh community. Document says "these eight men some of great social influence and all men of mark have thus in the most solemn and public manner adjured kukasim."
Letter No. 175 dated 16th April 1872.
Guru Ram Singh and the Kuka Sikh Book III, p. 14.
25. *Home Department Judicial A Proceedings,* March 1872, No. 235.
26. *Ibid.*
27. *Judicial A Proceedings,* March 1872, No. 235.
28. *Mutfarka Munsaikhana No. 1362 Jeend State,* See Appendix O.
29. *Ibid.*
30. Khazan Singh, Kaid Singh, Sham Singh, Gharib Singh, Deva Singh, Shobha Singh and several other numberadars of village Mandi Kalan area Belopur filled a petition in the form of *Munchalka.* See Appendix 'P'.
31. *Mutfarka Munshikhana 1362 Jeend State.* Also see for greater details in Chapter III.
32. *Foreign Department Political A,* February 1868, No. 202-203.
33. This aspect has already been discussed earlier. See also *Mad No. 1-86 of 1923 Foreign Deptt.,* Patiala.
34. *Home Judicial A Proceedings,* June 1872, No. 107-11.
35. *Ibid.*
36. *Home Judicial Proceedings,* 29th July 1871, No. 45-61.
37. *Home Judicial Proceedings,* March 1872, No. 235.
38. *Kuka Movement,* p. 188.

7

External Relations of the Namdharis

In this chapter an attempt has been made to trace the relations of Namdharis with external states and countries. It is significant to note that Namdharis, besides, having considerable influence in Punjab had extended the same beyond the frontiers of Punjab. Such influence is evident especially with important states and countries like Kashmir, Nepal and Russia. Baba Ram Singh had initiated a reforms movement, which aimed to purify the degraded Sikh society. It also aimed at strengthening the Sikh character and arousing their morals.

Baba Ram Singh was known for his reform even to a distant place like Kabul. In February Captain Baillie brought to notice the fact "that a native gentleman of some note in Kabul by name Abdul Razak had sent his two sons on a mission to Bhainee, it is supposed to learn Ram Singh's doctrines. It was not found possible to elicit any particulars regarding the journey though it would have been interesting to know how the fame of a village carpenter had reached so far".[1] Baba Ram Singh is said to have himself sent an envoy to Kabul. Bishen Singh who was well versed in Arabic, Pushto and Persian was staying in Kabul and working for Kukaism and maintaining relations with Russia.[2]

After the annexation of Punjab, Kashmir was sold to Raja Gulab Singh by the Britishers. Meanwhile conditions in Europe had changed and after the Crimean war, Britain was afraid of Russian attack through Afghanistan and Kashmir. Now Britishers were more concerned about the protection of their Indian borders particularly the routes falling in the North West.

On the other side, in Kashmir Darbar there were two groups. One was pro-Britishers which was headed by Diwan Kirpa Ram and another group was led by Vedantee. Vedantee was the guru and consultant of Maharaja Ranbir Singh. Raja was a man of independent ideas and did not like British hold on Kashmir. He wanted to keep Kashmir out of British influence which was a difficult task.

Raja Ranbir Singh wanted to increase the number of his forces. He had already raised regular regiments of Bhattis and Dogurs.[3] Now he wanted to raise another battalion of strong people for which Punjab was the best place. One confidential report of 1866 says about "the advent of a Cashmere recruiting party."[4] A demi official letter from Srinagar dated 5th Oct. 1871 said "his orders to those whom he sent to the Punjab to recruit were to get men of fine physique and good family. His idea being that by having men of good family he could through their influence get their relatives in like manner to enlist for his service."[5]

Kuka Enlistment in Kashmir Forces

Baba Ram Singh on the advice of Suba Kahn Singh allowed his disciples to join the service of Maharaja of Kashmir. Rather he welcomed the suggestion of Suba Kahn Singh for sending the Kukas in the territory of Kashmir. It seems, it was a little convenient and safe to develop and consolidate the Kuka activity outside the territory of Punjab where it was under strict vigilance of the Britishers who were always apprehensive of their activities. After the butcher killings and attacks on Malodh and Malerkotla British Government did not want to enlist Kukas for their services nor could native states keep them in their services since they rallied on the support of British Government[6]. However Kukas and some other historians believe that Kukas did not take up job with the Britishers as it was a boycott of government services and a directive of Baba Ram Singh.[7]

Perhaps, Baba Ram Singh was seeking job avenues for his people out of Punjab. He thought that his men could be made good warriors at the expense of the other powers. He was indeed making an experiment. Had he been successful in his scheme it could have been carried out at other places also where the Kukas could have the military training without any fear. Since their drills and parades were prohibited in Punjab.

Thus "the enlistment of the Kukas in the Jumoo service was brought about by Suba Kahn Singh Mahant who persuaded Guru Ram Singh to send Heera Singh to the Maharaja as his (the Gurus) agent in order to propose the raising of a Kuka force and Sardar Heera Singh obtained an interview with the Maharaja through the good offices of Colonel"[8] Hukma Singh who thought well of the Kuka tenets. This led to the entry of the Kukas in the Kashmir state.

Kuka regiment in Kashmir

In 1868 Sardar Heera Singh who was a Jagirdar of Sudowrah in the Saharanpur district met Maharaja at Jumoo and was allowed to enlist a regiment of the Kukas. He was even appointed to command that force under the subordination of Colonel Hukma Singh.[9] Sardar Heera Singh took 175 Kukas with him to Jumoo where on the advice of Maharaja they were split into two new regiments.

Considering the piety of Kuka living, Maharaja told them to have an independent regiment because in Dogurs regiment they could not keep their religious traditions. "These men were formed into two companies and were for four months at Jammu learning their drill. They were then sent to garrison the fort of Nowshera where they remained for three months and from where they were sent to Kashmir where they remained for one year in the cantonment of Batmalloo".[10] After remaining in Batmalloo for some time the Kukas were stationed at Muzaffarabad Kathu fort and then sent to Doputta fort.

In the beginning Maharaja of Kashmir was quite happy with the Kukas and they had good relations with him, who had not only allowed them to have an easy access and position in the court but were much patted and pampered by him. One report of C. Girdlestone in 1871 reported from Kashmir "The two hundred men stayed at Jumoo for a while and were then transferred to Srinagar. During their stay there they were much pampered and patted. Presents were frequently bestowed on them irrespective of their pay and prominent place was assigned to anyone who liked to go to Darbar. It was not an uncommon thing for a party of them to attend Darbar after morning parade."[11] Thus the growing importance of the Kukas and some sort of special privilege enjoyed by them had already created hatred in the minds of the other group of Kashmir courtiers and nobles led by Diwan Kirpa Ram. They were protected and patronised by the Britishers.

British Anxiety

The rise of the Kukas in Kashmir was a matter of great concern for the Britishers. Though the number of Kukas there was about two hundred which was relatively much less from the other groups like Dogurs and Bhattis yet the presence of the Kukas seems to have remained on eye-sore to the Britishers because of their known commitments. Detailed enquiries from different sources were made to know "the number, pay, discipline and equipment of the regiment which was quite in an embryo condition at that time."[12] But the fact remains that they were quite aware of the fighting spirit of the Sikhs and correspondence between the Secretary of Punjab L.H. Griffin and L. Colonel Mac-Andrew, Inspector General of Punjab shows that Britishers were quite afraid of the Sikhs being in the army of their neighbouring states and wanted to stop enlistment from Punjab by legislation "Foreign Princes can easily enlist at present without drawing attention to their action by securing the services of one or two recruits in a number of separate villages and telling them to find their own way singly to their regiment. The only way to ensure information in such cases would be to make the nearest male relative in the family and the lumberdars of the village responsible for reporting the occurrence of such enrolments"[13] By another order even the entrance by any enlistment party in Punjab from a foreign state was supposed to be informed to the Government.[14]

Disbanding Process Begins

Diwan Kirpa Ram was always against the enlistment of the Kukas and had advised the king not to take them in his ranks. "He represented to the Maharaja that no object was served by employing men of this sect who were opposed to the Hindu religion. The men were accordingly dismissed. "Now that intelligence report has been received of the murders of the butchers by men of this sect the Maharaja has commended the foresight of Diwan Kirpa Ram and has ordered all Kukas to be dismissed."[15] Britishers were surprised at Maharaja employing men whom the British Government would not take into ranks. In the due course of time the Raja of Kashmir also started considering the Kukas as political liability and thought them as controversial people. Considering the Kukas neither useful nor helpful for the state the Raja decided to disband them.[16]

Immediate Cause of Disbanding

Events of butchers' murder which took place at Raikot and Amritsar were quite alarming for the native as well as foreign states and after this, Kuka relations with Kashmir were severed. When they were disbanded they had at least the arrears of ten month's salary due to the Kashmir government. "The regiment numbered once 125 men, they never had uniform issued to them and only twelve had firearms or swords, the remainder did duty with a lathie... Hira Singh of Sundowrah was the commandant of Rs. 30/-. Tara Singh Gujranwala adjutant on an equal pay. Lall Singh, Bahadur Singh, Moola Singh and Budh Singh all of Sudowrah held appointment of Rs. 15/-, 12/-, 11/- and 10/-. Jye Singh Nilmony Singh Kuka was the (Ilegible). The Kukas were stationed at the forts of Muzaffarabad Kuthai and Dessutta. Their nominal pay was Rs. 9 (or Rs. 5-10 queens coin) per mensem out of which they had to feed themselves, they were constantly in arrears and on dismissal owed ten months salary".[17]

The change in the attitude of Maharaja towards the Kukas was understood by them. As a result, even before the final dismissal by Maharaja they started leaving his jobs. "When Sardar Heera Singh returned from leave only 70 men remained, the rest having left in consequence of irregularity and being badly paid ... some of the men had returned to their homes and others were coming"[18]. Murder of butchers further hastened their removal from Kashmir forces. The Government of India considered Kukas as useless "the foolish Kukas were pre-mature in commencing disturbances and in the consequences of the butcher massacre their bad intentions became known too soon and led to the nucleus of the military assemblage or force in Kashmir territory being broken up, otherwise the numbers would have largely increased and been recruited by orders of the Guru Sahib Baba Ram Singh".[19]

Relation with Nepal

Nepal was an independent neighbouring state of India. Maharaja of Nepal who was then called Paanch Sarkar used to be the nominal head of the Nepal. Actual power was enjoyed by the Prime-Minister who was called Teen Sarkar.[20] Rana Jang Bahadur was then the Prime Minister. He was a shrewd politician. For some time he was at the Lahore Darbar with his maternal uncle General Matabar Singh Thapa at the time of Ranjit Singh.

In 1850, he attacked Tibet and defeated the Tibetans. In the peace treaty Jang Bahadur emphasised that "all the Sikh prisoners of Lahore Darbar should be handed over to Nepal. In this way the Sikhs not only reached in Nepal but they were made officers and instructors in the Nepali army. When British Government put restrictions on Namdharis in Punjab some of them went to stay in Nepal.

Sardar Moti Singh an adjutant in the Nepali forces was son of Hari Singh Nalva who had taken Namdhari *Amrit* in 1869 at Manawala village. He had taken several Kukas with him to Nepal. Rana Jang Bahadur was not happy with the Britishers because despite of his help rendered to them during the 1857, he was not given back the territory which the Britishers had taken from him by the treaty of Sagauli. So he was ready to have relations with anybody who was against the Britishers. He looked for all disgrunted persons around him. Kukas were found useful and he wanted to have some sort of relations with them which was appreciated by the Kukas. In the beginning, relations with Kukas started when the Rana requested them to send two buffaloes and two mules.[21]

Rana Jang Bahadur was well aware of the Kuka activities in Punjab as Colonel R.C. Lawrence, a Resident in Nepal in a confidential letter informed C.U. Aitchison, Secretary to the Government of India, Foreign Department: "The minister spoke openly and freely regarding these people. He said that he had several conversations with them about their leader Ram Singh and with reference to their number and position in the Punjab and His Excellency appeared to have been impressed with a sense of the strength and standing they had already obtained in the country and he remarked that unless well looked after they would probably prove a source of trouble to the British Government.[22] Rana was quite aware of the Kuka strength in Punjab when he said "this new sect which has so recently appeared in the Punjab already numbering about 300000 followers all professing implicit belief in their guru and ready to do his bidding whether for good or evil."[23]

Commercial Relations

When enquired about the mission of their visit Rana said he wanted to have some Punjabi buffaloes and he had commissioned a Sikh in the service of the *darbar* to purchase some animals for him. Kukas availed of this opportunity to visit Nepal.[24] It appears that both the sides had some desire to establish relationship. Rana graciously responded to the presents sent by Kuka and return gifts. They comprised one Tibetan horse, 50 yards of Banal cloth, 108 Garland of Mask, 2 Khukheries and Rs. 500/- in cash.

However, there is no mention of this return gifts in the official sources. This exchange of gifts show that Rana Jang Bahadur had respect for Baba Ram Singh and he wanted to assist him secretly without coming in the eyes of the Britishers because when he was asked about Kuka's enlistment in his armies he said "It is opposed to the policy of the Darbar to recruit the ranks of the Gorkha Army with aliens and the only foreigner they can enlist are men qualified to act as drill instructors or as artificers in their magazines."[25]

But the British Government was quite scared of the relations of Baba Ram Singh. "This attempt of Baba Ram Singh to get a party of his followers under arms in Kashmir and also a similar move in Nepal goes for to show that he is working outside the sphere of a mere Guru or religious teachers."[26]

Relations with Russia

About the relations of Kuka with Russia, the earliest available records are of 1882 A.D. Thus, it was only after the deportation of Baba Ram Singh to Mergui, that the Kukas thought of seeking active help from Russia. In some way Russia had always served as a place of shelter to politically uprooted people from India. "Maya Hindu believed to be a native of the Gujranwala District was a jamadar in a native regiment but absconded after the mutiny. He now lives in Shib-diwalas at different places in Russia and Afghan Turkstan".[27] Likewise, another document says that Jammu State sent two Mohammedans of Madari tribe in 1867 to meet General Revanasky as envoys from Kashmir.[28] Besides Kukas some other native states were also trying to seek Russian help after the mutiny. "In the year 1875, one Hira Lal alias Ram Chand, a Maratha of Gwalior presented himself before General Kaufman and stated that he was in service of the Maharaja of Gwalior and Bhurtpore and stated that his master together with several other rajas are ready to join with Russia".[29] Even the state of Ram Nagar was trying to have relations with Russia.[30] Because of the hostile attitude of England and Russia against each other especially after the Crimean War to Kukas.

Russia was looked upon by the Kukas as saviour. They believe that according to Sau-Sakhi "There will be a man by name Bishan Singh in the garb of a fakir in the Russian dominion. The Czar will have a dream in which Bishan Singh will tell him that the Mahan Malech opposes us considerably. Our rule has been subverted by the Malech. Restore it to us by some means or other. Russia will, therefore, write to Turkey to stop the war. Turkey will take little heed of the letters and be displeased. The princes, Prime Ministers and others also will disagree to the proposal of Russia. Turkey will refuse, whereupon Russia will be annoyed and issue orders to her servants. Turkey, Russia and the rest will fight but in spite of all their efforts Turkey will be defeated and Russia will be victorious. Afterwards, the forces of Russia will advance on the Punjab. Bishen Singh and other members of the Khalsa will all meet together."[31] At the annual

Baisakhi fair held at Amritsar in the spring of 1884 Bishen Singh was described as "the Guru's precious jewel and martyr who has a large following has entered into negotiations with others who have expressed their readiness to join him".[32]

However, it is interesting to note that Russian sources do not speak about Bishen Singh who was so highly esteemed by the Kukas. In January 1882 W.M. Young, Secretary to Punjab Government informed A.C. Lyall, Secretary to the Government of India "Communications have been addressed to you from time to time regarding the proceedings of one Gurcharan Singh, son of Attar Singh Virk jat of Chak Parana in the Sialkot district, who has been for many years in the habit of visiting Central Asia and has been suspected of conveying intelligence from the Russian authorities in Central Asia to members of the Kuka Sect."[33] Gurcharan Singh was a descendant of Bhai Parana, a companion and disciple of Guru Nanak who established a *dharamsala* at Kabul. Gurcharan Singh had some relations in Kabul and as a boy he used to visit the followers[34] of his ancestors at Kabul. When he was in Sikh army he visited Kabul to collect some information for Raja Lall Singh. He became a *Kuka* in 1867 and was made a Suba in 1868.[35]

It is quite likely that he was the master-mind behind the relations of Kukas and the Russians.[36] Even earlier, he was collecting information about Central Asia for Sikh rajas. He must have encouraged the Kukas to have some relations with Russia and to seek their help for the restoration of Sikh rule in Punjab. British Government was not only aware of his activities but they were also suspicious of his moves when they refer about him: "the Lieutenent Governor has arrived at the conclusions that it is not expedient that he should remain at liberty as he will certainly continue to act in future as the medium of communication between the Russian authorities in Central Asia and the disaffected Kukas."[37] Gurcharan Singh himself said to the Russian leaders "He was considered eminently suitable for the task not because he had been in Kabul several times, knew the way leading to the Russian domains and could interpoet to the Russians better than any other, the attitude of the Indian people towards the British rulers"[38], First information about him to the Government was supplied by British Spy Gulab Khan who helped in his imprisonment later on.

Central Asian Experience of Gurcharan Singh

About the Central Asian experience of Gurcharan Singh there is some evidence preserved in the Archives of the Uzbeg Socialist Soviet Republic. However, the British record mention "on the Ist May 1879 a Kuka named Gurcharan Singh of the Village of Chak-Chak (Chak Ram Dass) of the Gujranwala Sialkot district, a tall man with a white beard and about fifty years old arrived in Katta-Kurajhan from India"[39] Russian document also discloses that on 9th May 1879 the citizens of Katta Kurghan a border city of Russian Turkistan came across an old Indian Gurcharan Singh by name. He was carrying with him a letter addressed to Governor-General of Turkestan by the Chief Priest and leader of the Sikhs. It was handwritten in Gurmukhi Script and did not bear the signature of the sender.[40] But Gulab Khan was of the view that the letter was in Hindi and was sent by Baba Ram Singh *kuka* leader and signed by several other *kukas.*[41]

Gurcharan Singh Meets Russian Officer

Soon after Major General N.A. Ivanov the principal officer of the Jeravshansk circle came to know about him, he expressed his desire to meet Gurcharan Singh personally at Samarkand. It was difficult for Gurcharan Singh to convey the contents of the letter to Russians but there was one Indian trader who knew both Persian and Gurmukhi. He translated the letter into Persian and from Persian it was translated into Russian without difficulty.[42]

Letter contained[43] the so called prediction of Guru Gobind Singh mention "Sant Khalsa (Kukas) would emerge in 1238. We should then be free from Aurangzeb but the English would suddenly begin to tyrannise over us. Then a band of people called Russians would come and drive out the English. The Russian hero would win."[44] The letter said that the *Kukas* had 315,000 Sikh fighters and if required many more would be found. This was a clear invitation to the Russian to invade India[45] and to rule after the victory. Such letter was bound to create some anxiety among the Russian administrators of Turkestan. N.I. Korolkov, an assistant to the Chief of the Jeravshansk circle had a long discussion with Gurcharan Singh, who disclosed that after the arrest of Baba Ram Singh, the leadership of the Namdhari sect passed on to his brother Baba Budh Singh who was aware of all the happenings in and around India.[46] The apprehension of both the British Government and the Sikhs about the possibility of Russian interference in Panjab, is not confirmed by the Russian sources. However, the *Kukas* believed that after the defeat of the English, the Russians would transfer the administration of the Punjab to the hands of Dalip Singh the off-spring of Maharaja Ranjit Singh.[47] Ivanov forwarded the letter of Baba Ram Singh together with the notes about the discussion which he had with Gurcharan Singh to K.P. Kayufman the Governor General of Turkestan. Kayufman consulted I.P. Minacov who was a specialist on Indian affairs at that time. He was aware of the rise of Namdhari sect and their suppression by the British rulers.[48] In his opinion there was nothing unusual in sending a person to enlist Russian support in the liberation movement launched by the *Kukas*. However, he also pointed out that Baba Nanak the first Sikh prophet lived in the 15th Century and could not be the author of the prediction, concerning the arrival of the Russians in Punjab. It was of contemporaneous origin and attributed to him to serve the need of the hour.[49]

However, "Kayufman decided to proceed with caution and made no departure from the policy of non intervention in British affairs.[50]

Kuka Envoy was Honoured.

However, Gurcharan Singh was received with great honour by the Russian and on the "12th June he received about Rs. 700 in Russian notes and three *chogas* of silk. A Shikarpuri merchant named Jawalla was ordered to entertain him."[51] However, another letter of Gulab Khan says "Gurcharan Singh later received 7 *chogas* and 2,500 *tangas* and was told to return to the Punjab and strengthen the friendship between the Russian and the *Kukas*."[52]

Gurcharan Singh was given a letter also to be delivered to Baba Ram Singh, which mentioned "Greetings from the

Commander-in-Chief and Governor General to Baba Ram Singh and Baba Budh Singh". It further recorded thanks for the informative communication but it is desirable to have details, more fresh news about the affairs and situation in India. The prophecy of Guru Govind Singh and Baba Nanak was noted for information. Everything will happen according to the will of God. The prophet knows the best when the hour will strike."[53]

The Russian document record the return journey of Gurcharan Singh in October 1879. N.A. Khalfins the Soviet Historian says that Gurcharan Singh reached safely the land of his birth but Namdharis or Kukas did not make any further attempt to renew their relations with Russia. About this incident P.C. Roy said that N.A. Khalfin was not aware of what the English records had to tell as to how Gulab Khan the British agent in Central Asia dogged the foot-steps of the *Kuka* patriot to contrive his arrest and detention soon after his arrival in India.[54] According to Mr. C. Brown's narration Gurcharan Singh after leaving Peshawar went to Hazro in the Rawalpindi District thence through Rawalpindi to his home Chak Parana and on 19th December he reached Lahore. He was ordered by the police not to leave the place without permission but on 21st December he went away secretly.[55] Nevertheless he was caught and imprisoned in the Anarkali prison as a political detenu under regulations III of 1818.

He was kept under surveillance in Multan till 1887, when he was allowed to return to his home in Sialkot on the condition that he would neither leave the district without the permission of the local authorities nor would make an attempt to cross the frontier.[56]

Kukas did try to have all sorts of help from Russians as they were sending the letters to Russia. The British Government was so alert that their no letter could reach to the hands of the Russian authorities. British sources themselves speak about some letters sent by *Kukas* to the Russians.[57] These letters were giving latest information about the British borders of North West and Eastern regions. In one of the letters taken by one Maya to the Russian recorded that British army had marched from Kabul for Balkh and that Sardar Wali Muhammed Khan was already on the Balkh side of Bamion with the advance guard.[58] Another letter speaks about

Burma, Rangoon, etc. that as to how people of Rangoon have submitted to Baba Ram Singh. In all the letters Russians are assured of the truthfulness of the predictions of *Sau-Sakhi*. Consequently, they not only invited the Russians to invade India but were given the assurance of full help from the Kukas and other Sikhs of Punjab.

British espionage system was quite strong to undo all attempts of the Kukas and watch their schemes to seek help from the other corners. It is quite likely that these letters never reached Russians and were always intercepted.

As far as the relations of the Kukas with neighbouring powers were concerned the same may be seen briefly. Ahluwalia thinks "so far as Kashmir and Nepal were concerned they were the least inspired by the noble sentiments of the Namdhari cause." The political attitude of the ruling dynasty of Kashmir was considered as betrayal to the Sikh cause. It could never lend any support to this movement, directed against the paramount power.[59]

About the change in the attitude of the Maharaja of Kashmir towards the Kukas it may be mentioned that the Maharaja was raising the battalion of Kukas not to please them or to help. He wanted to have different regiments and as he had already had two that of Dogras and Battis, "he pampered the Kukas and then threw them out to please his British masters".[60]

Almost same was the case with Nepal. It could not annoy the Britishers at any cost. Immediately after the Malerkotla incident when 49 Kukas were blown away with guns some of the Nepali Generals supported the Britishers. Official records show that General Babbur Jang offered his services to the British government to suppress the *Kukas* insurrections.

On the basis of whatever little material is available on the relations of the *Kukas* with the countries outside India, it can be mentioned that in spite of the fact that *Kukas* were enthusiastic in extending their area of influence to those countries, they could hardly find any favourable response from them.

In this connection the attitude of Russia deserves a special mention, as in spite of its hostility with Britishers, it could neither found any substance in the irritation of *Kukas* nor the political condition of India which could have made their intervention possible.

It may also be pointed out that while the Namdharis were very keen to have relation with the external powers, the Nirankaris had no such political ambitions.

REFERENCES

1. *Foreign Department Political A Proceedings,* February 1868, No. 202-203.
2. *Baba Ram Singh Namdhari,* p. 86.
   Jaswant Singh Jas.
3. *Home Department Judicial, Jan. 13-1872,* No. 56.
4. *Home Department Judicial, Feb. 1872,* No. 46.
5. *Home Department Judicial, Jan. 13-1872,* No. 56.
6. *Firman of Puttiala Raja,* 1-86-Mad. 1923, B.K.
7. For details see Baba Ram Singh Namdhari Jaswant Singh Jas Kuka Movement Fauja Singh.
8. *Home Department Judicial, Jan. 13-1872,* No. 58.
9. *Ibid.*
10. *Home Department Judicial, Jan. 13-1872,* No. 58.
11. *Home Department Judicial, Jan. 13-1872,* No. 56.
12. *Foreign Department Political A, Feb. 1872,* No. 44.
13. *Ibid.*
14. No. 43.
15. *Home Department Judicial, 13 Jan. 1872,* No. 56.
16. *Ibid.*
17. *Home Department Judical, 13 Jan. 1872,* No. 59.
    According to Jaswant Singh Jas and Nahar Singh the salary of each *kuka* solider was Rs. 10 or 10 Chilkies (Kasmiri coin equal to Rs. 1) where as the salary of other soldiers was one rupee less than the *kuka* soliders and they were getting only Rs. 9 a month.
    i) Baba Ram Singh Namdhari, p. 86.
    ii) Namdhari Itihas Pratham Bhag, p. 108, Nahar Singh.
18. *Home Department Judical, 13 Jan. 1872,* No. 58.
19. *Ibid.*
20. Namdhari Ithihas, Pratham Bhag, p. 109, Nahar Singh.
21. Prof. Ganda Singh feels it surprising and not understandable as to why mules were asked from Punjab as region was not known for the mules.
22. Foreign Deptt. Political, *A* Feb 1872, No. 39.
23. *Ibid.*
24. Jaswant Singh says "Rana sent a message to Baba Ram Singh to send him two buffaloes and two mules as a friendly gift. As soon as he got the message Suba Kahn Singh and Suba Sahib Singh were sent to purchase these animals from

village Ratol in the district of Firuzpur and Suba Sahib Singh purchased two horses from district Lahore." Both the Subas and four other Namdharis were accordingly sent to Nepal.

i) Baba Ram Singh Namdhari, p. 90, Jaswant Singh Jas.

25. Foreign Department Political A, February 1872, No. 39.
26. Home Deptt Judicial, January 13-1872, No. 58.
27. Foreign Department Secret Proceedings, No. 586, January 1882.
28. K.W. Secret F, August 1882, No. 114-115.
29. Confidential Foreign Department Secret F.K.W. No. 114-155, August 1889.
30. *Ibid.*
31. Confidential K.W., Foreign Department Secret F, No. 114-115, August 1889.
32. *Ibid.*
33. Foreign Department Secret F, January 1882, No. 568.
34. See Appendix-U.
35. Foreign Department Secret, January, 1982, No. 578, Enclosure No. 9.
36. *Indian Historical Records Commission Proceedings,* Volume XXXIV, Part II, Trivendrum, December 1958, P.C. Roy, pp. 87.
37. *Foreign Department Secret Proceedings, No. 568,* January, 1882.
38. *Foreign Department Secret Proceedings, No. 571,* January 1882. Described as item No. 462 in the consular fonds of the Turkestan Governor General it bears the title "The ambassador from the priest of the Punjab Sikhs arrives in Samarkand (1879)". This document has been searched by Soviet Historian N.A. Khalfin and contains the original copy of the letter sent by Kuka Guru and a copy of the reply sent by the Russians.
39. *Indian Historical Records Commission Proceedings* B, Volume XXXIV, Part II. Trivendrum Dec., 1958. Article Gurcharan Singh *Mission in Central Asia.* P.C. Roy, p. 85-86.
40. *Foreign Department Secret Proceedings, No. 571, January, 1882.*
41. *Indian Historical Records Commission Proceedings, Volume* XXXIV, *p. 86.* Trivendrum Dec., 1958. Article Gurcharan Singh *Mission in Central Asia.* P.C. Roy, p. 85-86.
42. The content of the letter is in fact reproduction of the *Sau-Sakhi.*
43. Indian Historical Records Commission Proceedings, Volume XXXIV, p. 86.
44. *Foreign Department Secret Proceedings No. 571, January 1882.*
45. *Foreign Department Secret Proceedings No. 571, January 1882.*
46. *Indian Historical Records Commission Proceedings,* Volume XXXIV, Part II.
47. *Indian Historical Records Commission Proceedings,* Vol. XXXIV, Part II. Trivendrum Dec.. 1958. Article Gurcharan Singh *Mission in Central Asia.* P.C. Roy, p. 88.
48. *Ibid.*
49. *Indian Historical Records Commission Proceedings.*
50. Foreign Department Secret Proceeding, No. 571, Enclosure No. 2, January, 1882.
51. *Ibid* Enclosure No. 3, Proceeding No. 571.

52. C.G.I.A. Uzbekskoii S.S.R. F 1 op 34 D 462 quoted in N.A. Khalfins "Posolstovo Baba Ram Singhkha B Turkestan B 1879 Godu" published in *Sovestkoe Vostokoveadenie* No. 2, 1957, p. 158. Quoted by P.C. Roy.
53. *Indian Historical Records Commission Proceedings, Volume* XXXIV Part II, Trivandrum 1958 *article Gurcharan Singh's Mission in Central Asia,* P.C. Roy, p. 89.
54. *Foreign Department Secret Proceedings, January 1882, No. 575.*
55. *Foreign Department Secret Proceedings F, August 1889, Nos. 114-115.*
56. *Foreign Department Secret Proceedings 572, January 1882, No. 574, 589, 591, 592.*
57. *Foreign Department Secret Proceedings,* January 1882, No. 572.
58. Ahluwalia, M.M. Kukas the freedom fighters of Punjab, p. 114, Allied Publishers, 1965 Delhi.
59. *Ahluwalia, M.M. Kukas the Freedom Fighters,* p. 114.
60. Foreign Department Political B Proceeding, Feb. 1872, 132-133.

8

Conclusion

In the preceding chapters an attempt has been made to discuss various features of two important Sikh movements of Punjab during the nineteenth century.

Nineteenth century was a period of social awareness and it witnessed a number of important socio-religious movements throughout Northern India and Punjab was no exception to it. The main objective of these two movements, was essentially to restore Sikhism to its basic principles and save it from the growing influence of Brahmanism. The contribution of these two movements to the socio-religious life of the Sikh society of Punjab during the nineteenth century is the scope of the present work.

The political role of the *Kukas* has been covered by various other scholars. I have no intention to enter into the debate whether the *Kukas* activities were mainly political or not as I have confined my emphasis to the socio-religious activities of both the movements which so far has remained out of the preview of scholarly research. This aspect has been taken in the present work to greater details. Some new sources have also been consulted on this aspect.

While dealing with the character of the Namdhari movement, Prof. Fauja Singh and others have reached a definite conclusion that it was basically a political movement. In this connection they have even gone to the extent of calling the *Kukas* as the first freedom fighters or their movement as the first war of Independence or the first revolt against British rule in Punjab. In their view, the Namdharis had evolved some definite political programme in an organized manner. These scholars have enumerated the political programmes of the *Kukas* as follows: (i) Boycott of the Government managed educational institutions, (ii) Boycott of the Government services, (iii) Setting up of independent judicial and postal services by *Kukas*, giving a semblance of a parallel government and (iv) Boycott of British manufactured cloth.

Thus, according to them this movement advocated cooperation and pleaded for Swadeshi.

However, Prof. Ganda Singh, a very senior scholar of Sikh history has strongly rebutted the political programme, attributed to the *Kukas* by Prof. Fauja Singh and others. Prof. Ganda Singh has relied upon information, contained in the *Singha Namdharian da Sahid Bilas* and *Namdhari Panth Parkash* written in 1913 and 1914 AD respectively by Bhai Kala Singh Namdhari.

If the views of Prof. Fauja Singh and others are examined in the light of the opinion expressed by Prof. Ganda Singh 'Kuka (Namdhari) Lahr in *Bhai Jodh Singh Abhinandan Granth* (pp. 115-21) the following facts deserve mention. As far as the educational institutions managed by the government are concerned, it may be pointed out that, when Baba Ram Singh started his missionary work there were hardly any government schools where English was taught. There were no government schools at the village level. Only in the districts one could find some schools. Upto December 1862 AD in Punjab including (frontier regions of Sindh, Baluchistan and Jammu & Kashmir) and the other native states there were only eight students who had passed Matric examination and that too from the Calcutta University. A government college was established in Lahore only as late as 1864 AD. The Punjab University was established in 1882 AD, i.e., about eleven years after the exile of Baba Ram Singh. When there were no Hindu or Sikh private schools and the *Kukas* also did not try to open some schools, children could go only to the native, local schools. It does not seem to be true that Baba Ram Singh had forbidden his followers to take up education or they were as such ever to remain uneducated. Perhaps, no social reformer would ever ask his followers to boycott the prevailing education system without providing any alternative to it.

Prof. Ganda Singh further said that it would be against the historical evidence to consider that Baba Ram Singh had forbidden the *Kukas* to join government service. Because boycott was a later development which started with Mahatma Gandhi's Swadeshi and non-cooperation movement. At the time of Baba Ram Singh, there were few government services which Punjabis could take up. Till then, the Indians were only as peons and at best clerks. They were usually Bengalis, Biharis or belonging to other eastern regions. Punjabis and particularly Sikhs used to get service only in the army or police and at such places, there were *Kukas.* In the police service by 1869, there were fifty-four *Kukas.* In 1870, there were forty-seven and upto January 1872, there were forty-eight *Kukas* in police.

With regard to Baba Ram Singh's order to boycott the courts, Prof. Ganda Singh states that by that time there were not many courts and even law was not very complicated. There were *Panchayats* and the Government had given judicial rights to native *Sardars* and *Jagirdars.* When a local agency for administering justice was available there was not much need of government courts. Therefore, the question of their boycott did not arise. Even then if the *Kukas* had to appear before any court, they did it and never refused to give the statements. Baba Ram Singh had never issued an order to this effect. He himself was a law abiding person and could even compromise at a place like Amritsar and Anandpur. When he was interred at Bhaini Sahib by the Government he obeyed the orders. Even when he was sent to exile, he made no attempt to escape or go underground.

So far the boycott of foreign cloth was concerned there was no need to give such an order as by that time imported foreign cloth had not reached Punjab. *Khaddar* was mainly popular among the masses while *Malmal* and silk was used by the rich. Rich *Kukas* were using only silk considering it to be a pure cloth. Even much later *Kukas* used silk, imported from Burma, Malaya and China.

In the light of these facts the views of Prof. Fauja Singh and others do need a serious reconsideration.

Two different movements, i.e., Nirankari and Namdhari, which started in two different regions of Punjab at different times, but covered the whole nineteenth century, have been studied here. They had to a great extent helped in the revival of Sikh religion and saved the Sikh society from further decay and degeneration.

Nirankaris originated in 1808-9 AD in the north-western region of Punjab at Rawalpindi under the leadership of Baba Dayal. Namdhari movement was started in 1857 AD by Baba Ram Singh at Bhaini District, Ludhiana in the eastern regions of Punjab. The Nirankaris believed in one God who is *Nirankar* or formless. Namdharis were called *Kukas* or sant Khalsa. They were called Namdharis because they had taken the *Nam* or God's name as the base of religion. The word *Kukas* is related to shrieks or cries (*kuks)* for God. Because of the pure saintly character, they were also called as *Sant Khalsa.*

Baba Dayal belonged to the business community and lived at Ralwalpindi while, Baba Ram Singh was a carpenter by caste and had settled at Bhaini as a farmer after leaving in the Khalsa army.

Both the leaders knew *Gurumukhi* well and this helped them to read and interpret the *Adi Grunth* themselves. Whereas Baba Dayal started impressing and influencing people by his discourses at *Bardari Gurudwara* at Rawalpindi, Baba Ram Singh even before initiating the movement was respectfully called as *Bhai* and his regiment as *Bhagtan di regiment.*

One basic difference between them is that whereas Namdhari claim that Ram Singh got spiritual powers from Baba Balak Singh of Hazro and was the twelth *Guru* in succession to the mortal *Gurus* of the Sikhs, on the other hand Nirankaris do not associate the origin of Baba Dayal to any *Guru*. They said that if he had some spiritual power it was because of that omnipotent, *Nirankar* who had given that power to Nanak and to other Sikh *Gurus.*

Nirankaris and Namdharis essentially had a socio-religious reform programme. However, to achieve it they had to face extreme opposition from Sikhs and as well as non-Sikhs. This led the Nirankaris to build up different centres for themselves well-known as *Nirankari Darbar* and *Dayal Sar.*

The second leader of the Nirankaris Darbara Singh had to work hard to consolidate the propagation work of his mission. He issued a *Hukumnama* (decree), popularly known as *Nirankari-chalan-da Chitha* or a code of conduct for the *Nirankaris.* It was to be read every fortnightly in each and every Nirankari Sangat. Namdhari Guru Baba Ram Singh did not issue one single code of conudct. But at the time of initiation certain teachings were given. From his letters written from exile one can know about his various teachings which he wanted his followers to adopt in practice.

It is important that whereas anybody could be a Nirankari without changing his social status position or caste, it was not the case with Namdharis. While Nirankaris had no specific ceremony of baptism or initiation, Namdharis had a specific system of initiation. Anybody willing to be taken in the fraternity had to take *Guru-Manar* from Baba Ram Singh.

Nirankaris and Namdharis took special care to consolidate and expand their mission. The Nirankaris established forty centres known as Biras. Every village had a *Sangat* with a Nirankari *Gurudwara.* Each had a coloured flag, a copy of *Hukumnama* and *parwana* of Sahib Ratta Ji.

The Namdharis under Baba Ram Singh also undertook vigorous steps for the consolidation of their movement. He established twenty-two *subas* each in different districts with two *jathedars* in every tehsil and a *grunthi* in every village. Each Namdhari gurudwars had a white flag. Baba Ram Singh's interest in setting up a judicial system on the lines of panchayati judicial system and some sort of postal system was also attributed to this movement.

These movements can be called as the puritan and protestant Sikh movements aiming at the revival of Sikhism. The Nirankaris as well as Namdharis emphasized on constantly remembering the name of God. Both of them emphasized on the supreme position of *Adi Grunth,* but the Namdharis gave equal importance to *Dasam Grunth, Chandee Path, Havan hom* and *Jyoti,* etc. Perhaps this was the reason why the Namdharis could not attract a much larger section of the Sikh society. It is still astonishing to note that, while they were against idol worship they did not do away with practices like *Havan,* etc.

The Nirankaris were also against idol worship. Regarding salvation they believed that Nanak was their saviour and that meditation would lead them to salvation. However, the Namdharis were quiet on this point. The Nirankaris and Namdharis both emphasized on evening prayers. Baba Ram Singh laid extra stress on the personal hygiene and sanitation. Nirankaris on the other did not lay much stress on this.

Pilgrimage was discouraged by the Nirankaris. The reason

for this perhaps was that the treatment given to the Nirankaris and Namdharis at such places was not a favourable one. The Nirankaris believed that pilgrimage is the name of God. Namdharis originally had a favourable attitude towards pilgrimage, but later on they developed their own centers and gave more importance to them. If the Nirankaris had developed a parallel Darbar Sahib, the Namdhari leader Baba Ram Singh wished his followers to call Bhaini Sahib as Ramdas Pura.

Another important aspect of these movements was their protest against the Brahmanic practices and a challenge to the unchallenged authority of the Brahmins in the Sikh society. Brahmins were very critical of these movements, because their pivotal position and religious monopoly was being rejected by the followers of these movements. The Nirankaris were strictly against the dogmatic and ritualistic position of the Brahmins. Resolutions were passed against them. They were boycotted from public, cremation grounds and other social functions, but Nirankaris did not deviate from the path of *Sat Nirankar, Jap Nirankar* and *Dhan Nirankar.*

Namdharis had also opposed the Brahmins, but their practices reflected some elements of Brahmanical beliefs. This might have been due to the fact that their following hailed mainly from rural background.

Nirankaris were neither in favour of animal worship nor against it, but somehow the Namdharis got entangled with the British Government on the issue of cow slaughter. This might again have been a result of Brahmanic influence on them. Though they did not worship the cow yet its sanctity for them could not be denied.

This issue had even given a violent touch to the Namdhari Movement which is related to the killing of butchers at Amritsar and Raikot. Later on this issue got merged with the incidents of Malodh and Malerkotla.

The Nirankaris had started a new system of *Charnamrit.* Although it was a Hindu practice, but the idea and the spirit behind it was that God does not reside in an idol, but he resides in every soul so true *Charnamrit* is one which has got the touch of all living gods (men). Later, the Nirankaris started worshipping the slippers of Baba Dayal, which was nothing less than idol worship. And in fact the negation of their very principle of opposing idol worship.

The Nirankaris did not lay much stress on the ceremonial or conventional part of the religion. Although for them the *Adi-Grunth* had supreme position, yet they did not lay any stress on its being read constantly, without break till it was read all the way through. It was known as *Akhand Path.* Baba Ram Singh not only emphasized *Akhand Path,* but gave an elaborate system to its performance. To the Nirankaris, His name was more a matter of personal reverence than a visual expression. They adopted the spirit of *Gurbani* instead of superficial practices.

The *Kukas* differed from the Nirankaris and other Sikhs on the practice of *Sootra* or *wajed* or state of ecstasy. The *Kukas* in this state used to forget even the general norms to be followed at a public place. For this Baba Ram Singh was seriously questioned by the priests of the *Akal Takht.*

In both the fraternities conversions were done from various classes but, whereas the Nirankaris had more following from urban areas, the *Kukas* had the majority of there following from the lower orders of rural masses. Thus, the Nirankaris were mainly from amongst shopkeepers or petty traders, the Namdharis predominantly influenced the agriculturist class.

Baba Ram Singh was known as *Guru, Satguru,* and *Sachapadshah.* Although the line of mortal Gurus was sealed by Guru Gobind Singh, when the Adi-Grunth was given the supreme position. It seems in due course of time, these movements ultimately concentrated their major efforts in retaining their identity, which to them perhaps became relatively more important than to the principles to which they essentially and initially subscribed.

Despite being essentially religious in character, these movements aimed at reforming the society at large also. Both were concious of various superstitions, ceremonies, dogmas, rituals and other social taboos. The *Nirankaris Chalan da Chitha* included all the ceremonies to be performed from birth to death besides expressing views on matters like polygamy, widow-remarriage, caste and untouchability etc. They did not believe in *sootak* at the time of birth or death.

The Nirankaris and Namdharis did pioneering work in introducing Anand marriage among the Sikhs, which was to be performed according to the prescribed methods. Till then, marriages were performed by Brahmins according to the *Vedic* rites.

There is a dispute among the Nirankaris and Namdharis as to who performed the first Anand Marriage. Chronologically speaking the Nirankaris were obviously the first to perform such a marriage. But the Namdharis also helped in making it popular afterwards. However, the Namdharis differed in some of its practices. For instance, they circumscribed around the *Vedi* and not the *Adi Grunth* as the Nirankaris did. In this connection, the major contribution of the Namdharis was making the marriages inexpensive which was otherwise costly when performed according to Brahminical practices.

Both movements advocated the remarriage of the widows. Prostitution was also opposed by leaders of both.

As far as, the rites to be performed after one's death were concerned, no ceremonies were attached with it by the Nirankaris, while the Namdharis believed in giving offerings to Brahmins in the form of money and clothing.

The Namdharis were silent on the issue of *Saradhs.* The Nirankaris strongly condemned it by quoting from the *Gurbani.* Both the movements believed in charity not only as an act of virtue but also as the demand of the time and circumstances.

The Namdharis gave a revolutionary message for the education of men and women alike thus, improving the social status of women. Women were baptized and appointed as *Subas* for the missionary work. This was indeed a revolutionary step, keeping in view the contemporary social setup.

Both these leaders were not only taking the women out of the gulf of age long taboos and stigmas, but at the same time they were offering them higher status in life and society. They tried to create social consciousness, through religious principles which was likely to be more effective.

The socio-religious programme of the Nirankaris and Namdharis had earned opposition for them from various sections of society. Whereas the Nirankaris had to face the opposition of the Brahmins, the Sikh priests and the social elite only, the Namdharis had to face the opposition of the authorities of the time like the British Government, native states, Chiefs and the officials. Most of the native Sikhs states of Punjab were hostile to the Namdharis. This led to their harassment and even expulsion from services. It was difficult for the *Kukas* to live peacefully without undertakings and guarantees.

The priestly class was particularly annoyed and disliked the Nirankaris and Namdharis because they had posed a challenge to their authority and existence. Both of them (Brahmins and Sikh priests) considered these reforms as an attack on them. While these reforms had an adverse effect on the Brahmins financially, they posed a more serious challenge to the authority of the Sikh priestly class. Both the movements questioned their authority in matters of the teachings and interpretation of *Adi Grunth,* besides many other issues. When Baba Ram Singh was sent to exile and a ban on *Kuka* activities was imposed this class passed resolutions, applauding the action of the British Government.

Both these movements were popular among the masses. However, some of the violent incidents of the Namdharis had given them a setback. These even led to renouncing of some of their followers. There are references to statements and evidences of the followers, denouncing *Kukaism* individually and collectively often under pressure of the Government or even otherwise. It gradually led to the isolation of the Namdharis. It also reduced their impact on the Sikh society in general. To avoid harassment, the Namdharis changed even the peculiar mode of their turban and wore the woollen rosary under their clothes. This was done on the instruction of their Guru, Baba Budh Singh (Hari Singh) after the exile of Baba Ram Singh.

By the last quarter of the nineteenth century, both the movements started declining. Subsequently, another movement after those of the Nirankaris and Namdharis had started in the form of the Singh Sabha movement. The Nirankaris and Namdhari movements were not accepted as the custodians of Sikh ethics as their *Gurus* become the real motivating force instead of the teachings of the ten Sikh *Gurus.*

However the fact can not be denied that these two movements were first of these kind, which aimed at reviving the Sikh religion through an organized system. In fact, sustained efforts of these movements later led to the rise of the *Khalsa Diwan,* the Singh Sabha movement and the Shiromani Gurudwara Prabandhak Committee. They all were basically inspired by these two movements and worked almost for the similar socio-religious programme, initiated by them, i.e., restoration of the Sikh religious practices to their original principles, during the twentieth century.

APPENDIX A

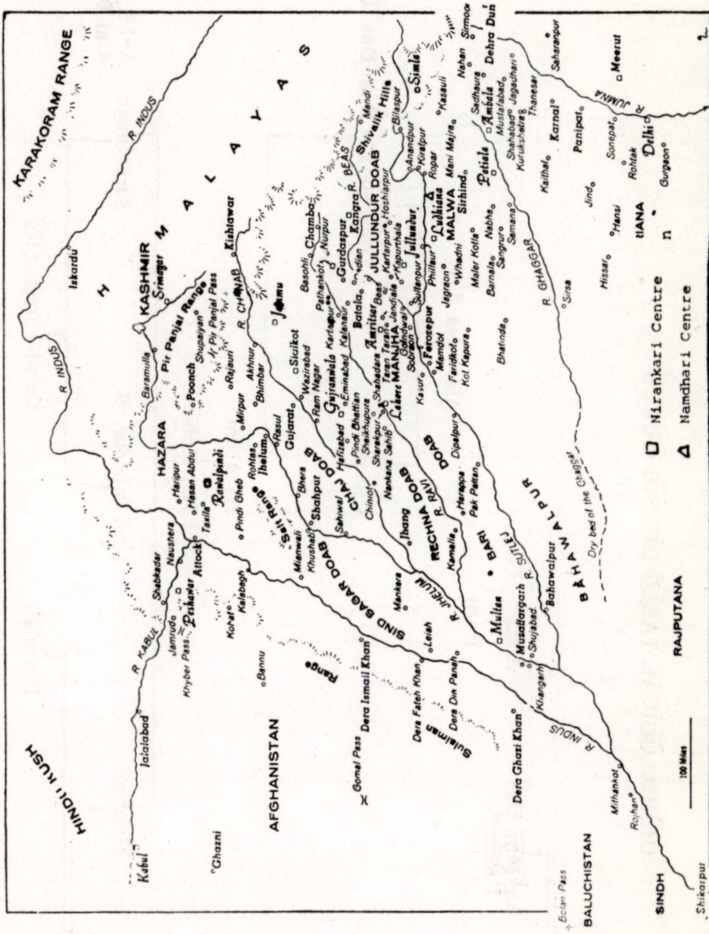

THE PUNJAB

APPENDIX B

GENEALOGICAL TABLE OF THE GURUS

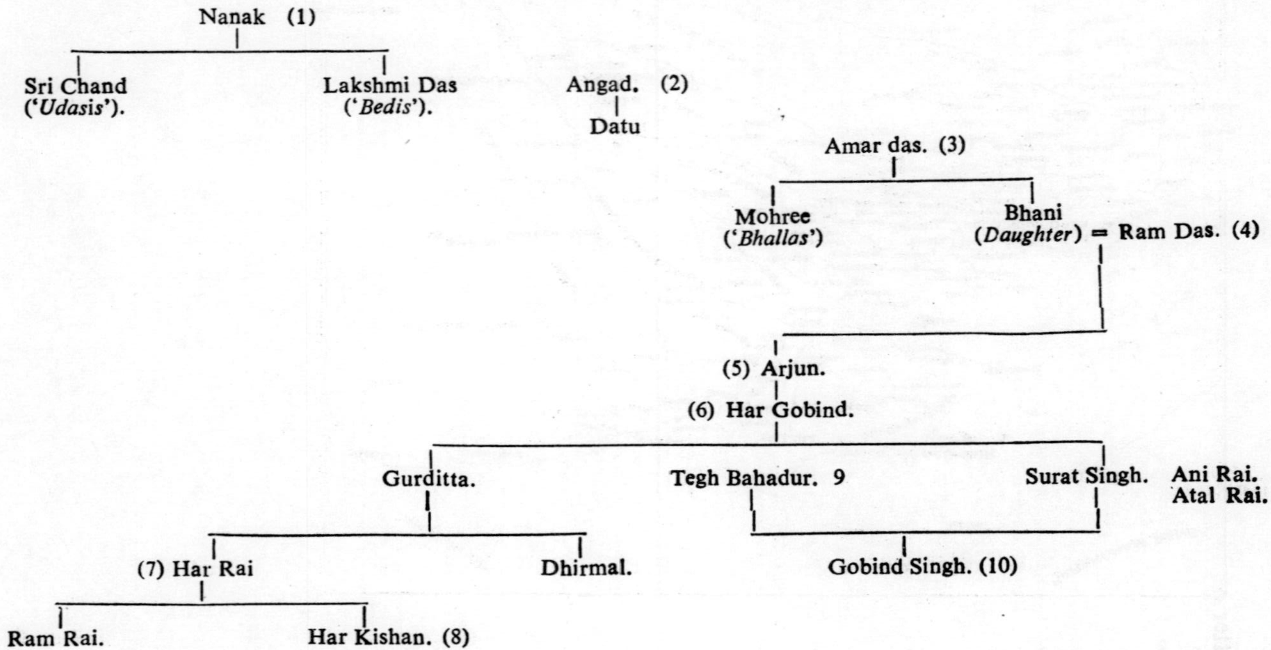

APPENDIX C

Letter of Baba Khem Singh Bedi

(ਸ੍ਰੀ ਮਾਨ ਬਾਬਾ ਖੇਮ ਸਿੰਘ ਜੀ ਬੇਦੀ ਦੀ ਚਿੱਠੀ, ਜੋ ਉਨ੍ਹਾਂ ਆਪਣੇ ਸੇਵਕਾਂ ਪ੍ਰਤੀ ਲਿਖੀ)

ੴ ਸਤਿਗੁਰ ਪ੍ਰਸਾਦਿ ॥

ਲਿਖਤੁਮ ਸ੍ਰੀ ਸਾਹਿਬ ਬਾਬਾ ਖੇਮ ਸਿਘ ਜੀ, ਥਾਨਾ ਮਾਕਣ ਜੋਗ ਵਸਾਖੀ ਸਹਿਗਲ ਜੋਗ ਖੁਸ਼ੀ ਵਾਚਣੀ। ਆਪ ਦਾ ਲਿਖਿਆ ਪਹੁੰਚਿਆ ਹੈ। ਚੰਗੀ ਬਾੜ ਕਰੀ ਹੈ। ਪਰ ਫੇਰ ਦੁਬਿਧਾ ਮਲੂਮ ਹੋਈ ਹੈ ਸਾਨੂੰ। ਜੋ ਬਰਾਹਮਣ ਵਿਚੋਂ ਉਠ ਗਏ ਹੈਨ। ਤੁਸੀਂ ਓਹਿ ਬਾਤ ਕਰੋ ਜਿਸ ਤੇ ਦੁਬਿਧਾ ਦੂਰ ਹੋਵੇ ਸਾਡੀ ਮਨਸ਼ਾ ਇਹ ਹੈ। ਕਾਮ ਕ੍ਰੋਧ ਆਦਿ ਖੋਟੇ ਕਰਮ ਤਿਆਗਣੇ ਆਏ ਹਨ। ਗੁਰੂ ਕਾ ਵਾਕ ਹੈ। "ਸ਼ੁਭ ਕਰਮਨ ਤੇ ਨਾਹਿ ਟਰੋ।" ਹੋਰ ਤੁਸਾਂ ਨੇ ਵਿਆਹ ਦੀ ਤੇ ਮਰਨੇ ਦੀ ਬਾਤ ਪੁਛੀ ਹੈ। ਸੋ ਅਜੇ ਤਜਵੀਜ਼ ਹੋਂਦੀ ਹੈ ਮੁਕਰਰਾ ਕੋਈ ਨਹੀਂ। ਜਿਸ ਵਕਤ ਮੁਕਰਰਾ ਹੋਵੇਗੀ, ਸਾਡਾ ਹੁਕਮਨਾਵਾਂ ਸਾਰੇ ਦੇਸ਼ ਵਿਚ ਚਲੁ ਜਾਇਗਾ। ਅਜੇ ਜਿਸ ਤਉਰ ਪਿਛੇ ਰੀਤਾਂ ਹੈਨ। ਸੋ ਕਰਨੀ ਤੁਹਾਨੂੰ ਬਣਦੀ ਬਣਦੀ ਹੈ। ਦੁਬਧਾ ਮਿਟਾਵਣੀ ਅੱਛੀ ਹੈ। ਹੋਰ ਸਿਠਣੀਆਂ ਨਹੀਂ ਦੇਣੀਆਂ ਤੇ ਸ਼ਬਦ ਸਾਖੀ ਵਿਆਹ ਵਿਚ ਬੇਸ਼ਕ ਪੜ੍ਹਨਾ ਤੇ **ਪਿਛਲੀ ਹੋਰ ਸਰਬ ਵੇਦ ਰੀਤ ਮਰਯਾਦਾ ਕਰਨੀ।** ਸਰਬ ਜੋਗ ਖੁਸ਼ੀ ਵਾਚਣੀ ਜਨਮ ਸਵਾਰਨਾ ਵਾਹਿਗੁਰੂ ਕਾ ਜਾਪੁ ਕਰਨਾ। ਤਾਰੀਕ ਸਾਵਣ ਦਿਨੇ ਪਹਿਲੀ।

APPENDIX D

An order of Baba Darbara Singh about the Code of Conduct of the Nirankaris which includes various instructions for the practisce to be followed accorning to Sikh Scripture Adi Grunth. It is popularly known as Hukamnama or Nirankari Chalan Da Chitha.

ਨਿਰੰਕਾਰੀ ਚਲਨ ਦਾ ਚਿੱਠਾ

(ਕ੍ਰਿਤ–ਸ੍ਰੀ ਮਾਨ ਭਾਈ ਰੂਪ ਸਿੰਘ ਜੀ)

ੴ ਸਤਿਗੁਰ ਪ੍ਰਸਾਦਿ ॥

ਧੰਨ ਨਿਰੰਕਾਰ, ਸਤਿ ਨਿਰੰਕਾਰ, ਜਪੁ ਨਿਰੰਕਾਰ, ਧੰਨ ਧੰਨ ਸ੍ਰੀ ਸਤਿਗੁਰੂ ਦਇਆਲ ਜੀ ।

ਹੁਕਮਨਾਮਾ ਅਕਾਲ ਪੁਰਖ ਜੀ ਕਾ ਸਭ ਸਿੱਖਾਂ ਪ੍ਰਤਿ

ਏਕ ਸਮੇਂ ਸ੍ਰੀ ਸਤਿਗੁਰੂ ਦਇਆਲ ਨਿਰੰਕਾਰ ਦੇ ਦੇਸ ਨੂੰ ਗਏ । ਅਗੇ ਦੀਵਾਨ ਲਗਾ ਹੋਇਆ ਸੀ । ਗੁਰੂ ਨਾਨਕ ਜੀ ਥੀਂ ਆਦਿ ਦਸੇ ਗੁਰੂ ਬੈਠੇ ਸਨ, ਤਾਂ ਸੰਗਤ ਉਠ ਖੜੀ ਹੋਈ, ਤਾਂ ਹੁਕਮ ਹੋਇਆ, ਨਿਰੰਕਾਰ ਜੀ ਦੇ ਪੁਰਖਾ, ਸਭ ਸਿੱਖਾਂ ਤਾਈਂ ਜਾਇਕੇ ਰਹਿਤ ਦਸ । ਜੋ ਦਸ ਪਾਤਸ਼ਾਹੀਆਂ ਤਕ ਸਿਖ ਹੋਇ ਹੈਨ ਸੋ ਤੇਰੇ ਹਵਾਲੇ । ਤਾਂ ਅਗੋਂ

ਸਤਿਗੁਰੂ ਦਇਆਲ ਅਰਦਾਸ ਕੀਤੀ, ਜੀ ਮੇਰੀ ਕੀ ਸ਼ਕਤ ਹੈ? ਤਾਂ ਹੁਕਮ ਹੋਇਆ ਪੁਰਖਾ, ਜੋ ਤੇਰਾ ਫੁਰਮਾਨ ਮੰਨੇਗਾ, ਸੋ ਮੋਖ ਪਦਵੀ ਨੂੰ ਪ੍ਰਾਪਤ ਹੋਵੇਗਾ, ਸਚ ਖੰਡ ਮੈਂ ਵਾਸਾ ਪਾਵੇਗਾ। ਅੱਗੇ ਜਗਤ ਵਿਚ ਬ੍ਰਾਹਮਣਾਂ ਸਭ ਨੂੰ ਭੁਲਾਇਕੇ ਨਰਕ ਗਾਮੀ ਕੀਤਾ ਹੈ। ਤੁਸੀ ਨਾਮ ਦਾ ਚਲਣ ਚਲਾਉ। ਤਾਂ ਦਰਗਾਹ ਥੀਂ ਹੁਕਮ ਲੈ ਕੇ ਮਾਤ ਲੋਕ ਵਿਚ ਆਏ!

ਇਕ ਸਮੇਂ ਸ੍ਰੀ ਸਤਿਗੁਰੂ ਦਰਬਾਰਾ ਸਿੰਘ ਜੀ ਦੀਵਾਨ ਲਾਏ ਬੈਠੇ ਹੋਇ ਸਨ। ਸ਼ਬਦ ਦਾ ਵੀਚਾਰ ਹੋਂਦਾ ਸੀ ਤਾਂ ਪੰਜਾਬ ਦੇਸ ਥੀਂ ਇਕ ਸਿਖ ਆਇਆ! ਸਿਖ ਨੇ ਆਇਕੇ ਅਰਦਾਸ ਕੀਤੀ, ਜੀ ਸਚੇ ਪਾਤਸ਼ਾਹ ਜੇ ਅਸਾਨੂੰ ਬ੍ਰਾਹਮਣ ਲੋਕ ਕਰਮ ਕਾਂਡ ਵਿਚ ਫਸਾਂਵਦੇ ਹਨ। ਅਸਾਨੂੰ ਕ੍ਰਿਪਾ ਕਰਕੇ ਜੋ ਸ਼ਬਦ ਦੇ ਅਨੁਸਾਰ ਰੀਤ ਜ਼ਨਮ ਮਰਨ ਵਿਆਹ ਸ਼ਾਦੀ ਜੋ ਕੁਛ ਗੁਰੂ ਕਾ ਹੁਕਮ ਹੈ ਸੋ ਸਭ ਸੁਣਾਈਐ ਜੀ। ਤਬ ਸੰਗਤ ਨੂੰ ਹੁਕਮ ਹੋਇਆ ਜੋ ਸਭ ਸਿੱਖਾਂ ਨੂੰ ਸਾਂਝਾ ਉਤਦੇਸ਼ ਹੈ ਜੋ ਨਿਰੰਕਾਰ ਜੀ ਦਾ ਜਾਪ ਜਪੁਣਾ ਤੇ ਜੋ ਕੋਈ ਤੁਸਾਨੂੰ ਮਨ੍ਹੈ ਕਰੈ, ਬਾਣੀ ਸ੍ਰੀ ਨਿਰੰਕਾਰ ਜੀ ਕੀ ਸ਼ਬਦ ਵਿਚ ਦੋ ਆਦਿ ਜਪੁ ਸਾਹਿਬ ਵਿਚ ਲਿਖਿਆ ਹੈ :—

"ਸਚ ਖੰਡਿ ਵਸੈ ਨਿਰੰਕਾਰੁ। ਕਰਿ ਕਰਿ ਵੇਖੈ ਨਦਰਿ ਨਿਹਾਲ॥"

ਸੁਖਮਨੀ ਸਾਹਿਬ ਵਿਚ ਲਿਖਿਆ ਹੈ :—

"ਜਨ ਲਾਗਾ ਹਰਿ ਏਕੈ ਨਾਇ। ਤਿਸ ਕੀ ਆਸ ਨ ਬਿਰਥੀ ਜਾਇ।
ਸੇਵਕ ਕਉ ਸੇਵਾ ਬਨਿ ਆਈ। ਹੁਕਮੁ ਬੂਝਿ ਪਰਮ ਪਦੁ ਪਾਈ।
ਇਸ ਤੇ ਊਪਰਿ ਨਹੀ ਬੀਚਾਰੁ। ਜਾਕੈ ਮਨਿ ਵਸਿਆ ਨਿਰੰਕਾਰੁ।
ਬੰਧਨ ਤੋਰ ਭਏ ਨਿਰਵੈਰ। ਅਨ ਦਿਨੁ ਪੂਜਹੁ ਗੁਰਕੇ ਪੈਰ।
ਇਹ ਲੋਕ ਸੁਖੀਏ ਪਰਲੋਕ ਸੁਹੇਲੇ। ਨਾਨਕ ਹਰਿ ਪ੍ਰਭਿ ਆਪੇ ਮੇਲੇ॥ ੧॥"
(ਸੁਖਮਨੀ)

'ਸਦਾ ਸਦਾ ਸਦਾ ਦਇਆਲ। ਸਿਮਰਿ ਸਿਮਰਿ ਨਾਨਕ ਭਏ ਨਿਹਾਲ।'
'ਸਤਿਗੁਰ ਦਇਆਲ ਹਰਿਨਾਮ ਦ੍ਰਿੜਾਇਆ ਹਰਿ ਪਾਧਰ ਹਰਿ ਪ੍ਰਭ ਕੇਰਾ।'
ਸਬਦ ਵਿਚਦੋ ਗੁਰੂ ਖੋਜ ਲੈਣਾ। ਗੁਰੂ ਨਿਰੰਕਾਰ ਹੈ।
'ਸਰਨ ਪਰੇ ਕੀ ਰਾਖੁ ਦਇਆਲਾ। ਨਾਨਕ ਤੁਮਰੇ ਬਾਲ ਗੁਪਾਲਾ।

ਸ੍ਰੀ ਸਤਿਗੁਰੂ ਦਇਆਲ ਬਾਬਾ ਜੀ ਗੁਰੂ ਗਰੰਥ ਸਾਹਿਬ ਜੀ ਸੂਬੱਤ ਸੰਗਤ ਕੀ ਸਰਬੱਤ ਸਾਧ ਸੰਗਤ ਸਿੱਖਾਂ ਅਗੇ ਧੰਨ ਧੰਨ ਨਿਰੰਕਾਰ ਵਾਚਣੀ। ਧੰਨ ਨਿਰੰਕਾਰ ਦਾ ਜਾਪ ਜਪੁਣਾ ਅਗੇ ਵਰਤਣ ਗੁਰੂ ਗਰੰਥ ਸਾਹਿਬ ਦੇ ਅਨੁਸਾਰ—

ਜੇ ਬਾਲਕ ਜਨਮਦਾ ਹੈ ਬੇਟਾ ਅਥਵਾ ਬੇਟੀ, ਤਾਂ ਸਬਦ ਗੁਰੂ ਜੀ ਦਾ ਗਾਂਵਦੇ ਹਾਂ। ਬਾਲਕ ਜਨਮ ਦੇ ਵੇਲੇ ਕੜਾਹ ਗੁਰੂ ਜੀ ਦਾ ਕਰਾਂਵਦੇ ਹਾਂ। ਭਾਈ ਜੀ ਸੂਤਕ ਕੋਈ ਨਹੀਂ, ਕਿਉਂ ਜੋ ਗੁਰੂ ਨਾਨਕ ਜੀ ਆਸਾ ਦੀ ਵਾਰ ਵਿਚ ਮਨ੍ਹੇ ਕਰਦੇ ਹਨ :—

ਸਲੋਕ ਮ: ੧—'ਜੇ ਕਰਿ ਸੂਤਕੁ ਮੰਨੀਐ ਸਭਤੈ ਸੂਤਕੁ ਹੋਇ।'

''ਸਭੋ ਸੂਤਕੁ ਭਰਮੁ ਹੈ ਦੂਜੇ ਲਗੈ ਜਾਇ।
ਜੰਮਣੁ ਮਰਣਾ ਹੁਕਮੁ ਹੈ ਭਾਣੈ ਆਵੈ ਜਾਇ।
ਖਾਣਾ ਪੀਣਾ ਪਵਿਤ੍ਰੁ ਹੈ ਦਿਤੋਨੁ ਰਿਜ਼ਕੁ ਸੰਬਾਹਿ।
ਨਾਨਕ ਜਿਨੀ ਗੁਰਮੁਖਿ ਬੁਝਿਆ ਤਿਨਾ ਸੂਤਕ ਨਾਹਿ॥ ੩॥'

ਤੇ ਸ਼ਬਦ ਇਹੋ ਪੜ੍ਹਦੇ ਹਾਂ :—

ਆਸਾ ਮਹਲਾ ੫॥

ਸਤਿਗੁਰ ਸਾਚੇ ਦੀਆ ਭੇਜਿ। ਚਿਰੁਜੀਵਨ ਉਪਜਿਆ ਸੰਜੋਗ।
ਉਦਰੈ ਮਾਹਿ ਆਇ ਕੀਆ ਨਿਵਾਸੁ। ਮਾਤਾ ਕੈ ਮਨਿ ਬਹੁਤ ਬਿਗਾਸੁ॥ ੧॥
ਜੰਮਿਆ ਪੂਤ ਭਗਤੁ ਗੋਵਿੰਦ ਕਾ॥

ਰਾਗ ਰਤਨ ਪਰਵਾਰ ਪਰੀਆ ਸਬਦ ਗਾਵਣ ਆਈਆ।
ਸਬਦੋ ਤ ਗਾਵਹੁ ਹਰੀ ਕੇਰਾ ਮਨਿ ਜਿਨੀ ਵਸਾਇਆ
ਕਹੈ ਨਾਕਕੁ ਅਨੰਦੁ ਹੋਆ ਸਤਿਗੁਰੂ ਮੈ ਪਾਇਆ॥ ੧॥

ਗੁਰੂ ਦਇਆਲ ਸਮਰਥ ਗੁਧੂ ਦਰਬਾਰ ਸਾਹਿਬ ਹੈ। ਹੋਰ ਸਾਹ ਨਹੀਂ ਪੁਛਦੇ ਜੋ ਬ੍ਰਾਹਮਣ ਆਪਣੇ ਲੋਭ ਵਾਸਤੇ ਭਰਮ ਪਾਏ ਦੇਂਦੇ ਹਨ। ਗੁਰੂ ਜੀ ਕਹਿਆ ਹੈ :—

ਆਸਾ ਦੀ ਵਾਰ ਸਲੋਕ

''ਲੈ ਭਾੜਿ ਕਰੇ ਵੀਆਹੁ॥ ਕਢਿ ਕਾਗਲੁ ਦਸੇ ਰਾਹੁ॥
ਸੁਣਿ ਵੇਖਹੁ ਲੋਕਾ ਏਹੁ ਵਿਡਾਣੁ। ਮਨਿ ਅੰਧਾ ਨਾਉ ਸੁਜਾਣੁ॥੪॥

ਮੂੰਹੋਂ ਕਹਿੰਦਾ ਹੈ ਜੋ ਧੀਆਂ ਦੇ ਘਰ ਦਾ ਖਾਣਾ ਨਿੰਦ ਹੈ। ਆਪ ਲਾਗ ਲੈ ਕੇ ਵਿਵਾਂਹੁ ਕਰਾਂਵਦਾ ਹੈ ਤੇਪਟੀ ਵਿਚ ਵੀ ਲਿਖਿਆ ਹੈ :—

''ਸਸੈ ਸੰਜਮੁ ਗਇਓ ਮੂੜੇ ਏਕੁ ਦਾਨੁ ਤੁਧੁ ਕੁਥਾਇ ਲਇਆ।
ਸਾਈ ਪੁਤ੍ਰੀ ਜਜਮਾਨ ਕੀ ਸਾ ਤੇਰੀ ਏਤੁ ਧਾਨਿ ਖਾਧੈ ਤੇਰਾ ਜਨਮੁ ਜਇਆ॥੬॥''

(ਰਾਗੁ ਆਸਾ ਮ: ੩ ਪਟੀ)

ਭਾਈ ਜੀ ਗੁਰੂ ਗਰੰਥ ਸਾਹਿਬ ਜੀ ਦੇ ਅਨੁਸਾਰ ਜਿਸਦਾ ਜਨਮ ਗਿਆ ਉਨ੍ਹਾਂ ਨਾਲ ਅਸਾਡਿਆਂ ਗੁਰੂ ਕੇ ਸਿੱਖਾਂ ਦਾ ਕੀ ਵਾਸਤਾ ਹੈ। ਕਿਉਂ ਜੋ ਗੁਰੂ ਜੀ ਦਾ ਸ਼ਬਦ ਨਾ ਮੰਨੀਏ ਤਾਂ ਗੁਰੂ ਪਾਸੋਂ ਬੇਮੁਖ ਹੋਵੀਦਾ ਹੈ। ਗੁਰੂ ਦੇ ਸਿੱਖਾਂ ਨੂੰ ਗੁਰੂ ਦਾ ਸ਼ਬਦ ਮੰਨਣਾ ਜੋਗ ਹੈ। ਤੇ ਜਪੁ ਸਾਹਿਬ ਵਿਚ ਭੀ ਲਿਖਿਆ ਹੈ :—

"ਵੇਲ ਨ ਪਾਈਆ ਪੰਡਤੀ ਜਿ ਹੋਵੈ ਲੇਖੁ ਪੁਰਾਣੁ।
ਵਖਤੁ ਨ ਪਾਇਓ ਕਾਦੀਆ ਜਿ ਲਿਖਨਿ ਲੇਖੁ ਕੁਰਾਣੁ।"

ਭਾਈ ਜੀ ਜਿਨ ਵੇਲ ਨ ਪਾਇਆ ਤਿਨ੍ਹਾਂ ਨੂੰ ਕੀ ਪੁਛਣਾ ਹੈ। ਹਥੋਂ ਭਰਮ ਪਾਏ ਦੇਂਦੇ ਹਨ ਤਾਂ ਤੇ ਖੋਟੀ ਰਾਸ ਨੂੰ ਤਿਆਗਣਾ ਧਰਮ ਹੈ।

ਤੇ ਸਾਹਿਬਾਂ ਭੀ ਕਹਿਆ ਹੈ :—

"ਸਾਸਾ ਗਣਹਿ ਨ ਕਰਹਿ ਬੀਚਾਰੁ। ਸਾਹੇ ਊਪਰਿ ਏਕੰਕਾਰ।"

(ਰਾਮਕਲੀ ਮ: ੧ ਛੰਤ)

ਇਸ ਵਾਸਤੇ ਸ੍ਰੀ ਸਤਿਗੁਰੂ ਦਇਆਲ ਚਲਣ ਨਾਮ ਦਾ ਰਖਿਆ ਹੈ। ਕਿਸ ਵਾਸਤੇ ਜੋ ਸਾਰੀ ਸ੍ਰਿਸ਼ਟੀ ਦਾ ਉਧਾਰ ਹੋਵੈ। ਫਰੀਦ ਸਾਹਿਬ ਜੀ ਕਹਿਆ ਹੈ :—

"ਜਿਤੁ ਦਿਹਾੜੈ ਧਨ ਵਰੀ ਸਾਹੇ ਲਏ ਲਿਖਾਇ ॥"
"ਸਾਹੇ ਲਿਖੇ ਨ ਚਲਨੀ ਜਿੰਦੂ ਕਿ ਸਮਝਾਇ ॥"

ਗੁਰੂ ਜੀ ਕਾ ਸ਼ਬਦ ਪੜ੍ਹੋ ਅਥਵਾ ਸੁਣੋ ਤੇ ਸ਼ਬਦ ਉਪਰ ਚਲਣਾ। ਜੋ ਸ਼ਬਦ ਆਖੇ ਸੋ ਮੰਨਣਾ। ਗੁਰੂ ਨਾਨਕ ਜੀ ਥੀਂ ਆਦਿ ਲੈ ਕਰਕੇ ਸਾਰਿਆਂ ਗੁਰੂਆਂ ਨੇ ਅਸਾਂ ਜੀਵਾਂ ਵਾਸਤੇ ਕੇਡੀ ਘਾਲ ਕੀਤੀ ਹੈ। ਸੋ ਅਸਾਨੂੰ ਸ਼ਰਮ ਨਹੀਂ ਆਉਂਦੀ ਜੋ ਅਸੀਂ

ਪ੍ਰਗਟਿਆ ਸਭ ਮਹਿ ਲਿਖਿਆ ਧੁਰਕਾ ॥ ੧ ॥ ਰਹਾਉ ॥
ਦਸੀ ਮਾਸੀ ਹੁਕਮਿ ਬਾਲਕ ਜਨਮੁ ਲੀਆ।
ਮਿਟਿਆ ਸੋਗੁ ਮਹਾ ਅਨੰਦੁ ਥੀਆ।
ਗੁਰਬਾਣੀ ਸਖੀ ਅਨੰਦੁ ਗਾਵੈ ॥ ਸਾਚੇ ਸਾਹਿਬ ਕੈ ਮਨਿ ਭਾਵੈ ॥ ੨ ॥
ਵਧੀ ਵੇਲਿ ਬਹੁ ਪੀੜੀ ਚਾਲੀ। ਧਰਮ ਕਲਾ ਹਰਿ ਬੰਧਿ ਬਹਾਲੀ।
ਮਨ ਚਿੰਦਿਆ ਸਤਿਗੁਰੂ ਦਿਵਾਇਆ।
ਭਏ ਅਚਿੰਤ ਏਕ ਲਿਵ ਲਾਇਆ ॥ ੩ ॥
ਜਿਉ ਬਾਲਕੁ ਪਿਤਾ ਊਪਰ ਕਰੇ ਬਰੇ ਬਹੁ ਮਾਣੁ।
ਬੁਲਾਇਆ ਬੋਲੈ ਗੁਰ ਕੈ ਭਾਣਿ।
ਗੁਝੀ ਛੰਨੀ ਨਾਹੀ ਬਾਤ ॥ ਗੁਰ ਨਾਨਕੁ ਤੁਠਾ ਕੀਨੀ ਦਾਤਿ ॥ ੪ ॥

ਤੇ ਪਿਛੋਂ ਦਿਨਾਂ ਚਾਲੀਆਂ ਨੂੰ ਮਾਤਾ ਬਾਲਕ ਸਮੇਤ ਦਰਬਾਰ ਸਾਹਿਬ ਵਿਚ ਆਉਂਦੀ ਹੈ। ਕੜਾਹ ਪ੍ਰਸਾਦ ਗੁਰੂ ਜੀ ਕਾ ਕਰਾਂਵਦੇ ਹਾਂ। ਬਾਲਕ ਦਾ ਨਾਮ ਗੁਰੂ ਗ੍ਰੰਥ ਸਾਹਿਬ ਵਿਚੋਂ ਰਖਦੇ ਹਾਂ। ਇਹੁ ਰੀਤ ਬਾਲਕ ਦੇ ਜਨਮ ਦੀ ਹੈ।

ਜਦੋਂ ਨਿਰੰਕਾਰ ਬਾਲਕ ਨੂੰ ਖਬਰਦਾਰ ਕਰਦਾ ਹੈ ਤੇ ਜਿਸ ਵੇਲੇ ਬਾਲਕ ਦਾ ਮੰਗੇਵਾ ਕਰਦੇ ਹਾਂ ਤਾਂ ਇਹ ਸ਼ਬਦ ਪੜ੍ਹਨੇ ਹਾਂ :—

*ਰਾਗ ਰਾਮਕਲੀ ਮਹਲਾ ੫ ॥

ਸਾਧ ਸੰਙ ਇਕਤ੍ਰ ਬਾਲਕ ਕਰੇ ਮੰਗੇਵਾ।
ਲਦੇ ਸੋ ਜਨ ਕੁੜਮ ਭਲੇ ਵੰਡੇ ਅੰਮ੍ਰਿਤ ਮੇਵਾ।

ਤੇ ਕੜਾਹ ਪ੍ਰਸਾਦ ਕਰਾਂਵਦੇ ਹਾਂ ਤੇ ਗੁਰੂ ਰਾਮ ਦਾਸ ਜੀ ਕਹਿਆ ਹੈ :—

"ਸਤੁ ਸੰਤੋਖੁ ਕਰਿ ਭਾਉ ਕੁੜਮ ਕੁੜਮਾਈ ਆਇਆ ਬਲਿਰਾਮ ਜੀਉ।
ਸੰਤ ਜਨਾ ਕਰਿ ਮੇਲੁ ਗੁਰਬਾਣੀ ਗਾਵਾਈਆ ਬਲਿਰਾਮ ਜੀਉ।"

ਸੂਹੀ ਮ: ੪ ॥ ਛੰਤੁ

ਸ਼ਬਦ ਗਾਂਵਦੇ ਹਾਂ ਦਰਬਾਰ ਸਾਹਿਬ ਵਿਚੋਂ। ਇਹੁ ਰੀਤ ਕੁੜਮਾਈ ਦੀ ਹੈ ਗੁਰੂ ਜੀ ਦੇ ਸ਼ਬਦ ਅਨੁਸਾਰ।

ਜਿਸ ਵੇਲੇ ਕਾਜ ਹੁੰਦਾ ਹੈ ਤਦ ਸਬਦ ਗੁਰੂ ਜੀ ਦਾ ਮੰਗਲਾਚਾਰ ਹੋਂਦਾ ਰਹਿੰਦਾ ਹੈ। ਮਾਈਆਂ ਤਥਾ ਸਿੱਖ ਪੜ੍ਹਦੇ ਹਨ :—

ਰਾਮਕਲੀ ਮਹਲਾ ੩ ॥ ਅਨੰਦ ॥

ਅਨੰਦੁ ਭਇਆ ਮੇਰੀ ਮਾਇ ਸਤਿਗੁਰੂ ਮੈ ਪਾਇਆ ॥
ਸਤਿਗੁਰ ਤ ਪਾਇਆ ਸਹਜ ਸੇਤੀ ਮਨਿ ਵਜੀਆ ਵਾਧਾਈਆ।

ਅਜਾਮਲ ਪਾਪੀ ਤੇ ਬਾਲਮੀਕ ਬਟਵਾਰੇ ਦਾ ਉਧਾਰ ਨਾਮ ਨੇ ਹੀ ਕੀਤਾ ਹੈ। ਤੇ ਅਸੀਂ ਤੇ ਤੁਸੀਂ ਸਿੱਖ ਪੁਤ੍ਰ ਅਖਵਾਂਦੇ ਹਾਂ। ਭਾਈ ਜੀ ਉਨ੍ਹਾਂ ਪਾਪੀਆਂ ਜੀਆਂ ਦਾ ਉਧਾਰ ਨਾਮ ਨੇ ਕੀਤਾ ਹੈ। ਤੇ ਬਾਵੇ ਭਾਈ ਸਾਧਾਂ ਤੇ ਸਿੱਖਾਂ ਦਾ ਉਧਾਰ ਨ ਹੋਇਆ। ਜੋ ਫੇਰ ਬ੍ਰਾਹਮਣਾਂ ਅਗੇ ਪਗਾਂ ਲਾਹ ਕੇ ਬਹਿਨੇ ਹਾਂ। ਅਸਾਨੂੰ ਲਜਾ ਨਹੀਂ ਆਉਂਦੀ। ਜੋ ਐਸੇ ਸਚੇ ਪਾਤਸ਼ਾਹ ਗੁਰੂ ਨਾਨਕ ਜੀ ਦੇ ਪੁਤ੍ਰ ਹੋਇਕੇ ਤੇ ਸਿੱਖ ਹੋਇਕੇ ਫੇਰ ਪੰਡਿਆਂ ਪਾਸ ਜਾਂਦੇ ਹਨ। ਤੇ ਜਿਸ ਵੇਲੇ ਗੁਰੂ ਨਾਨਕ ਨਿਰੰਕਾਰ ਗਇਆ ਦਾ ਉਧਾਰ ਕਰਨ ਕੋ ਗਏ

* ਇਹ ਸ਼ਬਦ ਭਾਈ ਬੰਨੋ ਜੀ ਦੀ ਬੀੜ ਵਿਚ ਹੈ। ਉਸ ਸਮੇਂ ਪਛਮੀ ਪੰਜਾਬ ਵਿਚ ਇਹੀ ਉਤਾਰੇ ਲਿਖਤੀ ਪ੍ਰਚਲਤ ਸਨ।

ਸਨ। ਤਾਂ ਪਾਂਡਿਆਂ ਨੇ ਕਹਿਆ ਜੋ ਤੁਸੀਂ ਪ੍ਰਦੇਸ ਫਿਰਦੇ ਹੋ ਤੁਸੀਂ ਪਿੰਡ ਪਤਲ ਕਰਵਾ ਛਡੋ। ੜਾਂ ਸ੍ਰੀ ਬਾਬੇ ਨਾਨਕ ਜੀ ਆਖਿਆ : ਅਸਾਂ ਆਪਣਾ ਤਥਾਂ ਪਿਤਰਾਂ ਦਾ ਜਗਿਆ-ਸੂਆਂ ਸਿੱਖਾਂ ਦਾ ਕਰ ਛਡਿਆ ਹੈ। ਅਸਾਂ ਨਾਮ ਦਾ ਪਿੰਡ ਕੀਤਾ ਹੈ। ਜੋ ਛਿਝਦਾ ਨਹੀਂ। ਤਬ ਸਭ ਪਾਂਡੇ ਸ੍ਰੀ ਗੁਰੂ ਨਾਨਕ ਜੀ ਦੀ ਸਰਨੀ ਪਏ। ਤਾਂ ਉਨ੍ਹਾਂ ਨੂੰ ਭੀ ਸਤਿਨਾਮ ਦਾ ਉਪਦੇਸ ਦਿਤਾ। ਤੇ ਭਾਈ ਜੀ, ਗੁਰੂ ਆਪ ਜੇ ਸਾਰੀ ਪੰਡ ਚਾ ਲੀਤੀ ਤਾਂ ਅਸਾਡਾ ਕੀ ਵਾਸਤਾ ਹੈ। ਜੋ ਪਾਖੰਡ ਕਰਕੇ ਨਰਕਾਂ ਨੂੰ ਜਾਈਐ। ਐਸਾ ਸਮਰਥ ਗੁਰੂ ਨਾਨਕ ਸਾਹਿਬ ਹੈ।

ਉਪ੍ਰੰਤ ਤੀਰਥਾਂ ਦਾ ਵਿਚਾਰ ਭਾਈ ਜੀ ਏਹੁ ਹੈ, ਜੋ ਕਬੀਰ ਸਾਹਿਬ ਜੀ ਕਹਿਆ ਹੈ :—

"ਕਬੀਰ ਗੰਗਾ ਤੀਰ ਜੁ ਘਰੁ ਕਰਹਿ ਪੀਵਹਿ ਨਿਰਮਲ ਨੀਰੁ।
ਬਿਨੁ ਹਰਿਭਗਤਿ ਨ ਮੁਕਤਿ ਹੋਇ ਇਉ ਕਹਿ ਰਮੇ ਕਬੀਰ ॥ ੫੪ ॥"

ਸ੍ਰੀ ਗੁਰੂ ਨਾਨਕ ਸਾਹਿਬ ਕਹਿਆ ਹੈ :—

"ਤੀਰਥਿ ਨਾਵਣ ਜਾਉ ਤੀਰਥੁ ਨਾਮੁ ਹੈ।
ਤੀਰਥੁ ਸਬਦ ਬੀਚਾਰੁ ਅੰਤਰਿ ਗਿਆਨੁ ਹੈ।"

ਤੇ ਕਬੀਰ ਸਾਹਿਬ ਕਹਿਆ ਹੈ :—

"ਨਾਵਣ ਕਉ ਤੀਰਥ ਘਨੇ ਮਨ ਬਉਰਾ ਰੇ, ਪੂਜਨ ਕਉ ਬਹੁ ਦੇਵ।
ਕਹੁ ਕਈਰ ਛੂਟਨੁ ਨਹੀਂ ਮਨ ਬੱਉਰਾ ਰੇਂ, ਛੂਟਨੁ ਹਰਿ ਕੀ ਸੇਵ ॥ ੪ ॥"

ਤੇ ਫੇਰ ਕਬੀਰ ਜੀ ਕਹਿਆ ਹੈ :—

ਜੀਵਤਿ ਪਿਤਰ ਨ ਮਾਨੈ ਕੋਊ ਮੂਏ ਸਿਰਾਧ ਕਰਾਹੀ।
ਪਿਤਰ ਭੀ ਬਪੁਰੇ ਕਹੁ ਕਿਉ ਪਾਵਹਿ ਕਊਆ ਕੂਕਰ ਖਾਹੀ।"

ਭਾਈ ਜੀ, ਸਰਾਧਾਂ ਵਿਚ ਬ੍ਰਾਹਮਣ ਲੋਕ ਖਤਰੀਆਂ ਦੇ ਪਿਤਰਾਂ ਨੂੰ ਕਾਂ, ਕੁੱਤਾ, ਸੱਪ, ਗਊ, ਡੱਡੂ ਬਣਾਂਵਦੇ ਹੈਨ। ਉਨ੍ਹਾਂ ਵਾਸਤੇ ਹੰਦੇ ਰਖਵਾਂਦੇ ਹੈਨ। ਗੁਰੂ ਕੇ ਸਿੱਖਾਂ ਨੂੰ ਇਹ ਗਲ ਨਹੀਂ ਚਾਹੀਦੀ। ਗੁਰੂ ਕੇ ਸਿੱਖਾਂ ਦਾ ਰਾਹੁ ਸ਼ਬਦ ਹੈ। ਭਾਈ ਜੀ ਜਿਸ ਵੇਲੇ ਕੋਈ ਪ੍ਰਾਨੀ ਚਲਦਾ ਹੈ ਤਾਂ ਸੋਗ ਨਹੀਂ ਕਰਦੇ। ਜੋ ਗੁਰੂ ਗਰੰਥ ਸਾਹਿਬ ਮਨਾ ਕਰਦਾ ਹੈ। ਕਬੀਰ ਜੀ ਕਹਿਆ ਹੈ :—

"ਅਵਰ ਮੂਏ ਕਿਆ ਸੋਗੁ ਕਰੀਜੈ।
ਤਉ ਕੀਜੈ ਜਉ ਆਪਨ ਜੀਜੈ।"

ਪੁਨਾ :—

''ਕਬੀਰ ਸੰਤ ਮੂਏ ਕਿਆ ਰੋਈਐ ਜੋ ਅਪੁਨੇ ਗ੍ਰਿਹਿ ਜਾਇ।
ਰੋਵਹੁ ਸਾਕਤ ਬਾਪੁਰੇ ਜੁ ਹਾਟੈ ਹਾਟ ਬਿਕਾਇ। ੧੯।

ਸੋਗ ਕਰਦੇ ਨਹੀਂ। ਸੋ ਸੁਖਮਨੀ ਸਾਹਿਬ ਵਿਚ ਭੀ ਸ੍ਰੀ ਗੁਰੂ ਅਰਜਨ ਸਾਹਿਬ ਜੀ ਨੇ ਕਹਿਆ ਹੈ :—

''ਅਪਨੀ ਅਮਾਨ ਕਛੁ ਬਹੁਰਿ ਸਾਹੁ ਲੇਇ।
ਅਗਿਆਨੀ ਮਨਿ ਰੋਸੁ ਕਰੇਇ।''

ਭਾਈ ਜੀ, ਜਿਸ ਵੇਲੇ ਕੋਈ ਨਿਰੰਕਾਰ ਦੇ ਦੇਸ਼ ਨੂੰ ਜਾਂਦਾ ਹੈ ਤਦ ਸ੍ਰੀ ਸਤਿਗੁਰੂ ਅਬਿਨਾਸ਼ੀ ਜੀ ਕਾ ਸਦਕਾ ਕਪੜੇ ਚਿਟੇ ਦੁਧ ਪਾਇਕੇ ਹਟੀ ਉਤੇ ਜਾਇ ਬਹਿਨੇ ਹਾਂ! ਵੂੜੀ ਪਾਂਦੇ ਨਹੀਂ। ਬਾਕੀ ਦਿਨਾਂ ਪੰਜਾਂ ਪਿਛੈ ਸ਼ਬਦ ਗਾਂਵਦੇ ਜਾਂਦੇ ਹਾਂ। ਅਸਤੀਆਂ ਤਥਾ ਭਸਮ ਮੇਲ ਕੇ ਜਲ ਵਿਚ ਪ੍ਰਵਾਹਿ ਦੇਂਦੇ ਹਾਂ। ਗੁਰੂ ਜੀ ਦਾ ਸਦਕਾ ਗੁਰੂ ਹੀ ਕਰਾਂਵਦਾ ਹੈ।

''ਨਾਮੁ ਵਰਤਣਿ ਨਾਮ ਵਾਲੇਵਾ ਨਾਮ ਨਾਨਕ ਪ੍ਰਾਨ ਅਧਾਰਾ।''
''ਹਰਿ ਧਨੁ ਸੰਚਨੁ ਹਰਿ ਨਾਮੁ ਭੋਜਨੁ ਇਹੁ ਨਾਨਕ ਕੀਨੋ ਚੋਲਾ।''

ਧੰਨ ਧੰਨ ਗੁਰਦੇਵ ਜਿਨ ਭਰਮ ਗੜ ਤੋੜਿਆ। ਜੀਆਂ ਦੇ ਮਾਰਨ ਵਾਲਾ ਤੇ ਜੀਵਾਵਣ ਵਾਲਾ ਸ੍ਰੀ ਨਿਰੰਕਾਰ ਹੈ। ਗੁਰੂ ਕੇ ਸਿੱਖਾਂ ਨੂੰ ਭਰਮ ਕੋਈ ਨਹੀਂ ਹੈ।

''ਸਰਬ ਸੁਖਾ ਬਨੇ ਤੇਰੈ ਓਲ੍ਹੈ। ਭ੍ਰਮ ਕੇ ਪਰਦੇ ਸਤਿਗੁਰ ਖੋਲ੍ਹੈ।''

ਪੁਨਾ :—

''ਜਿਉ ਜਿਉ ਤੇਰਾ ਹੁਕਮੁ ਤਿਵੈ ਤਿਉ ਹੋਵਣਾ॥
ਜਹ ਜਹ ਰਖਹਿ ਆਪਿ ਤਹ ਜਾਇ ਖੜੋਵਣਾ॥
ਨਾਮ ਤੇਰੈ ਕੈ ਰੰਗਿ ਦੁਰਮਤਿ ਧੋਵਣਾ॥
ਜਪਿ ਜਪਿ ਤੁਧੁ ਨਿਰੰਕਾਰ ਭਰਮੁ ਭਉ ਖੋਵਣਾ॥
ਜੋ ਤੇਰੈ ਰੰਗਿ ਰਤੇ ਸੇ ਜੋਨਿ ਨ ਜੋਵਣਾ॥''

ਪੁਨਾ :—

''ਬੇਦ ਪੁਰਾਨ ਸਿਮ੍ਰਿਤ ਸੁਨੇ ਬਹੁਬਿਧਿ ਕਰਉ ਬੀਚਾਰੁ॥
ਪਤਤਿ ਉਧਾਰਮ ਭੈ ਹਰਨ ਸੁਖ ਸਾਗਰ ਨਿਰੰਕਾਰ॥''

ਪਾਪੀਆਂ ਦਾ ਉਧਾਰ ਕਰਨ ਵਾਲਾ ਨਿਰੰਕਾਰ ਹੈ। ''ਅਜਾਮਲ ਗਜ ਗਨਿਕਾ ਪਤਤਿ ਕਰਮ ਕੀਨੇ। ਤੇਊ ਉਤਰਿ ਪਾਰਿ ਪਰੇ ਰਾਮ ਨਾਮ ਲੀਨੇ।' ਹੋਰ ਭਾਈ ਜੀ ਧੰਨ ਨਿਰੰਕਾਰ ਦਾਂ ਜਾਪੁ ਜਪਣਾ ਤੇ ਜਪੁਵਾਣਾ ਤੇ ਮਾਈਆਂ ਪਾਸੋਂ ਸ਼ਬਦ ਗਵਾਵਣੇ ਤੇ

ਪੜ੍ਹਨੇ। ਸ੍ਰੀ ਗੁਰੂ ਅਰਜਨ ਸਾਹਿਬ ਜੀ ਨੇ ਸੁਖਮਨੀ ਸਾਹਿਬ ਵਿਚ ਨਾਮ ਦਾ ਮਹਾਤਮ ਰਖਿਆ ਹੈ।

"ਸਲੋਕ ॥ ਬਹੁ ਸਾਸਤ੍ਰ ਬਹੁ ਸਿਮਿਪ੍ਰੀ ਪੇਖੇ ਸਰਬ ਢਢੋਲਿ।
ਪੂਜਸਿ ਨਾਹੀ ਹਰਿ ਹਰੇ ਨਾਨਕ ਨਾਮ ਅਮੋਲ।

ਅਸਟਪਦੀ ॥ ਜਾਪ ਤਾਪ ਗਿਆਨ ਸਭਿ ਧਿਆਨ।
ਖਟ ਸਾਸਤ੍ਰ ਸਿਮ੍ਰਿਤਿ ਵਖਿਆਨ।
ਜੋਗ ਅਭਿਆਸ਼ ਕਰਮ ਧ੍ਰਮ ਕਿਰਿਆ।
ਸਗਲ ਤਿਆਗਿ ਬਨ ਮਧੇ ਫਿਰਿਆ।
ਅਨਿਕ ਪ੍ਰਕਾਰ ਕੀਨੇ ਬਹੁ ਜਤਨਾ। ਪੁਨ ਦਾਨ ਹੋਮੇ ਬਹੁ ਰਤਨਾ।
ਸਰੀਰੁ ਕਟਾਇ ਹੋਮੈ ਕਰਿ ਰਾਤੀ। ਵਰਤ ਨੇਮ ਕਰੈ ਬਹੁ ਭਾਤੀ।
ਨਹੀ ਤੁਲਿ ਰਾਮ ਨਾਮ ਬੀਚਾਰ।
ਨਾਨਕ ਗੁਰਮੁਖਿ ਨਾਮੁ ਜਪੀਐ ਇਕ ਬਾਰ।"

ਪੁਨਾ :—

"ਕਰਮ ਧਰਮ ਪਾਖੰਡ ਜੋ ਦੀਸਹਿ ਤਿਨ ਜਮੁ ਜਗਾਤੀ ਲੂਟੇ!
ਨਿਰਬਾਣ ਕੀਰਤਨੁ ਗਾਵਹੁ ਕਰਤੇ ਕਾ ਨਿਮਖ ਸਿਮਰਤ ਜਿਤੁ ਛੂਟੇ।"

(ਸੂਹੀ ਮ: ੫)

ਹੋਰ ਭਾਈ ਜੀ ਕਰਮ ਧਹਮ ਸਭ ਝੂਠੇ ਹੈਨ ਤੇ ਤੁਸਾਂ ਨਾਮ ਜਪੁਣਾ। ਹੋਰ ਭਾਈ ਜੀ ਤੁਸੀ ਤਾਰੇ ਦਾ ਵੀਚਾਰ ਕੋਈ ਨਹੀਂ ਕਰਨਾ। "ਨਾਮੁ ਜਪਤ ਕੋਟਿ ਸੂਰ ਉਜਾਰਾ ਬਿਨਸੈ ਅੰਧੇਰਾ।" ਹੋਰ ਭਾਈ ਜੀ ਸਭ ਬ੍ਰਾਹਮਣਾਂ ਦੇ ਲਾਲਚ ਵਾਸਤੇ ਸਾਰ਼ਾ ਪਾਖੰਡ ਹੈ। ਭਾਈ ਜੀ ਤਾਰਾ ਚੜ੍ਹ ਪਿਆ ਤਾਂ ਕੀ ਹੋਏ ਗਿਆ ਤੇ ਡੁਬ ਗਿਆ ਤਾਂ ਸਾਨੂੰ ਕੀ ਹੈ।

"ਕਬੀਰ ਨਾ ਹਮ ਕੀਆ ਨ ਕਰਹਿਗੇ ਨਾ ਕਰਿ ਸਕੈ ਸਰੀਰੁ।
ਕਿਆ ਜਾਨਹੁ ਕਿਛੁ ਹਰਿ ਕੀਆ ਭਇਓ ਕਬੀਰੁ ਕਬੀਰੁ। ੬੨।"

"ਜਿਸ ਕਾ ਕਾਰਜ ਤਿਨ ਹੀ ਕੀਆ ਮਾਨਸੁ ਕਿਆ ਵੇਚਾਰਾ ਰਾਮ।
ਭਗਤ ਸੋਹਨਿ ਹਰਿਕੇ ਗੁਣ ਗਾਵਹਿ ਸਦਾ ਕਰਹਿ ਜੈਕਾਰਾ ਰਾਮ।"

ਅਸੀਂ ਕਵਣ ਜੀਵ ਹਾਂ। ਸ੍ਰੀ ਗੁਰੂ ਆਪ ਕਾਰਜ ਕਰਨ ਵਾਲਾ ਹੈ। ਮਨੁਖਾਂ ਦੀ ਕੀ ਸ਼ਕਤੀ ਹੈ। ਅਗੇ ਸਦਕਾ ਸ੍ਰੀ ਨਿਰੰਕਾਰ ਜੀ ਦਾ ਅਸੀਂ ਦਰਬਾਰ ਸ਼ਾਹਿਬ ਵਿਚ

ਸਰਬੱਤ ਸਾਧ ਸੰਗਤ ਦੇ ਚਰਨ ਧੋਂਦੇ ਹਾਂ। ਗੁਰੂ ਨਾਨਕ ਜੀ ਪ੍ਰਗਟ ਹੋਇ ਸਨ ਉਸ ਵਕਤ ਇਹੁ ਸਬਦ ਭਾਈ ਗੁਰਦਾਸ ਜੀ ਕਹਿਆ ਸੀ :—

"ਸਤਿਗੁਰ ਨਾਨਕ ਪ੍ਰਗਟਿਆ ਮਿੱਟੀ ਧੁੰਧ ਜਗ ਚਾਨਣ ਹੋਆ।
ਜਿਉਂ ਕਰ ਸੂਰਜ ਨਿਕਲਿਆ ਤਾਰੇ ਛਪੇ ਅੰਧੇਰ ਪਲੋਆ।"

ਅਗੈ ਸਾਧ ਸੰਗਤ ਵਿਚ ਗੁਰੂ ਨਾਨਕ ਇਕ ਰੀਤ ਰਖੀ ਹੈ।

ਪਉੜੀ। "ਸੁਣੀ ਪੁਕਾਰ ਦਾਤਾਰੁ ਪ੍ਰਭ ਗੁਰ ਨਾਨਕ ਜਗ ਮਾਹਿੰ ਪਠਾਯਾ।
ਚਰਨ ਧੋਇ ਰਹਿਰਾਸ ਕਰ ਚਰਨਾਮ੍ਰਿਤ ਸਿਖਾਂ ਪੀਲਾਯਾ।
.........ਕਲ ਤਾਰਣ ਗੁਰ ਨਾਨਕ ਆਯਾ।"

ਉਪ੍ਰੰਤ ਸ੍ਰੀ ਗੁਰੂ ਅਰਜਨ ਸਾਹਿਬ ਜੀ ਕਹਿਆ ਹੈ :—

"ਚਰਨ ਸਾਧ ਕੇ ਧੋਇ ਧੋਇ ਪੀਉ। ਅਰਪਿ ਸਾਧ ਕਉ ਅਪਨਾ ਜੀਉ।
ਸਾਧ ਕੀ ਧੂਰ ਕਰਹੁ ਇਸਨਾਨੁ। ਸਾਧ ਊਪਰਿ ਜਾਈਐ ਕੁਰਬਾਨੁ।"

(ਸੁਖਮਨੀ)

ਤਾਂ ਤੇ ਤੁਸਾਂ ਭੀ ਇਹ ਰੀਤ ਕਰਨੀ। ਜੋ ਗੁਰੂ ਗਰੰਥ ਸਾਹਿਬ ਜੀ ਦੀ ਸੰਗਤ ਕਰਨੀ ਤੇ ਸੰਗਤ ਦੇ ਚਰਨ ਧੋਣੇ। ਅਗੈ ਸ੍ਰੀ ਨਿਰੰਕਾਰ ਜੀ ਦਾ ਸਦਕਾ ਅਸੀਂ ਜੋੜੇ ਦਰਬਾਰ ਸਾਹਿਬ ਵਿਚ ਝਾੜਦੇ ਹਾਂ। ਕਿਉਂ ਜੋ ਗੂਰੂ ਨਾਨਕ ਜੀ ਕਹਿਆ ਹੈ।

ਜੋ ਰਾਜਾ ਦੇਵ ਲੂਤ ਸਭ ਰਾਖਸ਼ਾਂ ਨੂੰ ਨਾਲ ਲੈ ਕੇ ਸ੍ਰੀ ਗੁਰੂ ਨਾਨਕ ਜੀ ਦੀ ਸਰਨੀ ਆਇ ਸਨ ਜੋ ਸਚੇ ਪਾਤਸਾਹ ਜੀ ਅਸਾਡਾ ਉਧਾਰ ਹੋਵੈ ਤੇ ਰਾਖਸ਼ੀ ਜੂਨ ਕਟੀਐ। ਤਾਂ ਗੁਰੂ ਨਾਨਕ ਸਾਹਿਬ ਬਚਨ ਕੀਤਾ ਜੋ ਭਾਈ ਜੀ ਤੁਸਾਂ ਧਰਮਸਾਲਾ ਬਣਵਾਨੀ ਤੇ ਜੋੜੇ ਝਾੜਨੇ, ਪ੍ਰਸਾਦ ਦਾ ਕਿਣਕਾ ਡਿਗਾ ਮੂੰਹ ਪਾਵਣਾ। ਜਿਉਂ ਜਿਉਂ ਤੁਸੀਂ ਮੂੰਹ ਪਾਵੋਗੇ ਤਿਉਂ ਤਿਉਂ ਤੁਸਾਡੀ ਰਾਖਸ਼ੀ ਜੂਨ ਕਟੀ ਜਾਵੇਗੀ।

ਭਾਈ ਜੀ ਗੁਰੂ ਜੀ ਦਾ ਬਚਨ ਰਾਖਸ਼ਾਂ ਤਥਾ ਪਸ਼ੂਆਂ ਨੇ ਮੰਨਿਆ। ਤੁਸੀਂ ਤੇ ਅਸੀਂ ਤਾਂ ਸਿਖ ਪੁਤ੍ਰ ਅਖਵਾਂਦੇ ਹਾਂ। ਤੁਸਾਨੂੰ ਤੇ ਅਸਾਂਨੂੰ ਲਜਾ ਨਹੀਂ ਆਉਂਦੀ?

ਅਗੇ ਉਪਦੇਸ਼ ਤ੍ਰੈ ਹੈਨ। ਸ੍ਰੀ ਗੁਰੂ ਨਾਨਕ ਅਬਨਾਸ਼ੀ ਤੇ ਸ੍ਰੀ ਸਤਿਗੁਰੂ ਦਇਆਲ ਜੀ ਕਹੈ ਹੈਨ। ਜੋ ਭਜਨ ਨਿਰੰਕਾਰ ਜੀ ਦਾ ਕਰਨਾ।੧। ਮਾਤਾ ਪਿਤਾ ਦੀ ਟਹਿਲ।੨। ਕਿਰਤ ਕਰਕੇ ਖਾਵਣੀ ਸਦਕਾ ਸ੍ਰੀ ਨਿਰੰਕਾਰ ਜੀ ਦਾ ਤੇ ਵਿਕਾਰਾਂ ਦਾ ਤਿਆਗ ਕਰਨਾ।੩। ਜੋ ਕਬੀਰ ਜੀ ਦਾ ਬਚਨ ਹੈ :—

"ਕਬੀਰ ਭਾਂਗ ਮਾਛੁਲੀ ਸੁਰਾਪਾਨਿ ਜੋ ਜੋ ਪ੍ਰਾਨੀ ਖਾਂਹਿ ।
ਤੀਰਥ ਬਰਤ ਨੇਮ ਕੀਏ ਤੇ ਸਭੈ ਰਸਾਤਲ ਜਾਂਹਿ ।" ੨੩੩ ।

ਇਹਨਾਂ ਤ੍ਰੈਆਂ ਬਚਨਾਂ ਦਾ ਬੀਚਾਰ ਏਹੁ ਹੈ । ਜੋ ਭਜਨ ਨਿਰੰਕਾਰ ਜੀ । ਇਸ ਵਾਸਤੇ ਜੋ ਜਨਮ ਮਰਨ ਕਟਿਆ ਜਾਵੈ । ਮਾਤਾ ਪਿਤਾ ਦੀ ਟਹਿਲ ਇਸ ਵਾਸਤੇ ਜੋ ਮਾਤਾ ਦਸ ਮਹੀਨੇ ਆਪਣੇ ਗਰਭ ਵਿਚ ਰਖਦੀ ਹੈ । ਤ ਫੇਰ ਇਸ ਨੂੰ ਨਿਰੰਕਾਰ ਬਾਹਰ ਲੈਆਂਵਦਾ ਹੈ ਤਦ ਸਾਰੀ ਪੰਡ ਨਾਤਾ ਪਿਤਾ ਦੇ ਸਿਰ ਹੋਂਦੀ ਹੈ । ਕਿਰਤ ਕਰਕੇ ਖਾਵਣਾ ਇਸ ਵਾਸਤੇ ਜੋ ਮੁਥਾਜ ਕਿਸੇ ਦਾ ਨਾ ਹੋਵੈ ।

ਇਹਨਾਂ ਤ੍ਰੈਆਂ ਬਚਨਾਂ ਥੀਂ ਬਿਨਾ ਹੋਰ ਕੋਈ ਪਾਖੰਡ ਵਿਚ ਪਾਵੈ ਤਦ ਤੁਸਾਂ ਨਹੀਂ ਨਹੀਂ ਮੰਨਣਾ । ਇਹੁ ਉਪਦੇਸ਼ ਆਪ ਸ੍ਰੀ ਸਤਿਗੁਰੂ ਨਾਨਕ ਜੀ ਸ੍ਰੀ ਸਤਿਗੁਰੂ ਦਇਆਲ ਜੀ ਕਹੈ ਹੈਨ ।

"ਇਸ ਉ ਊਪਰਿ ਨਹੀਂ ਬੀਚਾਰੁ । ਜਾਕੈ ਮਨਿ ਬਸਿਆ ਨਿਰੰਕਾਰੁ ।"
"ਸਦਾ ਸਦਾ ਦਇਆਲ । ਸਿਮਰਿ ਸਿਮਰਿ ਨਾਨਕ ਭਏ ਨਿਹਾਲ ।"

ਇਹ ਬਚਨ ਸੁਣਕੇ ਉਹ ਸਿਖ ਚਰਨਾਂ ਤੇ ਡਿਗ ਪਿਆ । ਜੋ ਮੈਨੂੰ ਸਿਖ ਕਰੀਏ । ਤਾਂ ਬਚਨ ਹੋਇਆ ਇਹੀ ਸਿਖਿਆ ਹੈ ਜੋ ਗੁਰੂ ਸਬਦ ਬਿਨਾ ਹੋਰਸ ਦੀ ਪੂਜਾ ਨਹੀਂ ਕਰਨੀ । ਨਿਰੰਕਾਰ ਦਾ ਜਾਪੁ ਜਪੁਣਾ ।

ਇਹ ਅਰਦਾਸ ਸ੍ਰੀ ਨਿਰੰਕਾਰ ਜੀ ਦੀ ਕਿਰਪਾ ਨਾਲ ਹੋਈ । ਪਹੁੰਚੇ ਗੁਰੂ ਗਰੰਥ ਸਾਹਿਬ ਪਾਸ । ਧੰਨ ਧੰਨ ਨਿਰੰਕਾਰ । ਧੰਨ ਧੰਨ ਸ੍ਰੀ ਸਤਿਗੁਰੂ ਦਇਆਲ ਅਬਨਾਸ਼ੀ ਸਾਹਿਬ ਸਚਾ ਪਾਤਸ਼ਾਹ ਜੀ ਜਿਸ ਏਹੁ ਨਾਮ ਦਾ ਚਲਣ ਕਢਿਆ ਤੇ ।

ਸੰਮਾਪਤੰ ।

ਸੰਮਤ ੧੯੧੩ ਵਿਚ ਇਹੁ ਚਿਠਾ ਚਲਣ ਦਾ ਤਿਆਰ ਹੋਇਆ ਰਾਵਲ ਪਿੰਡੀ ਹਰਿਮੰਦਰ ਸਾਹਿਬ ਵਿਚ ਮਹੀਨਾ ਨਿਰੰਕਾਰ ਅਬਨਾਸ਼ੀ ਜੀ ਦਾ ॥

ਚੌਪਈ :—ਵਾਸੀ ਰਾਜੜ ਕੀ ਤੁਮ ਜਾਨੋ । ਰੂਪ ਸਿੰਘ ਤੁਮ ਨਾਮ ਪਛਾਨੋ ।
ਗੁਰੂ ਦਇਆਲ ਜਬ ਕਿਰਪਾ ਧਾਰੀ । ਚਿਠੇ ਕੀ ਤਬ ਕਰੀ ਤਿਆਰੀ । ੧ ।
ਚਲਣ ਲਿਖ ਗੁਰੂਅਨ ਕੇ ਸਾਰੇ । ਕਿਰਪਾ ਕੀਤੀ ਦਇਆਲ ਮੁਹਾਰੇ ।
ਜੋ ਕੋਈ ਐਸੀ ਰੀਤ ਕਰਾਵੈ । ਜਨਮ ਮਰਨ ਮੈ ਫੇਰ ਨ ਆਵੈ । ੨ ।

ਦੋਹਿਰਾ :—ਕਿਰਤ ਕਰੇ ਜੋ ਧਰਮ ਦੀ ਟਹਿਲ ਕਰੈ ਦਰਬਾਰ ।
ਦਇਆਲ ਗੁਰੂ ਕਿਰਪਾ ਕਰੇ ਦਰਬਾਰਾ ਸਿੰਘ ਬਲਿਹਾਰ । ੩ ।
ਐਸੇ ਗੁਰ ਕੋ ਜੋ ਨਰ ਤਿਆਗੈ । ਈਹਾ ਖੇਦ ਨਰਕ ਤਿਹ ਆਗੈ ।
ਧੰਨ ਧੰਨ ਸ੍ਰੀ ਸਤਿਗੁਰੂ ਦਇਆਲ ਜੀ ।
ਧੰਨ ਧੰਨ ਸ੍ਰੀ ਸਤਿਗੁਰੂ ਦਰਬਾਰਾ ਸਿੰਘ ਸਾਹਿਬ ਜੀ ।

ਦੋਹਿਰਾ :—ਅਖਰ ਵਾਧੇ ਘਾਟ ਜੋ ਪੜ੍ਹ ਪੜ੍ਹ ਕਰੋ ਬੀਚਾਰ ।
ਹਮ ਕੋ ਦੋਸ ਨ ਦੀਜੀਐ ਹਮ ਖਿਨ ਖਿਨ ਭੂਲਨਹਾਰ ।

ਧੰਨ ਧੰਨ ਨਿਰੰਕਾਰ ਜੀ

ਨੋਟ :—੧. ਜਿਹੜਾ ਹੁਕਮ ਨਾਮਾ (ਚਲਣ ਦਾ ਚਿਠਾ) ਸ੍ਰੀ ਦਰਬਾਰ ਸਾਹਿਬ ਨਿਰੰਕਾਰੀ ਰਾਵਲਪਿੰਡੀ ਵਿਖੈ ਮੌਜੂਦ ਸੀ ਤੇ ਜਿਸ ਦੀ ਕਾਪੀ ਉਤਾਰਾ ਗੁਰਦਵਾਰਾ ਨਿਰੰਕਾਰੀ ਗੋਲੜਾ ਦੀ ਪ੍ਰਾਪਤ ਹੋਈ ਹੈ, ਉਸਦੇ ਅਖੀਰ ਚੌਪਈ ਨਹੀਂ ਲਿਖੀ ਹੋਈ ਤੇ ਇਸ ਦੀ ਥਾਂ ਕੁੰਡਲੀਆ ਲਿਖਿਆ ਹੋਇਆ ਹੈ ।

ਕੁੰਡਲੀਆ :—ਵਾਸੀ ਰਾਜੜ ਜਾਨੀਐ ਰੂਪ ਸਿੰਘ ਜਹਿ ਨਾਮ ।
ਦਇਆਲ ਗੁਰੂ ਕ੍ਰਿਪਾਂ ਕਰੀ ਚਿਠੇ ਕੀਣ ਬਖਾਨ ।
ਚਿਠੇ ਕੀਨ ਬਖਾਨ ਲਿਖੇ ਚਲਣ ਗੁਰ ਸਾਰੇ ।
ਕ੍ਰਿਪਾ ਕੀਨੀ ਦਇਆਲ ਗੁਰੂ ਜੀ ਸਿੰਘ ਦਰਬਾਰੇ ।
ਟਹਿਲ ਕਰੈ ਜੋ ਪ੍ਰੀਤ ਕਰ ਕਰੈ ਕਿਰਤ ਸੁਭ ਕਾਮ ।
ਦਇਆਲ ਗੁਰੂ ਕੀ ਕ੍ਰਿਪਾ ਤੇ ਪ੍ਰਾਪਤ ਹੋਵੈ ਨਾਮ ।

ਸ੍ਰੀ ਗੁਰੂ ਦਇਆਲ ਬਾਬਾ ਜੀ ਲਿਖਾਰੀ ਪਿੰਗਲ ਦਾਸ ਕੀ ਭੁਲ ਚੁਕ ਬਖਸ਼ਣੀ । ਵਿਸਾਖੋ ੨੧ । ਸੰਮਤ ੧੯੪੧ । ਬੁੱਧਵਾਰ ਸੰਪੂਰਨੰ ।

੨:—ਇਸ ਹੁਕਮ ਨਾਮਾ (ਚਲਣ ਦਾ ਚਿਠਾ) ਵਿਚ ਲਿਖਿਆ ਹੋਇਆ ਹੈ —

ਹੋਰ ਜਿਸ ਜਗਾ ਦਰਬਾਰ ਸਾਹਿਬ ਨਾਂ ਹੋਵੈ ਤਾਂ ਪੰਜ ਗਰੰਥੀ ਪੋਥੀ ਭਾਵੇਂ ਚਾਰ ਲਾਵਾਂ ਲਿਖਕੇ ਚੌਕੀ ਉਤੇ ਰਖਕੇ ਦੀਵਾਨ ਲਗਾਇ ਕਰ ਫੇਰੇ ਦੇ ਦੇਣੇ ।"

੩ :—ਇਕ ਨਿਰੰਕਾਰੀ ਜਲਣ ਦੇ ਚਿਠੇ ਦੀ ਕਾਪੀ ਗਿਆਨੀ ਹੀਰਾ ਸਿੰਘ ਜੀ ਪਾਸੋਂ ਪ੍ਰਾਪਤ ਹੋਈ ਸੀ ਜੋ ਅਸਲ ਚਿਠੇ ਦਾ ਉਤਾਰਾ ਨਹੀਂ । ਉਸ ਦੀ ਬੋਲੀ ਉਰਦੂ ਤੇ ਅਖਰ ਗੁਰਮੁਖੀ ਸਨ । ਚਿਠੇ ਦੇ ਅੰਤ ਵਿਚ ਲਿਖਾਰੀ ਦਾ ਨਾਮ ਨਹੀਂ, ਤੇ ਸੰਮਤ ਇਸ ਤਰ੍ਹਾਂ ਲਿਖਿਆ ਹੈ :

"ਸੰਮਤ ੧੯੨੩ ਮਿਤੀ ਮਾਗੋ ਦਿਨੇ ੨੫ ਮਹੀਨਾ ਗੁਰੂ ਨਾਨਕ ਸਾਹਿਬ ਜੀ ਦਾ । ਇਹੁ ਪੋਥੀ ਸੰਪੂਰਨ ਹੋਈ ਮੰਗਲਵਾਰੈ ।"

ਸਿਧਾਂਤ ਉਹੀ ਹੈ, ਜੋ ਫਾਈ ਰੂਪ ਸਿੰਘ ਜੀ ਨੇ ਵਰਨਨ ਕੀਤਾ ਹੈ, ਪਰ ਅੰਤ ਵਿਚ ਇਹ ਗਲ ਵਾਧੂ ਅੰਕਿਤ ਹੈ : –

"ਔਰ ਇਲਾਵੈ ਇਨਕੇ ਏਕ ਔਰ ਫੁਰਮਾਨ ਬਾਬਾ ਦਿਆਲ ਗੁਰੂ ਜੀ ਨੇ ਮੁਫ਼ੀਦ ਸਮਝ ਕਰ ਫੁਰਮਾਇਆ ਹੈ ਕਿ ਜਬ ਕਿਸੀ ਔਰਤ ਕਾ ਸ਼ੌਹਰ ਬਵੱਜਾ ਨਿਰੰਕਾਰ ਫ਼ੌਤ ਹੋਇ ਜਾਵੈ ਤੌ ਔਰ ਬੇਵੈ ਕੋ ਉਸ ਕੇ ਸ਼ਹੁਰ ਕੇ ਭਾਈ ਕੇ ਸਾਥ ਸ਼ਾਦੀ ਕਰ ਦੇਤੇ ਹੈਂ । ਅਗਰ ਔਰਤ ਕੀ ਸਾਹਮਰਾਇ ਦੇਵਰ ਅਪਨੇ ਕੇ ਨਾ ਹੋ ਤੌ ਦੂਸਰੇ ਖਾਨਦਾਨ ਅਪਨੇ ਰਿਸ਼ਤੇ ਮੇਂ ਸ਼ਾਦੀ ਕਰ ਦੇਤੇ ਹੈਂ ।

ਬਾਇਸ ਇਸ ਕਾ ਯੇ ਹੈ ਕਿ ਔਰਤ ਬੇਵੇ ਖਰਾਬ ਨਾ ਹੋ ਔਰ ਨਨੀਜੀ ਅਪਨੇ ਮਜ਼ਹਬ ਕੋ ਛੋੜ ਕਰ ਦੂਸਰੇ ਮਜ਼ਹਬ ਮੈ ਨਾ ਜਾਵੇ ।"

— — —

APPENDIX E

This order was issued by Saheb Rattaji to his all Nirankari followers to abide by the conduct as prescribed in the Nirankari Chalan da Chitha. It emphasised the importance of Chitha which was to be read every fortnightly in all the Nirankari Gurudwaras.

ਹੁਕਮ ਨਾਮਾ

ਸ੍ਰੀ ਸਤਿਗੁਰੂ ਸਾਹਿਬ ਰੱਤਾ ਜੀ ਮਹਾਰਾਜ

ੴ ਸਤਿਗੁਰ ਪ੍ਰਸਾਦਿ

ਧੰਨ ਧੰਨ ਨਿਰੰਕਾਰ ਅਬਨਾਸੀ ਸਾਹਿਬ ਸਚਾ ਪਾਤਸਾਹ ਜੀ ।
ਧੰਨ ਧੰਨ ਸ੍ਰੀ ਸਤਿਗੁਰੂ ਦਿਆਲ ਨਿਰੰਕਾਰ ਅਬਨਾਸੀ ਸਾਹਿਬ ਸਚਾਂ ਪਾਤਸਾਹੁ ਜੀ ।
ਧੰਨ ਧੰਨ ਸ੍ਰੀ ਸਤਿਗੁਰੂ ਦਰਡਾਰਾ ਸਿੰਘ ਨਿਰੰਕਾਰ ਅਬਨਾਸੀ ਸਹਿਬ ਸਚਾ ਪਾਤਸਾਹੁ ਜੀ ।

ਹੁਕਮ ਸ੍ਰੀ ਸਤਿਗੁਰੂ ਦਿਆਲ ਸ੍ਰੀ ਸਤਿਗੁਰੂ ਦਰਬਾਰਾ ਸਿੰਘ ਜੀ ਦੇ ਨਾਲ

ਪ੍ਰਵਾਨਾ ਲਿਖਿਆ

ਸ੍ਰਬਤ ਖਾਲਸਾ ਸੰਗਤ ਬੀੜਿਆਂ ਵਾਲਿਆਂ ਪਾਸ । ਜੋ ਸ੍ਰਬਤ ਬੀੜਿਆਂ ਵਾਲਿਆਂ ਜੋਗ ਮਲੂਮ ਹੋਵੇ ਜੋ ਤੁਸਾਂਨੂੰ ਹੁਕਮ-ਨਾਮਾਂ ਅਗੈ ਚਲਣ ਦੇ ਚਿੱਠੇ ਸ੍ਰਬਤ ਜੋਗ ਦਿਤੇ ਹੈਨ ਸੋ ਤੁਸਾਂ ਅੰਦਰ ਰੱਖ ਛੱਡੇ ਹਨ । ਨਾ ਆਪ ਪੜ੍ਹ ਕਰ ਕਮਾਂਵਦੇ ਹੋ ਤੇ ਨਾ ਹੋਰਨਾਂ ਨੂੰ ਪੜ੍ਹ ਕਰ ਸੁਣਾਂਵਦੇ ਹੋ । ਸੁ ਸਭ ਲੋਕ ਨਿਰੰਕਾਰੀਏ ਜਗਤ ਨਾਲ ਮੇਲਵਾਂ ਕੰਮ੍ਹ ਕਰਦੇ

ਹੋ । ਅੰਦਰੋਂ ਕਰਮ-ਕਾਂਡ ਤੇ ਚਿਤ ਕਰਦਾ ਹੈ ਤੇ ਬਾਹਰੋਂ ਨਿਰੰਕਾਰੀ ਸਦਾਂਵਦੇ ਹੋ । ਸੋ ਤੁਸਾਡੇ ਮਨ ਵਿਚ ਹੈ ਜੋ ਸਤਿਗੁਰੂ ਦਰਬਾਰਾ ਸਿੰਘ ਜੀ ਸਮਾਇ ਗਿਆ ਹੈ ਸੋ ਅਸੀਂ ਤਾਂ ਨਿਰੰਕਾਰ ਰੂਪ ਹੋਕਰ ਸੂਤ੍ਰ ਬੀੜਿਆਂ ਤੇ ਦੇਖਦੇ ਹਾਂ ਤੁਸਾਡੀ ਕਰਤੂਤ । ਤੁਸਾਡਾ ਚਿਤ ਹੋਵੇ ਜੋ ਜਗਤ ਨਾਲ ਅਸੀਂ ਮਿਲ ਜਾਵੀਏ ਸੋ ਅਸੀ ਐਸੀ ਕਰਾਂਗੇ ਜੋ ਨਿਰੰਕਾਰੀਆ ਹੋ ਕਰਮ ਕਰਮ-ਕਾਂਡ ਕਰੇਗਾ ਸੋ ਉਸਦਾ ਦੂਹਾਂ ਜਹਾਨਾਂ ਵਿਚ ਮੂੰਹ ਕਾਲਾ ਕਰਾਂਗੇ । ਜੇ ਕਰ ਤੁਮੀ ਇਹੁ ਪਰਵਾਨਾ ਪੜ੍ਹ ਕਰ ਸੁਣ ਕਰ ਮੰਨੋਗੇ ਤਾਂ ਪਿਛਲੇ ਗੁਨਾਹ ਤੁਸਾਡੇ ਸਭ ਬਖਸ਼ੇ । ਤੇ ਅਗੋਂ ਤੁਸੀਂ ਇਸ ਪਰਵਾਨੇ ਤੇ ਲਿਖ ਦੇਵੋ ਜੋ ਅਗੋਂ ਅਸੀਂ ਕੁਝ ਰਾਈ ਮਾਤ੍ਰ ਭੀ ਕਰਮ-ਕਾਂਡ ਕਰੀਏ ਤਾਂ ਬੇਮੁਖ ਹੋਵੀਏ । ਸਾਰਾ ਭਾਰ ਤੁਸਾਡਾ ਪਾਪਾਂ ਦਾ ਮੈਂ ਚੁਕਾਂ ਤੇ ਫੇਰ ਤੁਸੀਂ ਕਰਮ-ਕਾਂਡ ਕਰੋ । ਜੋ ਕੋਈ ਸਿਖ ਸ੍ਰੀ ਸਤਿਗੁਰੂ ਦਿਆਲ ਅਬਨਾਸੀ ਜੀ ਦਾ ਇਸ ਪ੍ਰਵਾਨੇ ਨੂੰ ਮੰਨੇਗਾ ਸੋ ਨਿਹਾਲ ਹੋਵੇਗਾ । ਇਹ ਪ੍ਰਵਾਨਾ ਸ੍ਰੀ ਸਤਿਗੁਰੂ ਦਿਆਲ ਸ੍ਰੀ ਸਤਿਗੁਰੂ ਦਰਬਾਰਾ ਸਿੰਘ ਜੀ ਦੇ ਹੁਕਮ ਨਾਲ ਲਿਖਿਆ ।

ਧੰਨ ਨਿਰੰਕਾਰ ।

ਸੰਮਤ ੧੯੩੦ ॥ ਮਹੀਨਾ ਗੁਰੂ ਰਾਮਦਾਸ ਜੀ ਦਾ । ਮਿਤੀ ਵਿਸਾਖ ਦਿਨੇ ਪਹਿਲੀ । ਤੇ ਜੇਹੜੇ ਚੱਲਣ ਦੇ ਚਿਠੇ ਤੁਸਾਡੇ ਪਾਸ ਹਨ ਸੋ ਪੰਦਰੇ ਦੇ ਪੰਦਰੇ ਦਿਨੇ ਪੜ੍ਹ ਕਰ ਸੂਬੱਤ ਸੰਗਤ ਨੂੰ ਰਾਤੀਂ ਕਥਾ ਕਰਕੇ ਸੁਣਾਵਣਾ । ਧੰਨ ਧੰਨ ਨਿਰੰਕਾਰ ।*

ਦਸਖੱਤ—ਗੁਲਾਮ ਰੱਤਾ

* ਅਸਲ ਦਸਤਖਤੀ ਹੁਕਮ ਨਾਮਾ ਸ੍ਰੀ ਦਰਬਾਰ ਸਾਹਿਬ ਨਿਰੰਕਾਰੀ ਰਾਵਲਪਿੰਡੀ ਵਿਖੇ ਮੌਜੂਦ ਸੀ ਹਜ਼ੂਰ ਬਾਬਾ ਜੀ ਪਾਸ ਹੈ ।

APPENDIX F

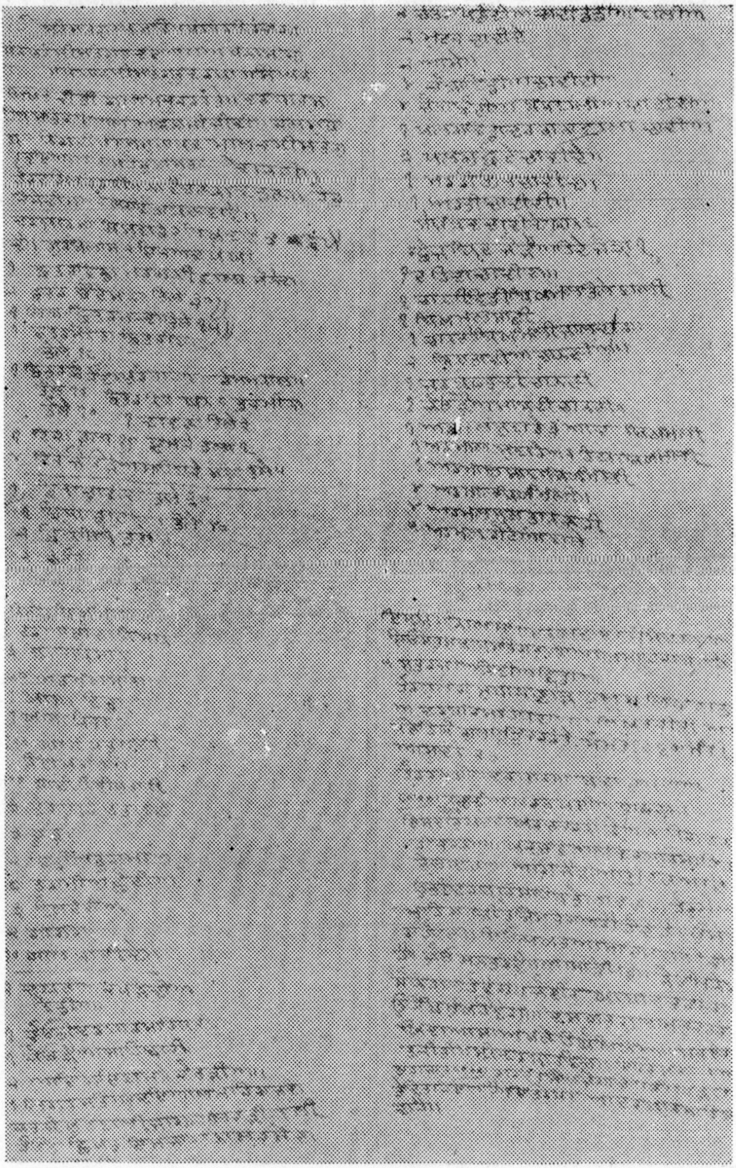

Reproduction of original WILL of Saheb Rattaji written by his own hands which makes it clear that all properties belong to the Darbar (Mission) and not to any individual or dynasty.

APPENDIX G

List of the Subas of Baba Ram Singh Namdhari

List showing names, parentage and other particulars of the Lieutenants of Ram Singh Kooka, who attended him during the late Dewalee fair at Umritsar:-

1st:- Labh Singh, son of Jeeta Singh cultivator (Vring) resident of Nawashahur District Jullundur is blind of both eyes, aged 40 years. This man preaches in Jullundur and Umritsar District.

2nd:- Lukkha Singh, son of Ram Singh, cultivator ("Surai") resident of Malloudh, District Loodiana, but at present residing in Bhainee, aged 28 years. This man preaches to make converts in the Hoshiarpore and Jullundur Districts.

3rd:- Rakjuss, son of Nanuck Chand, caste Brahmien resident of Jagraon, District Loodiana, 70 years, preaches in the Loodiana District.

4th:- Sahib Singh, son of Dial Singh, caste carpenter resident of Baiwaleepoor, District Umritsar, aged 34 years. This man always remains in personal attendance on Ram Singh, and is the Chief Lieutenant and reputed successor of the Gooroo.

5th:- Kanh Singh, son of Nutha Singh, caste cultivator ("Bopari"), resident of Chuck in the Mulair Kotla territory, aged 60 years, at present residing at Bilol, District Hoshiarpore. This man is a great Nahung, though a Kooka and preaches in Hoshiarpore, Umballa, Malwa and Kohistan.

6th:- Narain Singh, son of Sunt Singh, caste carpenter, resident of Kheyree, District Loodhiana, aged 32 years, preaches in Mukatsar and other places in the Ferozepur District.

7th:- Hookma Singh, son of Mohur Singh, caste cultivator ("man"), resident of Poonoo in the Nabha territory, aged 25 years, preaches in Loodiana and Manjha, and C.

8th:- Pahara Singh, son of Hema, caste cultivator, ("Boondheyr") resident of Millondh, District Loodiana, age 37 years, preaches in Loodiana, Goojranwalla and C.

9th:- Jowahir Singh, son of Dhul Singh, caste cultivator ("Sohun") resident of Bholeke, at present residing at Tukhtoopoora,

District Ferozepore, age 46 years, preaches at Farozepore and Adjacent places.

10th:- Sumund Singh, son of Wassawa Singh, caste cultivator ("Sidhoo"), resident of Khotee, District Ferozepore, aged 40 years, preaches in Ferozepur District.

11th:- Aroor Singh, son of Dyal Singh, caste carpenter, resident of Baiwaleepoor, District Umritsar, aged 40 years, preaches in Umritsar District.

12th:- Wassawa Singh, son of Khurruck Singh, caste cultivator ("Thong") resident of Anool, District Kurnal, aged 50 years, preaches in Kurnal and Umballa Districts.

13th:- Mussamut Hookmee, daughter of Ruttun Singh, cultivator, resident of village Varya, District Umritsar, aged 20 years. This woman, in company with Kanh Singh Nahung No. 5, preaches with great success in the Hoshiarpoor, Umritsar, and other Districts.

14th:- Jotha Singh, son of Rutna Singh, caste potter, resident of Debbee, District Sealkote, aged 35 years, preaches in Sealkote and Lahore Districts.

15th:- Gopal Singh, son of Sahib Singh, caste cultivator ("Dhareewal") resident of Mudhar in the Pattialla territory, aged 35 years, preaches in Loodiana and has a shop in Bhainee, in Ram Singh Mahunt's house.

16th:- Brema Singh, son of Gulab Singh, caste cultivator, resident of Koolana, District Umballa, aged 45 years, preaches in Jullundur, Goojranwalla, Lahore and Sealkote Districts.

17th:- Khuzan Singh, son of Manee caste carpenter, resident of Luddhiana District Jullundur, aged 35 years preaches in Lahore, Umritsar, & C.

18th: - Surmookh Singh, son of Vassawa Singh, caste carpenter, resident of Delho in the Pattialla territory, aged 30 years, preaches in and about the Pattialla territory.

19th:- Hurnam Singh, son of Asa Singh, caste cultivator, resident of Mundee in the Jheend territory, aged 28 years, preaches in the Jheend and Patialla States.

20th:- Jumeeyut Singh, son of Chunda Singh, caste cultivator, resident of village Gill, District Sealkote, aged 50 years, preaches in the Sealkote and adjacent Districts.

21st:- Mulook Singh, cultivator, resident of Bolaywal, District Ferozepure, aged 35 years, preaches in and around Ferozepore.

22nd:- Sadhoo Singh, resident of Ghanpur, District Loodhiana, caste Oodasee Sadh, aged 32 years, preaches in about the Loodhiana District.

Besides preaching in the Districts noted opposite each, these Lieutenants with the permission of Ram Singh are allowed to preach in many other places.

Foreign Department Political A. February 1868.

No. 202-203.

APPENDIX-H

Appendix 'H' covers an elaborate ceremony of the Akhand Path (complete reading of the Adi-grunth at a stretch without break) it seems from the document (next page) that Baba Ram Singh' had made it quite complicated and expensive affairs, Haven, Hom, Jayoti, Kumb (Pitcher) and coconut etc. had no relevance in the Sikh practices. This shows how for Namdharis were influenced by the brahmanical practices and despite their efforts for reform and revival of Sikh society they could not do away with some of the brahmanical practices.

ੴ ਸਤਿਗੁਰ ਪ੍ਰਸਾਦਿ

ਸ੍ਰੀ ਮੁਖ ਵਾਕ ਪਾਤਿਸ਼ਾਹੀ ੧੨

ਅਬ ਅਖੰਡ ਪਾਠ ਕੀ ਰੀਤੀ ਮ੍ਰਯਾਦਾ ॥

ਜਦ ਸ੍ਰੀ ਸਤਿਗੁਰੁ ਜੀ ਰੰਗੂਨ ਜਾਇ ਰਹੇ ਡਾਂ ਮਹਾਰਾਜ ਹਰੀ ਸਿੰਘ ਜੀ ਰਾਮਸਰ ਕੇ ਕੋਲ ਥੇ ਤਾਂ ਅਵਾਜਾ ਮਹਾਰਾਜਾ ਜੀ ਕੀ ਹੋ ਹੋਇਆ ਜੋ ਅਖੰਡ ਪਾਠ ਪੰਜ ਕਰਾਓ ਸਾਡੇ ਨਮਿਤ । ਤਾਂ ਮਹਾਰਾਜ ਹਰੀ ਸਿੰਘ ਜੀ ਅੰਦਰ ਪਾਠ ਕਰਨਾ ਕੋਠੜੀ ਕੇ ਸ਼ੁਰੂ ਕੀਤਾ ਤੋ ਤੀਨ ਪਾਠੀ ਏਕ ਧੂਪ ਪਾਉਣ ਵਾਲੇ ਤੇਲ ਦਾ ਦੀਵਾ ਪਾਠੀ ਕੇ ਅਗੇ ਜਗਦਾ ਰਹਿਆ ਧੂਪ ਪੈਦੀ ਰਹੀਆਂ ਧੂਪੀਆਂ ੧ ਮਾਲਾ ਫੇਰੇ, ਇਸਨਾਨ ਕਰਕੇ ਪਾਠੀ ਬੈਠੇ ਤਾਬਿਆ ਰਾਤ ਨੂੰ ਤਾਂ ਗੰਗਾ ਸਿੰਘ ਅਰ ਗੁਰਦਿਤ ਸਿੰਘ ਮਹੰਤ ਤੇ ਰਾਘੋ ਸਿੰਘ ਭੀ ॥ ਦਿਨ ਨੂੰ ਬਸੰਤ ਸਿੰਘ, ਨਰੈਣ ਸਿੰਘ ਦੋ ਤੇ ਲਾਵਣੇ ਪਾਠ ਤਾਪਾਏ ॥

ਏਸੇ ਤਰਾਂ ਫੇਰ ਸੌ ਭੋਗ ਕਾ ਸੰਕਲਪ ਅਖੰਡ ਪਾਠ ਤ੍ਰਾ ਆਰੰਭ ਕੀਆ ਹੈ ॥ ਸ੍ਰੀ ਸਤਿਗੁਰੂ ਜੀ ਨੇ ਰੀਤੀ ਲਿਖੀ ਕੇ ਜੀ ਏਸ ਰੀਤ ਸੇ ਪਾਠ ਕਰਦੇ ਹੈ ॥ ਸ੍ਰੀ ਸਤਿਗੁਰੂ ਦੀਨਾ ਕੇ ਦਿਆਲ ਕਿਰਪਾਲ ਬਚਨ ਕੀਤਾ ਬਾਰਵੇ

ਗੁਰੂ ਆਪਨੇ ਮੁਖਾਰਬਿੰਦ ਸੇ ਕੇ ਏਸ ਰੀਤੀ ਪਰ ਚਲ ॥ ਅਖੰਡ ਪਾਠ ਕੀ ਰੀਤੀ ॥ ਪ੍ਰਿਥਮੇ ਪਾਠ ਸੁਣਾਇ ਕੇ ਕਰਨਾ, ਜੇ ਚੀਤਾ ਛਡੇ ਤਾਂ ਗੋਡਿਆਂ ਤੋੜੀ ਲਤਾਂ ਤੇ ਅਰ ਅੇਰਕਾਂ ਤੋੜੀ ਬਾਵਾਂ ਤੇ ਚੁਲੇ ਕਰਨ। ਮੰਜੇ ਉਤੇ ਪਾਠੀ ਨਾ ਸੋਵਣ, ਗਰਿਸਤ ਨਾ ਵਰਤੇ ਜਿਤਨਾਂ ਚਿਰ ਪਾਠ ਕਰੇ। ਜਿਸ ਜਗਾ ਪਾਠ ਹੋਵੇ ਦੋ ਆਦਮੀ ਆਣ ਕੇ ਨਾ ਬਹਿਣ ਨਾ ਗਲਾਂ ਕਰੇ ॥ ਮੁੰਡਾ ਨਹੀਂ ਲਾਵਣਾ ॥ ਬਾਰਾਂ ਸਿੰਘਾਂ ਥੀਂ ਬਿਨਾਂ ਪਾਠ ਨਹੀਂ ਟੋਰਨਾਂ ਘਟ ਬਾਰਾਂ ਥੀਂ ਨਹੀਂ ਕਰਨੇ ॥ ਪਾਠੀ ਪੂਰੇ ਈ ਰਖੇ। ਥੋੜਾ ਛਕੇ, ਜਿਸ ਸੇ ਵੌਕਾਂ ਨਾ ਸਰੇ। ਅਬਲ ਤਾਂ ਚੌਦਾਂ ਪਾਠੀ ਚਾਹੀਏ, ਨਹੀਂ ਤੇ ਬਾਰਾਂ ਥੀਂ ਘਟ ਨ ਕਰੇ ਜਰੂਰ ॥ ਪਾਠ ਨਹੀਂ ਕਰਨਾਂ ਜੇ ਪਾਠੀ ਪੂਰੇ ਨ ਹੋਵਣਿ, ਚੋਲੀ ਰਮਾਲ ਧੋਇ ਲੈਣੇ ਕਪੜੇ ਕੀ ਜੇ ਹੋਵੇ ਤਾਂ ਧੋਵੇ ॥ ਘਿਉ ਦਾ ਦੀਵਾ ਕਰਨਾ, ਤੇਲ ਦਾ ਨਾ ਚਾਹੀਏ। ਤਾਂ ਫੇਰ ਤੇਲ ਦਾ ਦੀਵਾ ਬੰਧ ਘਿਉ ਕਾ ਜਲਨੇ ਲਗਾ ਹੈ।

ਸਵੇਗ ਸਿੱਘ ਮੁਰਾਣੇ ਕਾ ਨੌ ਦਿਨ ਰਹਿਓ, ਉਸ ਸ਼ਹਰ ਮੈ ਬਚਨ ਕੀਤਾ ਸੀ ਕਿ ਏਕ ਜਨਾ ਹਜ਼ੂਰ ਰਹਿਆ ਕਰੇ ਬਾਣਾ ਬਦਲ ਕੇ ਜਾਂਦੇ ਸੇ ਏਕ ਦਿਨ ਬਚਨ ਕੀਤਾ ਕਿ ਅਸੀਂ ਤਾਂ ਕਦੇ ਦੇ ਦੇਖਦੇ ਹਾਂ ਤੁਸੀਂ ਡੇਰ ਨਾ ਲਾਇਆ ਕਰੋ। ਨਾਵੇਂ ਦਿਨ ਜਹਾਜ ਪਰ ਚੜ ਕਰ ਚਲੇ ਆਏ ਹੁਕਮਨਾਮਾਂ ਰਾਮਦਾਸਪੁਰੇ ਭੀ ਸੁਣਿਆ ਤਾਂ ਏਸੇ ਰੀਤੀ ਪਰ ਲਗੇ ਪਾਠ ਅਖੰਡ ਹੋਣ, ਸੌ ਸੌ ਪਾਠ ਅਖੰਡ ਸਾਲ ਕਰਣੇ ਲਗੇ

ਧੂਪ ਕੀ ਬਿਪ

(੧) ਬਦਾਮ (੨(ਖੋਪਾ (੩) ਛੁਹਾਰੇ (੪) ਸੌਗੀ (੫) ਲਾਚੀ ਛੋਟੀ (੬) ਲੌਂਗ (੭) ਸੰਧੂਰ (੮) ਮੁਸ਼ਕ ਕਾਫੂਰ (੯) ਕਾਲਾ ਕਪੂਰ (੧੦) ਲਾਲ ਚੰਦਨ (੧੧) ਸੁਫੇਦ ਚੰਦਨ (੧੨) ਕੇਸਰ (੧੩) ਕਸਤੂਰੀ (੧੪) ਮੁਥਾ ਕਾਲੀ (੧੫) ਛੜ (੧੬) ਇੰਦੂ ਜੌ (੧੭) ਦੇਸੀ ਜੌ (੧੮) ਤਿਲ (੧੯) ਗੋਗਲ (੨੦) ਭੋਜ ਪਤ੍ਰ (੨੧) ਖੰਡ (੨੨) ਘਿਉ।

ਏਕ ਸਮੇਂ ਮਹਾਰਾਜ ਹਰੀ ਸਿੰਘ ਜੀ ਬਚਨ ਕੀਤਾ, ਕਿ ਭਾਈ ਪੈਲੇ ਭੋਗ ਅਖੰਡ ਪਾਠ ਇਕ ਧੂਪੀਜੇ ਨਾਲ ਪਾਠ ਕਰ ਲੈਂਦੇ ਸਾ। ਸ੍ਰੀ

ਸਤਿਗੁਰੂ ਜੀ ਰੀਤੀ ਲਿਖ ਕੇ ਭੇਜੀ ਉਸ ਰੀਤੀ ਨਾਲ ਪਾਠ ਕਰਨੇ ਲਗੇ ॥ ਪਾਂਚ ਪਾਠੀ, ਪਾਂਚ ਧੂਪੀਯੇ ਜਪ ਸਾਹਿਬ ਜੀ ਕੇ ਪਾਠੀ ॥ ਪਾਠੀ ਸੁਧ ਰਹਿਣ ਕਿਸੀ ਤਰਾਂ ਕੀ ਗਾਫਲੀ ਨਾ ਕਰਨ, ਸਾਰੇ ਧੂਪੀਕੇ ਪਾਠੀਆਂ ਕੇ ਸਾਥ ਬਦਲ ਜਾਵਨ, ਪਾਠੀਆਂ ਕੀਆਂ ਪੁਸ਼ਾਕਾਂ ਧੋ ਕੇ ਸੁਧ ਕਰੇ, ਕੇਸੀ ਅਸ਼ਨਾਨ ਦਹੀਂ ਸਾਥ ਕਰਨਾਂ ਪਾਠੀਆਂ ਨੇ ਲਾਂਗਰੀਆਂ ਸਮੇਤ ਅੰਮ੍ਰਿਤ ਛਕ ਕੇ ਲਗਨਾ, ਸਵਾ ਰੁਪੈਯੇ ਕਾ ਕੜਾਹ ਪ੍ਰਸ਼ਾਦਿ ਕਰਨਾ, ਗੁਰੂ ਗਰੰਥ ਸਾਹਿਬ ਜੀ ਕਾ ਪ੍ਰਕਾਸ਼ ਕੇ ਅਠਾ ਯਾ ਬਾਰਾ ਪਹਿਰਾਂ ਔਰ ਸੋਲਾਂ ਪਹਿਰਾਂ ਤੋਂ ਬਾਦ ਸਾਧਾਰਨ ਪਾਠ ਜੈਸਾ ਫਲ ਹੋ ਜਾਤਾ ਹੈ ਔਰ ਕੁੰਭ ਧਰਨਾ ਕੋਰੇ ਬਰਤਨ ਮੈ, ਉਪਰ ਕੋਰਾ ਮਾਫਾ ਧੋਇ ਕੈ ਰਖੈ, ਏਕ ਥਾਲ ਮੇਂ ਬੇਰੀ ਜਾਂ ਪਲਾਸ ਕੀ ਲਕੜੀ ਗਿਠ ਰਖ ਕਰ ਹੋਮ ਕਰੇ, ਜਪ ਸਾਹਿਬ ਜੀ ਕਾ ਪਾਠ ਸੰਚੀ ਤੋਂ ਕਰਨਾ, ਅਹੁਤੀ ਹਰ ਏਕ ਪੌੜੀ ਪਰ ਪੌਣੀ, ਲਕੜੀ ਜਲਦੀ ਰਹੇ ਔਰ ਧੂਪੀਏ ਕੋ ਤਿਨ ਚੀਜਾਂ ਕੀ ਊੜਦੀ ਹੈ, ਦੀਵੇ ਕੀ ਖਬਰ, ਧੂਪ ਔਰ ਜਪ ਸਾਹਿਬ ਕਾ ਪਾਠ ਕਰਨਾਂ ।

ਔਰ ਭਗੌਤੀ ਕਾ ਪਾਠ ਪਹਿਲੇ ਭੀ ਕਰਨਾ ਔਰ ਜਪ ਦਾ ਪਾਠ ਕਰ ਕੇ ਪੀਛੇ ਭੀ ਭਗੌਤੀ ਪੜਨੀ, ਔਰ ਇਸੀ ਤਰਾਂ ਪਾਠੀ ਨੇ ਭਗੌਤੀ ਅਰਦਾਸਾ ਸੋਧ ਕੇ ਲਗਨਾ ਔਰ ਅਰਦਾਸਾ ਸੋਧ ਕੇ ਹਟਨਾ । ਔਰ ਪਹਿਰੇਦਾਰ ਬਹੁਤ ਚੁਸਤ ਚਾਹੀਏ ਜਿਸ ਵਕਤ ਗਰੰਥੀ ਵਾ ਧੂਪੀਆ ਇਸ਼ਾਰਾ ਜਾਂ ਟਲੀ ਖੜਕਾਵੇ ਫੌਰਨ ਖਬਰ ਲੇਵੇ, ਗ੍ਰੰਥੀਆਂ ਕੀ ਬਦਲਾਈ ਕਰੇ ਜਾ ਕੋਇਲਿਆਂ ਕੀ ਖਵਰਦਾਰੀ ਰਖੇ ਔਰ ਮਾਲਾ ਫੇਰਦਾ ਰਹੇ ਔਰ ਦੀਵੇ ਦੀ ਧੂਨ ਦੀ ਖਬਰਦਾਰੀ ਰਖੇ ਔਰ ਆਏ ਮਨੁਖ ਨੂੰ ਅਟਕਾਵੇ, ਔਰ ਅਰਦਾਸੀਆ ਸੁਧ ਹੋ ਕੇ ਅਰਦਾਸਾ ਕਰੇ ਔਰ ਸਜੇ ਪਾਵੇ ਤਲੇ ਇਕ ਰੁਪੈਆ ਰਖੇ ਔਰ ਨਾਲੀਏਰ ਕੋ ਇਕ ਕੁੰਭ ਪਰ ਰਖੇ ਏਕ ਪੀਛੇ ਹੋਮ ਕਰੇ, ਕੁੰਭ ਵਾਲਾ ਨਿਰੀਅਲ ਝਟਕਾ ਕੇ ਵਰਤਾ ਦੇਵੇ ਅਰ ਅਗੇ ਕੋ ਹੋਰ ਤੋਰਨਾਂ ਹੋਵੇ ਤੇ ਉਸੇ ਕੜਾਹ ਪ੍ਰਸ਼ਾਦਿ ਨਾਲ ਤੋਰ ਦੇਨਾਂ ਕੁੰਭ ਨਾਲਯੇਰ ਆਦਿ ਸਭ ਚੀਜ਼ਾਂ ਥਾਂਉਂ ਥਾਂਖੀ ਪਈ ਰਹੇ ॥ ਪਾਠੀਆਂ ਦੀ ਬਹੁਤ ਸੇਵਾ ਕਰਨੀ ਘਿਉ ਦੁਧ ਆਦਿ ਬਹੁਤ ਛਕਾਵਨਾਂ, ਜੈਸੇ ਗੁਰੂ ਗਰੰਥ ਸਾਹਿਬ ਕੋ ਛਕਾਯਾ ਜੋ ਗਰੰਥੀ ਕੋ ਛਕੌਣਾ ਅਕਾਲ ਪੁਰਖ ਕੇ ਮੁਖ ਪੈਂਦਾ ਹੈ, ਜਿਤਨੀ ਫੁਰਸਤ ਹੋਵੇ ਉਤਨੀ ਹੀ ਭੇਟਾ ਦੇਵੇ । ਜਿਤਨੀ ਭੇਟਾ ਦੇਵੇ ਉਤਨੀ ਹੀ ਥੋੜ੍ਹੀ ਹੈ, ਅਮੋਲਕ ਪਾਠ ਹੈ । ਪਾਠੀ ਕੋ ਦੀਆ ਗੁਰੂ ਕੋ ਦੀਆ ਏਕ ਬਰਾਬਰ ਹੈ, ਫ਼ੁਰਸਤ ਵਾਲਾ ਤੋ ਜਿਤਨਾ ਦੇਵੇ ਉਤਨਾ ਹੀ ਥੋੜ੍ਹਾ ਹੈ, ਔਰ ਗ਼ਰੀਬ ਸਿੰਘ ਕੇ ਵਾਸਤੇ ਪਚੀ

ਰੁਪੈਯੇ ਮੇਂ ਅਖੰਡ ਪਾਠ ਦਾ ਭੋਗ ਪਾ ਦੇਣਾ, ਔਰ ਸਾਧਾਰਨ ਭੋਗ ਗ਼ਰੀਬੌਂ ਕੇ ਲੀਯੇ ਪੰਜ ਰੁਪੈਯੇ ਮੇਂ ਪਾ ਦੇਣਾ । ਔਰ ਅਗੇ ਨੂੰ ਜੇ ਪਾਠੀ ਜਾਂ ਧੂਪੀਆ ਹੋਰ ਲੈਣਾ ਹੋਵੇ ਤੋਂ ਅਰਦਾਸਾ ਕਰਕੇ ਕੁੰਭ ਵਿਚੋਂ ਅੰਮ੍ਰਿਤ ਕਢ ਕੇ ਛਕਾ ਦੇਣਾ ॥ ਅਖੰਡ ਪਾਠ ਸਰਬ ਕਾਰਜ ਕੀ ਸਿਧੀ ਦੇਣ ਵਾਲਾ ਹੈ, ਇਕੋਤ੍ਰ ਸੌ ਮੇਂ ਸਾਧਾਰਨ ਪਾਠ ਜੈਸਾ ਏਕ ਅਖੰਡ ਦਾ ਫਲ ਹੈ, ਮਹਾਤਮ ਬਹੁਤ ਹੈ, ਅਸਮੇਧ ਜਗ ਕਲਜੁਗ ਅਖੰਡ ਭੋਗ ਹੈ, ਪੰਜ ਕਕੇ ਕੀ ਰੀਤੀ ਬਿਨਾ ਪਾਠ ਨਹੀਂ ਕਰਨਾ, ਜਿਸ ਤਰਾਂ ਹੋ ਸਕੇ ਸ਼ੁਧ ਪਾਠ ਕਰਨਾਂ ॥ ਜਿਸ ਕਾਰਜ ਪਰ ਕਰੇ ਸੋ ਕਾਰਜ ਪੂਰਾ ਹੋ ਜਾਂਵੇਗਾ ॥ ਔਰ ਪਾਠੀ ਜਦ ਕੋਲ ਬੈਠੇ ਦਾਤਨ ਇਸ਼ਨਾਨ ਕਰ ਕੇ ਬੈਠੇ, ਪੁਸ਼ਾਕ ਪਾ ਕੇ ਜਿਤਨਾ ਹੋ ਸਕੇ ਸੁਧ ਸੁਚ ਨਾਲ ਕਰਨਾ, ਬਹੁਤ ਭਲਾ ਹੋਵੇਗਾ । ਸਚ ਕਰ ਮੰਨਣਾਂ ॥

APPENDIX I

The appendix depicts that Kukas were mainly from lower castes engaged in various occupations like cultivators, tailors, brass workers, carpenters, sweepers, masons, weavers, goldsmith, blacksmith, barber, jhiwar and at time there were patwaris and jagirdars also, but their number was negligible.

Appendix I (Contd.)

Home Judicial B 1881 No. 186-189

Circle	*Distt.*	*No. of Kukas Notable*	*Profession or Occupation*	*Antecedents Character and some Other Remakrs*
1	2	3	4	5
	Sirsa	1	Cultivator	He is a Kuka Suba appears to be in intimate terms with the Kuka of Patiala and Nabha.
Ambala	Ambala	9	5 Cultivators 1 worker in brass	
			1 Jagirdar	Sardar Mangal Singh was Ressaldar in the service of Patiala state the late Maharaja was his nephew.
			1 Lambardar 1 doing nothing	Of Village Jharmari Lalru Police Station (Patiala)

(Contd....)

1	2	3	4	5
		152 152	26 (None)	Bholi Musamat of Ludhiana "this woman is related to Guru Ram Singh and is consequently much respected by the sect who style her mai or mother. Her house is a rendezvous for visiting Ludhiana."
Ambala	Ludhiana		3 Tailor	One tailor Buta Singh of Raipur village carries messages for one *Kuka* to another.
			71 Cultivator	Chain Singh of Gujraws acts as a messenger. He was formerly employed as a Tehsil Chaprasi.
			9 Carpenter	
			2 Cook	One is Jaimal Singh of Bhaini who was formerly a

(Contd....)

1	2	3	4	5
				lambardar of Raipur Police Station Dhelon. Interestingly Baba Budh Singh younger brother of Ram Singh has also been mentioned as carpenter.
		1	Groom	
Ambala	Ludhiana	1	Makes rosaries	
		1	Mendicant	
		1	Sweeper	
		7	Granthee	
		4	Weavers	
		2	Mason	
		1	Goldsmith	
		1	Blacksmith	
		3	Merchant and petty shopkeepers	
		3	Barber	

(Contd....)

1	2	3	4	5
		3	Jhiwar	
		1	Daily labourer	
		2	Beggar	who work as messengers.
		1	Servant of Baba Budh Singh	Manna is employed as a carter and looks after the grain which members of the sect present to Budh Singh.
		1	Attendant on Baba Budh Singh	All cart drivers who are employed by Baba Budh Singh are under him.
Ambala	Ferozpur	17	1 Granthee	Joga Singh naib suba is mentioned well behaved and
			9 Cultivators	the one who supplies information to police.
			2 Jagirdar	Phula Singh and Hira Singh of Chogavan both own a third share in the Chowgava Jagir.
			1 land owner money-lender	Kharak Singh of Pehla is one of the richest man of

(Contd....)

1	2	3	4	5
				the village. He owns land
			1 Barber	near Bhatinda Patiala territory. He has established a village called Kharak Singhwalla.
			1 Patwari	Dhian Singh Suba of Chethiana is often absent from his patwari duties which are performed by his agents.
			1 Carpenter	
			1 Trader	
			1 None	
Lahore	Jallander	8	2 Cultivators	Mayya Singh Suba was formerly in Hoshiarpur Distt. Police. He resigned the service and returned to his home.

(Contd....)

1	2	3	4	5
			1 Granthee	
			2 None	Fateh Singh Sarghana of Moothada Kalan. He frequently visits Bhaini and his
			1 Lambardar	duties as Lambardar are carried on by his son Amar Singh.
			1 Blacksmith	Bhagwan Singh suba of Bengesh was formerly a Jamadar of Chaukidars.
			1 Swar in a regiment cavalry	Captain Nicheletts Distt. Supdt. of Police Punjab enlisted him in a cavalry regiment *Kukas* suspect him of giving information to Government.
Lahore	Lahore	14	Cultivator 6 1 owns a press	Buta Singh Diwan of Lahore City established a press in 1866 for publication of a law journal *Anwarful Shams.*

(Contd....)

1	2	3	4	5
			2 Lambardar 1 Carpenter 1 Granthee	In 1872, the first issue of the Aftab-I-Punjab was published by him. Since Guru Ram Singh's deportation and arrest he has not openly professed Kukaism but he secretly associates with members of the sect and is said to communicate Kabul news, etc., to Baba Budh Singh of Bhaini. He is very well to do men.
			2 None 2 were Cultivators and Bankers.	
Lahore	Montegomery	5	1 Halwai	1871-72, Mahal Singh Suba of Jethpur was employed in Commissariat Department at Mian Mir but then he left job

(Contd....)

1	2	3	4	5
				came to his village and opened the shop.
			1 Lambardar 1 2nd Grade Sergeant in Montgomery Police and Record keeper in Distt. Supdt. office	
			1 None	Sangat Singh of Montgomery is enlisted as none in occupation list. He was enlisted in the police on the 5th October, 1871 and for some time after behind quietly. Then resigned. Before leaving the lines he took to singing songs connected with the *Kuka* rising of 1872, in which

(Contd....)

1	2	3	4	5
				the action taken by Government was condemned and pronounced unjust.
Lahore	Hoshiarpur	28	Jagirdar	Man Singh is an earnest *Kuka* and frequently celebrates the *Bhog* and home ceremonies.
			Jagirdar	Chanda Singh does not believe that Guru Ram Singh will return but says that he will continue to be a *Kuka* as the members of the sect are as a rule peaceable and honest men. He possesses a license to carry arms for security purpose.
Lahore	Amritsar	10	6 Cultivators 2 Lambardar 1 sells Pakoras 1 None	

(Contd....)

1	2	3	4	5
Lahore	Gurdaspur	5	2 Cultivators 1 None 1 Carpenter 1 Priest	Kartar Singh suba is a priest at Dera Nanak. This man is a Bedi and descendant of Guru Nanak. He had gone to Patna also.
Rawalpindi	Sialkot	9	6 Cultivators 1 Priest	Prem Singh Mahant of Hamza Ghaus is a priest of well-known temple at Baba Ber and has great influence. Cultivator Gurcharan Singh (same reference as given in other files)
			1 Patwari 1 Banker	
Rawalpindi	Gujranwala	18	4 None	Lehna Singh of Garjakh

(Contd....)

1	2	3	4	5
				included in the list of name has been mentioned a Rai who is son-in-law of famous Sardar Hari Singh Nalwa. In 1871, he used to preside the *Kuka* meetings. Tara Singh of Mirsri Maini (None is the nephew of Colonel Main who was Governor of Peshawar in the time of Maharaja Ranjit Singh. Tara Singh is appointed adjustment of the two companies of *Kukas* which were raised by the Maharaja of Kashmir in 1872.
			2 Cultivators 1 Labourer 1 Shopkeeper	

(Contd....)

1	2	3	4	5
			1 Trader 1 Revenue Jaildar.	Anok Singh (Jaildar) of Chuharkhana is not openly a *Kuka* but his sympathies are with the sect.
Rawalpindi	Rawalpindi	1	Shopkeeper	Khan Singh Bhari of Hazre is nephew of Balak Singh who was Ram Singh's Guru. He is acknowledged head of the Hazre *Kukas*.

Appendix J

Correspondence of the Nirankari gurus concerning the Anand Marriage Act found in the three volumes entitled, Petitions Regarding the Anand Marriage Act, VII of 1909 (Part I), in the National Archives, New Delhi

No. 107/241

To

The Secretary to the Government of India
Legislative Department—Calcutta

Sir,

It has afforded me a great pleasure to learn about the proposed Anand Marriage Bill. Its need was very badly felt and the Hon'ble the Tikka Sahib of Nabha has placed the whole of the Sikh community including several thousands of my disciples and followers of the Nirankari Sect widely spread throughout the Province under gratitude and obligation by introducing the bill into the Legislatice [*sic*] Council.

My heartfelt thanks may kindly be communicated to His Excellency Viceroy and the Governor General of India for his graciously allowing the said bill being proposed.

I heartily approve of the bill and request that our benign Government may kindly be moved to pass it into an Act under the title of the Sikh Marriage Act.

I am Sir,
Your Sincerely
(Sd.) Baba Hara Singh
S/o Baba Gurdit Singhji
Guru of the Nirankari Sect of
the Sikh Community

Rawalpindi City
8th December, 1908

No. 24 of 1909

Sri Darbar Sahib Nirankari
Rawalpindi City
the 10 January 1909

To

The Secretary to the Government of India
Legislative Department, Calcutta.

Sir,

In continuation of my letter dated 8th December 1908 in which I respectfully requested that the Anand Marriage Act which received the approval of all the Nirankari Sikhs kindly be passed into law. I beg most submissively to add that the favourably decision of the Government is anxiously awaited.

2. I don't think it will be out of place to mention here that the ceremonies on the occasions of both the marriages and remarriages have been performed by all the Nirankaries [*sic*] according to *Anand* Riti (custom) from about 80 years when this sect was founded by our first Satguru Baba Dyal and that performance of ceremonies according to other rites is quite opposed to our religion.

Trusting to be excused for the trouble.

I am Sir,
Your most obedient servant
(Sd.) Gurdit Singh
Guru of Nirankari [*sic*] Sect
in the 4th place
Rawalpindi

Rawalpindi,
the 9th : January [*sic*] 1909
10th
BR 142 it
142

Telegram received 17-9-09

Appendix K

The Anand Marriage Act (VII of 1909) 22 October, 1909.

An act to remove doubts as to the validity of the marriage ceremony common among the Sikhs called Anand.

Where as it is expedient to remove any doubts as to the validity of the marriage ceremony common among the Sikhs called Anand. It is hereby enacted as follows.

Short title and Extent (1) This act may be called Anand Marriage Act 1909 and it extends to the whole of British India.

Validity of Anand Marriage (2) All marriage which may be or may have been duly solemnized according to the Sikhs marriage ceremony called Anand shall be and shall be deemed to have effect from the date of the solemnized of each respectively, good and valid in law.

Exemption of Certain marriage from act (3) Nothing in this act shall be apply to.

(a) Any marriage between persons not professing the Sikh religion.

(b) Any marriage which has been judicially declared null and void.

Saving of Marriages Solemnized according to other ceremonies (4) Nothing in this act shall effect the validity of any marriage dully solemnized according to any other marriage ceremonies customary among the Sikhs.

Non-validation of marriage without the prohibited degrees (5) Nothing in this act shall be deemed to validate any marriage between persons who are related to each other in any degree of consanguinity or affinity which would according to the customary law of the Sikhs render a marriage between them illegal.

Appendix—L

Text of an order of H.M. Lawrence engraved on a Copper Plate which prohibited the cow killing in Amritsar, thus maintaining the holiness of the Sarovar (Tank) and the Golden Temple.

(See opposite page 217)

Judicial Cn July 29.1.71

Commissioner, who at once consented to walk over with me and be present at the meeting which was held at 9 A. M. on the same date, the 9th.

Sirdar Soorut Singh Mujithia called upon me that morning and remained with me, pointed out that riots such as that of the night before were disgraceful, and would not occur if the Raises did their duty. I told them that I held them responsible for the quiet of the city. They promised all I required, and it was arranged that the police should keep them informed of any disturbance. Mr. Elsmie then proposed that the full bench of the Honorary Magistrates should try the riot case, and this was agreed to. Twenty-two Hindoo rioters were sent up by the police, and the case has not yet been decided. There has been no breach of the peace since Sirdar Mungul Singh Ram Ghurriah had, as I mentioned in my last letter, sent up the man who had taken the beef bone into the Sikh temple with a view to cause disturbance. This man I have kept still under enquiry and trial. He turns out not to be an *akali*, nor yet lunatic, but a religious fanatic and follower of Bhai Veer Singh, who was killed in battle (*vide* Griffin's Punjab Chiefs, pages 25 and 49) so far as I can gather. However, there is no reason to believe that any cause of dissatisfaction exists, except that which has been duly reported in my former letter. It is probable, however, that the antagonistic feeling between Hindoos and Mahomedans has spread from the Lower Provinces. During the past week one Native gentleman mentioned to me that the same thing had happened at Lucknow. I fancy he meant Rohilkund. It is perhaps fortunate, under the circumstances, that the Mahomedan portion of the population continues so quiet. It is not for want of provocation, for there is a dead set made against them by the Hindoos. The *kaseras*, or brass and copper-smiths, have banded together to refuse to sell their manufactures to Mahomedans, and specially to refuse to buy from them the second-hand vessels which their necessities lead them to dispose of, on the plea that they have been used for cooking beef. All this, I trust, will right itself in due course of trade without interference. But it is doubtless to the impoverished state of the Cashmerees that much of the quiet is attributable. The feeling of dislike is felt more towards them than towards the Punjabee Mahomedans. I have taken some pains to go over the whole of the correspondence and orders which have passed since annexation on the subject of the slaughter of kine and sale of beef. I find that there have been four previous occasions on which the subject came up for disposal before the Amritsar authorities, *viz.*, 20th May 1849, before M. C. Saunders; 7th May 1856, before Mr. F. Cooper; 28th May 1863, before Major Mercer; and November 1864, before Mr. D. Macnabb. The matter in 1863 was reported by Major Mercer to higher authority: and the Judicial Commissioner's judgment, on revision side, No. 128, dated 20th June 1863, if correctly copied, goes much further in giving liberty to the Mahomedans, than is sanctioned by the custom of Amritsar. I communicated to Rajah Sir Sahib Dyal your desire received on 12th instant in reply to the vernacular paper of demand from the Hindoos that they should be more explicit. He agreed to wait until your arrival, which I told him I daily expected. I think the Hindoos are too pretentious in asking for the sale of beef in the city to be stopped. Their disorderly conduct in marked contrast to that of the Mahomedans does not entitle them to any extra consideration.

In conclusion, I think I may report that the tendency to riot has been in great measure suppressed. To-day's fair, held close by the slaughter-houses, has passed off without accident, though extra police arrangements were made.

Copy of an order engraved on a copper-plate and placed at the entrance of the Sikh Temple called the Durbar Sahib.

The priest of Amritsar having complained of annoyances, this is to make known to all concerned that, by order of the Governor General, British subjects are forbidden to enter the temple called the Durbar at Amritsar, or its precincts, with their shoes on. Kine are not to be killed at Amritsar, nor are the Sikhs to be molested, or in any way to be interfered with. Shoes are to be taken off at the *Bhoonga* at the corner of the tank, and no person is to walk round the tank with his shoes on.

LAHORE; The 24th March 1849.

H. M. LAWRENCE,
Resident.

Translation of an Urdu address delivered by MAJOR W. G. DAVIES, *Officiating Commissioner, Amritsar Division, at a Durbar held in the Town Hall at Amritsar on the 3rd June 1871.*

For some time past there has been, as you are aware, a bad feeling between the Hindoos and Mahomedans of this city on the subject of the slaughter of kine, and the sale of its flesh, and some slight disturbances have taken place. Those who have infringed the orders of Government in this respect, as also those who have taken the law into their own hand, with the

Appendix—M

Plan of the residence of butchers and the slaughter house at Raikot.

(See page 219)

Appendix—N

Telegram sent and received by the Government about attack on the butchers of Raikot.

(See page 220)

Judicial July 29, 1871

No. 177, dated the 18th July 1871.

From—Deputy Commissioner, Ludiana.

To—The Commissioner and Superintendent, Umballa Division.

My telegrams and demi-official notes of the past two days will have informed you of the outrage perpetrated at Raikote, in this District, on the night of the 15th instant. I now proceed to give you a connected account of all the circumstances of this most lamentable affair which have as yet come to my knowledge, and of the steps taken for the discovery and apprehension of the offenders.

2. Between 9 and 10 A. M. on the 16th instant, I received a police report to the effect that on the previous night about 11 o'clock a body of men, estimated at from 15 to 20 in number, and armed with swords and *gundassas* (a sort of chopper for cutting fodder), had made a sudden attack on the butchers' quarter at Raikote—a town about 38 miles from Ludiana by road—and had killed two persons—a man and a woman—and wounded severely seven others, chiefly women and children.

3. I telegraphed this information to you and desired the Civil Surgeon to proceed as soon as possible to attend to the wounded, whose injuries were too severe to permit of their being moved. I also requested the District Superintendent of Police to give instructions to his Deputy Inspectors throughout the District to have the butchers' quarters in their respective towns watched during the night till further orders, and, before 12 noon, accompanied by Mr. Hutchill, Deputy Superintendent Police, I left Ludiana for Raikote.

4. There was some delay at Jugraon, where we left the metalled road in procuring carriage for the remaining 15 miles of *cutcha* road. It was nearly 5 P. M. when we left Jugraon, and we arrived too late at night to do much more than make general enquiries.

5. At daylight on the 17th I visited the butchers' mohulla. This is a small ragged hamlet, containing in all three habitable flat-roofed houses with the remains of court-yards, all of which have been allowed to decay till the place is quite exposed and unprotected; these huts are about ten paces from what, at this season, is a large pool of water, and at the edge of this water on one side are thrown the bones of the animals slaughtered; a sort of lane (flooded for a distance of 50 yards) lies in front of the houses.

The following gives a rough idea of the place.

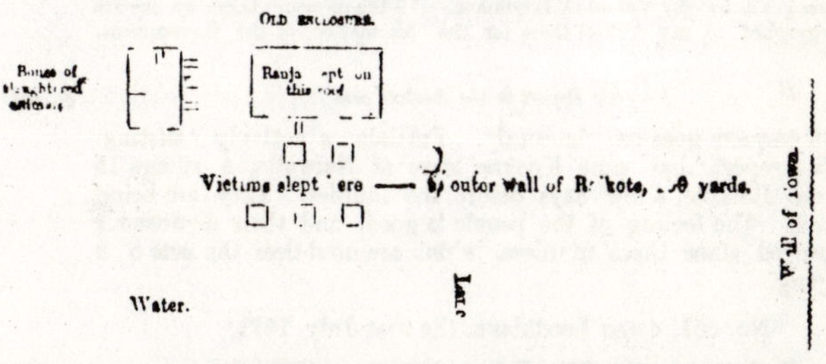

There are no other habitation near. Two butchers, named Ranja and Buta, with their families, live and follow their calling in this place. On the night of the 15th instant Buta was absent, having gone to Ludiana to appeal against a recent order of the Tehseeldar of Jugraon fining him Rs. 10 on the

( )

JUDICIAL.

Progs. No. and date.

HOME DEPT. PROCEEDINGS, JULY 29, 1871.

Telegram dated 20th July 1871. — July 29. No. 55

From—Loodhiana.	To—Simla.
From—Deputy Commissioner.	To—Home Secretary.

No (sd P) important clue has been discovered in the Raikote case. Puttiala and Nabha officials are assisting. More by post.

No. 908, dated Simla, the 21st July 1871. — No. 56.

From—L. H. Griffin, Esq., Offg. Secy. to the Govt. of the Punjab,

To—E. C. Bayley, Esq., C. S. I., Secy. to the Govt. of India.

I am desired to forward, for the information of His Excellency the Viceroy and Governor General in Council, copy of a telegram addressed to His Highness the Maharajah of Puttiala, and of his reply, in regard to the arrest of parties concerned in the recent murder of butchers at Raikote.

Telegram dated 19th July 1871.

From—Punjab.	To—Puttiala.
From—Offg. Secy. to Govt., Punjab.	To—His Highness the Maharajah.

A cruel and cowardly murder has been perpetrated at Raikote; two persons being killed and seven wounded, mostly women and children. The murderers have been traced to Cheemewalla, in Puttiala territory. His Honor the Lieutenant-Governor calls upon your Highness to take the most energetic measures for the arrest of these cowardly assassins.

Telegram dated 20th July 1871.

From—Puttiala.	To Punjab
From—His Highness the Maharajah	To Offg. Secy. to Govt., Punjab.

Previous to the receipt of your telegram, strict instructions were issued upon the Nazims to take energetic measures for the arrest of the murderers on the information given by my Vakeel at Loodhiana. All the measures taken by me are fully telegraphed to my Vakeel there for the information of the Government.

Progress Report in the Raikote case — No. 57

The enquiry goes on vigorously. Puttiala is actively assisting. There is a report that some Kookas were at Naiwalla, a village 15 miles from Raikote, a few days before the murder. They are being traced out. The feeling of the people is good, and their demeanour has improved since these murders, which are doubtless the acts of a single gang.

No. 551, dated Loodhiana, the 21st July 1871.

Endorsed by the Offg. Deputy Commr., Loodhiana.

Copy of the above forwarded to Home Secretary with the Viceroy

No. 918, dated Simla, the 22nd July 1871. — No. 58.

From—L. H. Griffin, Esq., Offg. Secy. to the Govt. of the Punjab

To—E C Bayley, Esq., C. S. I., Secy. to the Govt. of India.

The number of persons killed and wounded at Raikote, in the Loodhiana District, in the attack made on the residences of the butchers, are nine—

(1.) Dusaundi Guja, dead.
(2.) Rasa, wife of above, dead.
(3.) Ranja, child of above, dying

APPENDIX O

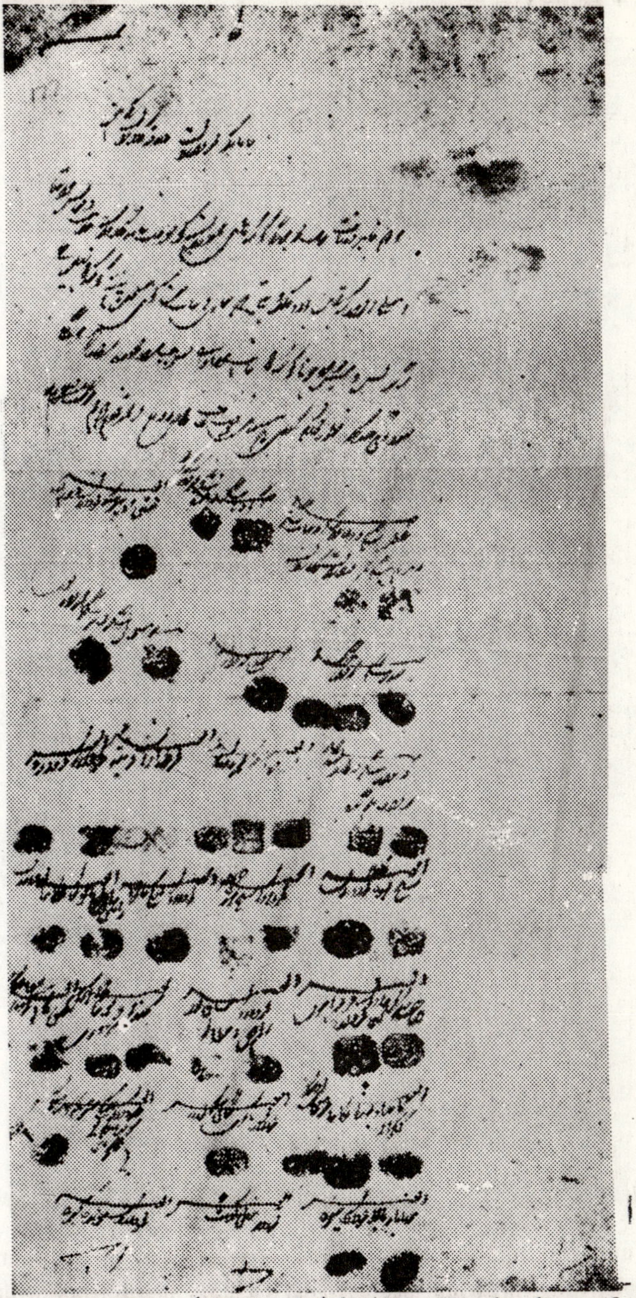

It is an undertaking (Mucha lka) by the Numberdars of region Kalaran whereby they declare that there will be no Kuka in their Villages and if some Kuka would be found they would be liable to punisment.

Mutfarka Munshi Khana, 1362 Jeend State.

APPENDIX P

An undertaking by the various Numberdars of Belapur area whereby they furnished security of Rs. 25/- in case they would fail to inform the police about the incoming and outgoing Kukas from their Villages. Importance of the document lies in the fact as to how restrictions were put on the movements of Kukas.

APPENDIX Q

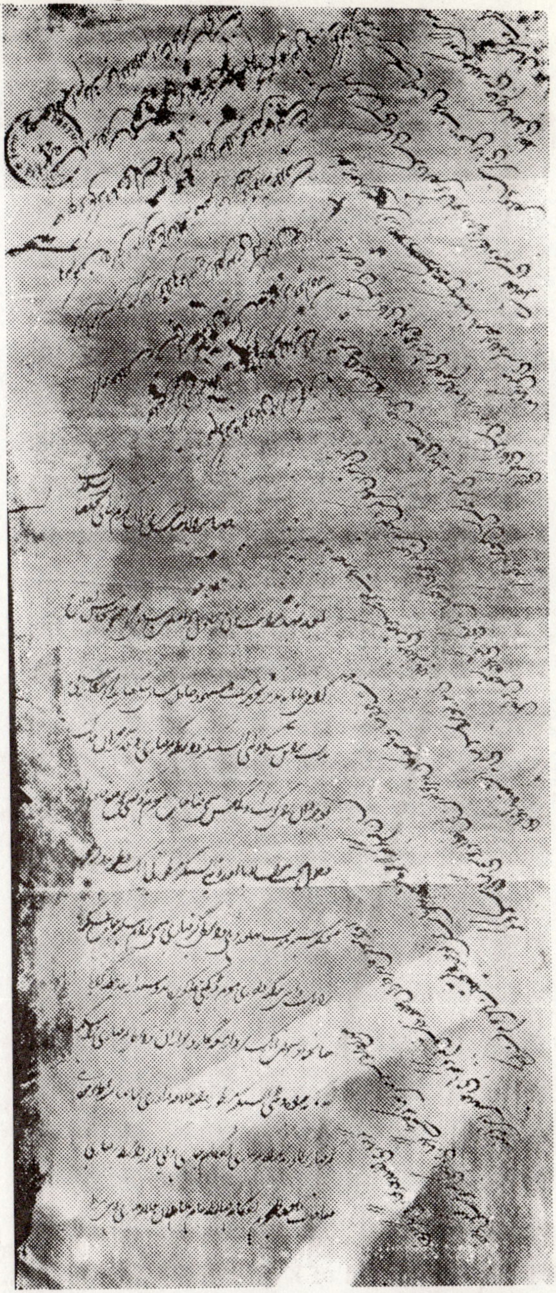

This document is in the form of an undertaking by the numberdars of region Kalaran by which they took the responsibility of informing the police about any Kuka which they would find in their areas.

Mutfarka Munshikhana, 1362 Jeend State.

APPENDIX Q I

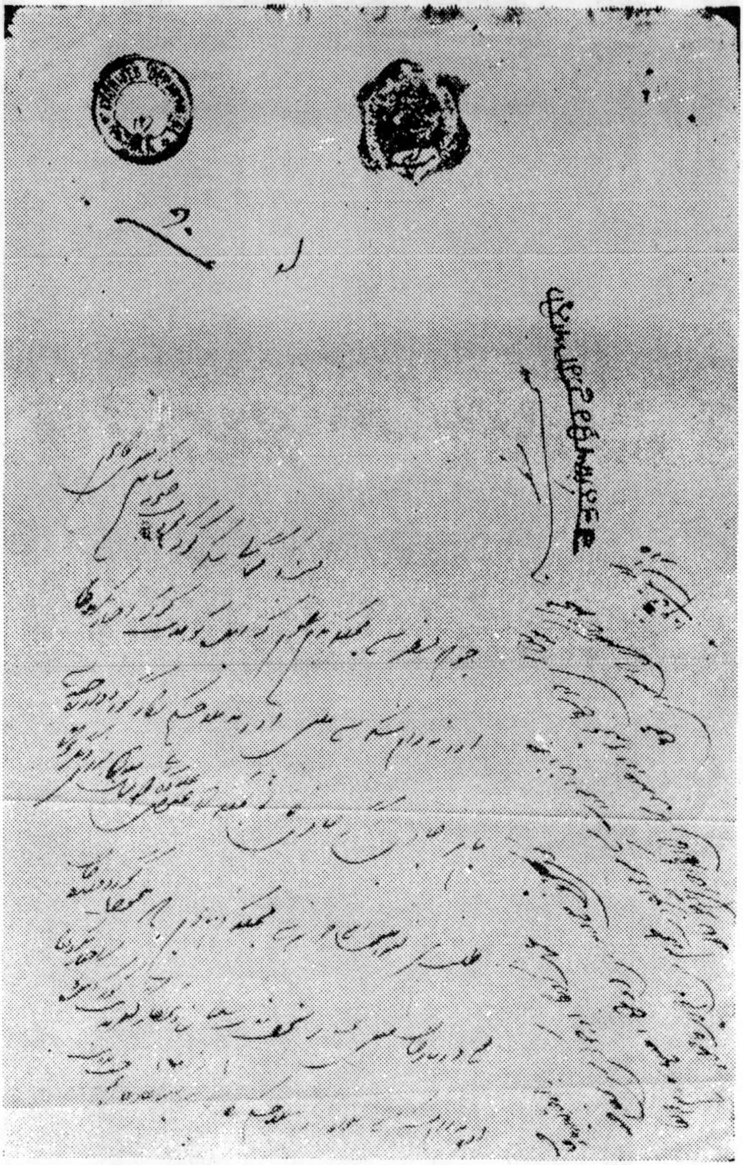

It is a statement given by one Kuka Giyani Ratan Singh that he would not follow the Creed of Kukas nor would meet Ram Singh. He writes "Therefore I am tendering this Muchalka with my blood" and would not depart by a hair's breadth from what he had said.

Mutfarka Munshikhana, 1362 Jeend State.

نقل مشولہ مثل نمبر 741 متعلقہ سنگین منشی خانہ ریاست جیند . بابت مقدمہ فساد برپا کرنے کوکہ ہائے بمقام کوٹلہ .

نمبر ۶۰۵ 5-6

داخل دفتر ہوا
۱۳ جنوری سنہ ۷۲ء

غریب پرور سلامت . ——— بعد القاب گذارش حال یہ ہے کہ امروز وقت
۸ بجے دن کے صاحب داخل کوٹلہ ہوئے ہیں اور ڈپٹی کمشنر بمقام موضع ملود ریاست
سردار ہت سنگھ واسطے دریافت حال گئے ہیں . اوسجگہ پر دنگہ فساد ہوا تھا . ہر ایک یعنی فرزند
سردار صاحب شمشیر کا زخم ہوا ہے . اسواسطے واسطے تحقیقات کے گئے ہیں . اور آج شام
تک داخل کوٹلہ ہونگے اور آمد ڈاک انگریزی سے یہ دریافت ہوا ہے کہ فوج معہ افسر پلس
بمقام موضع ڈیہلوں آگئے ہیں اور یہ بھی سنا گیا ہے کہ تھانہ دار موضع شیر پور علاقہ پٹیالہ
نے کوکہ ہائے کو گرفتار کر لیا ہے اور دروازہ کوٹلہ اب تک کشادہ نہیں ہوئے ہیں اور توپ بر سر
کرم خاں ناظم نے بر دیوان خانہ لگا دی ہیں اور آپ معہ ۲۰ بیس آدمی کے کہ
جس جگہ پر کوٹ شہر پناہ مسمار تھا اوسجگہ شب پہرہ دیا اور ایک طرف قاضی خدا بخش نے
پہرہ دیا مگر تمام شب بارش باران کے سبب سے عمل در آمد رہے اور اب یہ سنا جاتا ہے
کوکہ ہائے پھر کوٹلہ میں آوینگے . اسواسطے گذارش حضور ہے . زیادہ حد آداب . ملکم ...
آفتاب دولت کا تاباں رہے . مکرر عرض ہے . پاس فدوی کوئی ہرکارہ موجود نہیں ہے کہ
جس سے ہر وقت خبر روانہ حضوری کی جاوے . اب کرما ہرکارہ وقت ۱۱ بجے دن کے پاس فدوی
لوٹا ہوا تھا . سو اوسکے ہاتھ ڈاک دے کر روانہ حضور کیا گیا ہے . امیدوار ہوں کہ ہر چہار ہرکاران
کو اسجگہ واسطے دو چار روز کے روانہ فرماویں تاکہ ہر وقت خبر حضور والا میں کی جاوے .
زیادہ آداب . عرضی
فدوی نمک پروردہ قدیم گوپال ... محرر
ڈاکخانہ کوٹلہ . مورخہ ۱۲ ماہ جنوری سنہ ۷۲ء

These documents deal with various details of Kuka's attack on Malodh and Malerkotla. They speak about the Kukas who were blown away by the guns and Baba Ram Singh's deportation to Allahabad etc.

File No. 741 Mutalka Sangin Munshikhana, Jeend State.

صفحہ ۸۰۷

داخل دفتر ہو۔
۱۹ جنوری ۱۸۷۲ء

غریب پرور سلامت۔ خاکسار گذارش حال یہ ہے کہ ہمہ لنگری طرف
نواب سکندر علی خان صاحب قتل ہوئے اور سے لنگری کو قتل ہوئے ہیں۔ بعد دو گھنٹہ کے پھر کوکے
بھاگکر موضع رڑ علاقہ مہاراجہ پٹیالہ والہ داخل ہوئے ہیں اور یہاں نواب صاحب مذکور
واپس آگئے ہیں اور تھانہ دار مع بیس ۲۰ پچیس ۲۵ آدمی کے ہمراہ لیکر بمقام ڈیہلوں سے
واسطے مدد کے پہونچا تھا۔ پھر وہ بھاگ گئے۔ اب ایک شتر سوار بمقام لودیانہ سے اسوقت آیا ہے
کہ فوج کی مع صاحب بہادر واسطے گرفتاری کوکہ کے لمبے اوتے ہیں۔ سو اب تک بمقام کوٹلہ داخل
نہیں پہونچے ہیں اور تھانہ دار انگریزی نے چہار لنگری کوکہ بھی گرفتار کرے ہیں اور ایک عورت
بھی گرفتار ہوئی ہے۔ مگر اب تک تمام شہر کے دروازہ بھی کشادہ نہیں ہوئے ہیں۔ عرصہ چہار روز
گذر چکا ہے اور دو گھنٹہ تک ایسی شمشیر چلی کہ تحریر نہیں کیا جاتا ہے۔ اسواسطے گذارش ہے
کہ پاس فدوی ڈاک بعد ۳ بجے دن کے پہونچی تھی اور منگوانا ہرکارہ بھی ۳ بجے ڈاک لیکر واپس آیا تھا
اسوقت ڈاک دیگر روانہ حضور کیا گیا ہے۔ واجب تھا عرض کیا۔
ظل ہمیشہ حمد و یاد الہی آفتاب دولت تاباں و درخشاں رہے۔ زیادہ آداب۔

[signature]
فدوی نمک پروردہ قدیم گورہ دت
محرر ڈاکخانہ کوٹلہ۔ عرضی
۱۸ جنوری ۱۸۷۲ء
وقت ۴ بجے روانہ ہوا

صفحہ ۲۷

29

غریب پرور سلامت ۔ حسب الحال وقت ۱۰ بجے رات کے ایک مراسلہ بنام
حضور والا سردار اوتم سنگھ کے پاس فدوی بھیجا تھا ۔ سو اسوقت فدوی نے روانہ حضور
کیا ہے ۔ ملاحظہ اقدس سے گذرے گا ۔ اور امروز جو نفری گورکہائے از توپ ہائے
اوڑائے گئے ہیں اور مدت ۱۹ نفری باقی ہیں ۔ اونکے واسطے کل کا حکم دیا ہے ۔ اور
ملحہ نفری کو کہ سردار اوتم سنگھ محمد عمر خان از موضع ملوماجرہ سے پکڑ روبروئے صاحب بہادر
کر رہے تھے ۔ سو صاحب بہادر نے یہ حکم دیا ہے کہ کل کو ان کی روبکاری کی جاوے گی ۔
جیسا حکم ہوگا گزارش حضور کیا جاوے گا ۔ جو نسی ملحہ نفری سردار صاحب گرفتار کر کے لائے ہیں
اونکی تفصیل یہ ہے ۔ خوشحال سنگھ صوبا یک ۔ کماہ سنگھ نائب صوبا یک ۔ گورمکھ سنگھ یک

ہری سنگھ یک ۔ سو کل ملحہ نفری گرفتار کر کے لائے ہیں ۔ جسوقت توپ خانہ جاری ہوا ۔ اوسوقت
صاحب بہادر نے آپکی فوج بہت تعریف کری ۔ جس کا بیان نہیں ہو سکتا ہے ۔
زیادہ حد آداب طلبکم ہمہ دم یاد ۔

فدوی نمک پرورده قدیم گوری دت

صفحہ ۳۷

شامل مسل ریہہ ۲۲ جنوری سنہ ۱۸۷۲ء

غریب پرور سلامت : جناب عالی بشناگیب کرمنت

سوامان سرکار بشیار جو کوکا گرفتار ہوئے ہیں وہ مقام کوٹلہ اڑا دئے گئے

اور رام سنگھ بھی گرفتار ہو کر کس جگہ کو بھیجا گیا لیکن یہ ہے ۔

اس معاملہ میں فوج سرکار والا نے بھی مدد کری ہوگی ضرور مدد

مناسب ہے اور جو روز دوشنبہ دہلی سے نواب لفٹنٹ گورنر بہادر کا

کوچ ہے ۔ اطلاعاً عرض کیا ۔ الہیٰ آفتاب دولت و اقبال و ایامانباں رہے ۔

عرضی

فدوی جگت سنگھ وکیل تعلقہ پٹیالہ ۱۹ جنوری سنہ ۱۸۷۲ء

از دہلی

داخل دفتر ہوئی ۲۵ جنوری ۱۸۷۲ء

غریب پرور سلامت   جناب عالی۔ ایسا سننا گیا ہے کہ بھائی رام سنگھ

مذہب کوکاہا در قلعہ الہ آباد یعنی پراگ راج جی بافضل مقید ہے

لیکن پہر اوسکا چالان کہیں اور جگہ ہوگا اور کوکاہا نے جو شورش اوٹھایا تھا

سبہی بکیفر کردار خود پہونچ گئے۔ ابہی ایک دو روز نواب لفٹننٹ گورنر بہادر پنجاب

کا در دہلی مقام ہے۔ اور قواعد کمپوہا انگریزی کے متصل گوڑگانوں و محلہ صاحب

ہر روز بخوبی وجہ ہو رہی ہے۔ اطلاعاً عرض ہے۔ الہی آفتاب دولت در وعظمت و اقبال

ہمیشہ تاباں رہے۔

فدوی جگت سنگھ وکیل قصبہ لاہپور از دہلی۔

۲۲ جنوری سنہ ۷۲ء

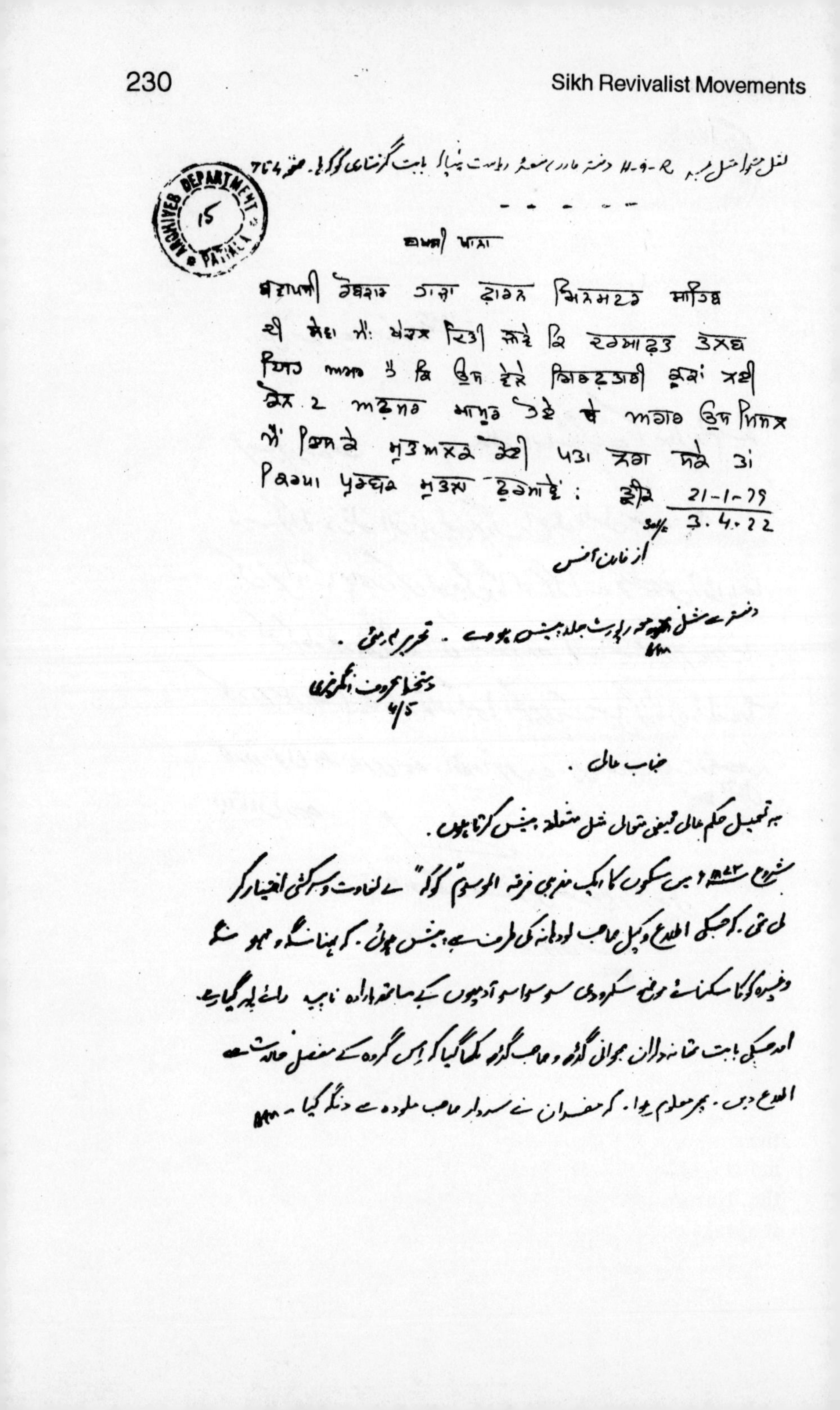

نقل مثل مشمولہ مثل نمبر R-9-11 دفتر مادر سمعھ ریاست پٹیالہ بابت گرفتاری کوکہ۔ صفحہ 764

- - - - -

[illegible]

[illegible]

ਫ਼ੈਰ [illegible] : 21-1-79
Sd/- 3.4.22

از فارن آفس

دفتر سے مثل ~~[illegible]~~ ہمراہ رپورٹ جلد پیش ہووے ۔ تحریر ۴ مئی ۔

دستخط حروف انگریزی
4/5

جناب عالی ۔

بہ تعمیل حکم عالی فیض متوال مثل متعلقہ پیش کرتا ہوں ۔

شروع سنہ ۱۸۷۲ء میں سکھوں کا ایک مذہبی فرقہ الموسوم "کوکہ" نے بغاوت و سرکشی اختیار کر لی تھی۔ کہ جسکی اطلاع وکیل صاحب لودہانہ کی طرف سے پیش ہوئی۔ کہ ہیرا سنگھ و لہنا سنگھ وغیرہ کوکا سکنائے موضع سکرودی سو سوا سو آدمیوں کے ساتھ بارادہ نابہ روانہ ہو گیا ہے۔ اور جسکی بابت تھانہ داران مجوال گڑھ و صاحب گڑھ لکھا گیا کہ اِس گروہ کے مفصل حالات سے اطلاع دیں۔ پھر معلوم ہوا۔ کہ مفسدان نے سردار صاحب ملودہ سے دنگہ کیا۔

صفحہ 47 تا 50

غریب پرور سلامت ۔ خیالحال ۔ حال فساد کوٹلہ کا اسطور پر سنا جاتا ہے

کہ جب گیانی سنگھ صوبہ کوکا ہے کا گرفتار ہوا تھا ۔ بوقت قلمبندی اظہارات اوس سے لکھا یا تھا کہ

میرے پھانسی دینے سے تمکو کچھ فائدہ حاصل نہوگا ۔ بلکہ ایک کس طرح کا تکلیف اوٹھانا ہوگا اور مجھکو

مار کر بنیاد قوم کوکا قطع ہو جاوے گی ۔ دس ہزار کوکا جی اپنے سر پر کفن بکٹے ہیں اور کل علاقہ

صوبہ ہمارے ہر یک ملک میں اپنا اپنا انتظام کرتے ہیں ۔ اور خاص نیپال میں بھی ہمارا صوبہ رہتا ہے ۔

چنانچہ صاحب مکناب صاحب کمشنر سابق نے یہ حکم فرمایا تھا کہ یہ بیان اُنکا صرف واسطے خوف

گورنمنٹ کے ہے ۔ مع ہمارے نزدیک ایسی سمنات واہیات کا خیال کرنا نہ چاہیئے ۔ چنانچہ

جب سے گیانی سنگھ کو پھانسی ہوئی تھی ۔ اوسوقت سے اُن کا ارادہ تھا کہ صوبہ کا سرکار انگریزی سے

بدلا لینا چاہیئے ۔ چنانچہ یہ بات قرار پائی تھی کہ ریاست کوٹلہ میں کوئی حاکم نہیں ہے ۔ اول دفعہ اپنا کوٹلہ

پر کرنا چاہیئے ۔ بعدہ سنگرور و نابھہ و پٹیالہ ہو کر انبالہ کو جانا چاہیئے ۔ چنانچہ کوٹلہ پر ارادہ کیا اور [illegible]

۲۳ شنبہ کو بعد مشورہ موضع بھینی سے باجازت گرو خود روانہ کوٹلہ ہوئے اور موضع ریسہ میں آکر روٹی کھائی

اور کسی جگہ کچھ کھانے کا انتظام نہوا اور بارش میں بھی برابر چلتے رہے ۔ اور رات کو کوٹلہ کا محاصرہ

کر لیا اور کوٹلہ میں سابق خبر پہونچی تھی کہ کوکا دھاوا کریں گے ۔ چنانچہ باہر شہر سے رود سواران مع [illegible]

اور اونکو جا بجا کوٹلہ چلتے تھے ۔ قبل از طرح کوکا ہے نے ۔ ایک عورت کو یہ بہانہ [illegible] کے شہر میں

بھیجا اور وہ ہر یک جگہ میں آکر سب حال معائنہ کر گئی اور صفدان پاس جاکر کہا کہ اب سب حاصل

ہیں ۔ چنانچہ وہ براستہ شکستہ کوٹ کے دھاوا کیا ۔ اول کوتوال شہر کو مارا بعدہ تو ویلہ میں جاکر

داروغہ کو مارا اور سلح خانہ تلاش کیا ۔ کچھ پتہ نہ لگا ۔ جب شہر میں غوغا ہوا تو بعضے بعضے آدمی نے

مقابلہ اونکا کیا ۔ اونکو مارا اور آپ بھی مر گئے ۔ اور پھر کوکا بسبب ملنے ملاحظات کے کوٹلہ سے باہر چلے

گئے اور موضع رڑ میں جاکر قیام پذیر ہوئے ۔ کیونکہ جو دو لٹری ہمرہ ہیرا سنگھ و سوبھا سنگھ سردار

اونکے تھے اونکے ہاتھہ کٹ گئے تھے ۔ اسواسطے وہ موضع رڑ سے آگے نہ چل سکے اور

This document gives various details of Kukas, their numbers, their influence in Nepal etc. It gives some details about the Kuka motive of attack on Malerkotla and how they were captured by the Nazim Niaz Ali when they were taking rest at village Rar. It speaks about the various arrangements done for the Kukas.

File No. 741 Mutalka Sangin Munshikhana, Jeend State.

نمبرداران موضع مذکور نے حکمت عملی سے مشورہ کرکے پاس مفسدان جاکر کہا کہ بھائی سکھو تم بڑے تھکے ہوئے ہوں گے۔ اسجگہ
پرشادہ تیار ہوتا ہے چھکلو۔ چنانچہ اونہوں نے منظور کیا۔ کیونکہ روزسے کچھ کھایا نہ تھا اور اون کو اسطور
گاؤں میں تقسیم کردیا کہ کسی گھر میں دو آدمی اور کسی گھر میں تین آدمی ہمشلہ دیئے۔ اور دو آدمی کو پاس ناظم
صاحب بھیج دیا۔ کہ اسجگہ کوکا فساد کرکے آئے ہیں۔ اور ہم نے علیحدہ علیحدہ کر رکھا ہے۔ چنانچہ نائب ناظم
مع سواران و پیادگان موضع مذکور حاضر ہوا اور ہر یک گھر سے اونکو گرفتار کرکے کوٹلہ میں حاضر کردیا۔ چنانچہ بضرب
توپ ہر یک کو اڑادیا گیا اور بعوض خدمتگزاری نائب ناظم کو ایک ہزار روپیہ عطائے ہوا اور باقی ہمراہیان کو
بقدر حیثیت انعام دیا گیا اور پانچ لشری کوکا جو عقب سے گرفتار ہوکر آئے تھے اونکو مقام لدھیانہ پھانسی
دی جاوے گی۔ اگرچہ مقام ملود اونکو پھانسی دی جاتی لیکن کرنل صاحب ملودیہ نے بسبب خوف اس بات کے
کہ اگر کوکا اس جگہ پھانسی دی گئی۔ پھر کہیں آکر فساد برپا نکریں۔ ملود میں پھانسی دینا منظور نکیا۔ امروز
آج صاحب کمشنر بہادر مع صاحب ڈپٹی کمشنر بہادر ملود سے لدھیانہ تشریف لے جاویں گے اور ایسا بھی سنا
گیا ہے کہ ریاست جیند و یا نابہ یا پٹیالہ سے کچھ فوج واسطے انتظام کوٹلہ میں چندے قیام پذیر رہیں
اور ملازمان کوٹلہ شاہ باد والا کو صاحب بہادر نے بہت ندامت کی بات سنائی کہ وہ اداس ہو رہے ہیں۔
اور بہت قوم کوکا گرفتار ہوکر لدھیانہ میں آئے ہیں۔ شاید اون کو بھی پھانسی دی جاوے۔ لہذا جو
کچھ سنا گیا بحضور انور گزارش کیا گیا۔ الہی آفتاب دولت و اقبال تاباں رہے۔

عرضی
بندہ فدوی کریم بخش وکیل کمشنری طرف انبالہ
مورخہ ۲۰ جنوری ۱۸۷۲ء
مقام ملود۔

مکرر عرض یہ ہے کہ ایسا بھی سنا گیا ہے کہ
رام سنگھ گرو کو سواری ریل طرف روانہ
کیا گیا۔ اصل حال اسکا پھر سے
گزارش حضور ہوگا۔ فقط

اور دو چار آدمی ان کے قتل کئے۔ اور انکی ایک دو گھوڑی لیکر کوٹلہ پہونچے۔ کوٹلہ میں [illegible]
جنگ وجدل کیا۔ سررشتہ ہذا میں باستماع ان خبروں کے متواتر احکامات تاکیدی ناظم صاحبان
اضلاع کے نام جاری کئے گئے۔ اور فوج بمقام کوٹلہ بھیجی گئی۔

دریں اثنا سید نیاز علی صاحب نائب ناظم امرگڈھ نے بمقام شیرپور سے رپورٹ کی
کہ بہ تقریب [illegible] وہ اس جگہ آیا ہوا تھا۔ کوکوں کی نسبت معلوم ہوا۔ کہ کوٹلہ و ملودھ میں دنگہ کرکے
موضع رڑ کے قریب قیام رکھتے ہیں۔ چنانچہ مع [illegible] سنگھ و اوتم سنگھ سواران و عمدار قلعہ شیرپور
مستان علی محرر فوجداری وہاں پہونچا۔ [illegible] اگرچہ جمعیت بہت
قلیل تھی۔ مگر دلیری سے ان کو کہا۔ کہ خبردار آگے نہ بڑھنا۔ میں مہاراج کا ناظم ہوں اور تمہارے
گرفتار کرنے کو آیا ہوں۔ مفسدوں نے ان کو محاصرہ کرلیا۔ بس یہ بھی ناچار ہتھیار سنبھال کر کھڑے
ہوگئے۔ اتنے میں سردار پنجاب سنگھ رائے پوریہ مع اپنے بھائی ہرتاپ سنگھ کے دونالی بندوقیں لئے ہوئے
مدد کو آپہونچے۔ کہ جس کے بعد باغیوں نے ہتھیار ڈال دیے۔ غرض 68 کس گرفتار ہوئے۔ کہ جس
میں 29 کس زخمی تھے۔ کہ جنکو شیرپور کی گڑھی میں لے جاکر خبرداری سے رکھا۔ اگلے روز
نظامت واحد گڈھ سے کسی قدر امداد اور بیڑیاں آگئیں۔ کہ جو ان کے ڈال گئیں۔ اس طرح سے
اس فساد کا سلسلہ رک گیا۔

گورنمنٹ پنجاب میں اس واقعہ کی اطلاع دی گئی۔ جہاں سے حسب ذیل انعام
خدمت اہلکاران گورنمنٹ ہذا وصول ہوا۔

سید نیاز علی صاحب — پنجاب سنگھ درباری — جیمل سنگھ مخبر — اوتم سنگھ — رتن سنگھ — گلاب سنگھ — ہرتاب سنگھ

مستان علی محرر

This document gives various details of the Kuka attack on Malodh Malerkotla and how Kukas were caught. All those involved in capturing the Kukas were richly rewarded in terms of money, clothes, titles and ranks etc.

File No. A-9-R Office Foreign Ministry, Patiala.

بحضور مہاراجہ مہندر سنگھ صاحب بہادر نے حسب ذیل انعامات بخشے :-

میر نیاز علی
[illegible] روپیہ
خلعت [illegible]
رقم [illegible]
[illegible]

بنجاب سنگھ [illegible]
بعہدہ رسالداری ترقی
یاب ہوا۔
معہ انعام
دوشالہ [illegible]
[illegible]

پرتاب سنگھ برادر
بنجاب سنگھ
دوشالہ

مستان علی محرر
بعہدہ تھانہ داری
ترقی یاب ہوا
دوشالہ قیمتی

فیض بخش محرر تھانہ شیرپور
دوشالہ

رتن سنگھ سوار
بعہدہ جمعداری
ترقی یاب ہوا
دوشالہ قیمتی

اوتم سنگھ سوار
بعہدہ جمعداری
ترقی یاب ہوا
دوشالہ

گلاب سنگھ جمعدار
قلعہ شیرپور کی تنخواہ
[illegible] دو چندگی
جاوے
دوشالہ

قاسم علی ملازم [illegible]
پسر نیاز علی
تبدیل سواران
مامور ہوا۔

دایر سنگھ سوار کو
دوشالہ [illegible] روپیہ
ادا [illegible]
دفعہ اور کیا جاوے

اوتم سنگھ تھانہ دار
شیرپور۔ دوشالہ
[illegible] ادا۔ عہدہ
ممبری رجمنٹ [illegible]
مامور ہوا۔

[illegible] ملازم
تبدیل [illegible] سواران
با سواران رجمنٹ
ملازم کیا جاوے۔

رحیم دل خان سپاہی
[illegible] سنگھ سپاہی
فی کس [illegible] روپیہ
خلعت [illegible]
اور سارجنٹ [illegible]
جاویں۔

فتح سنگھ سپاہی
پلٹن
کمیس

جواہر سنگھ۔ بہادر خان [illegible]
[illegible] چند [illegible]
قلعہ شیرپور کو کمیس فی
[illegible] روپیہ
نقد [illegible] روپیہ

جیمل سنگھ جس نے
پہلے اطلاع دی تھی
دوشالہ
[illegible]

رستم خان
سپاہی تھانہ
کمیس

روڑا [illegible]
نقد
[illegible]

[illegible] نائب ناظر
بجائے مستان علی
ترقی پاوے۔

عطر سنگھ۔ جواہر سنگھ۔ [illegible] سنگھ
محبوب سنگھ۔ مستان سنگھ [illegible]
نمبرداران شیرپور کو دوشالہ
فی کس روپیہ۔

محبوب سنگھ نمبردار
[illegible] کو
دوشالہ

عطر سنگھ شیام سنگھ
اوتم سنگھ نمبرداران
کو کمیس

خوشحال سنگھ ہریم سنگھ
نمبرداران [illegible]
کمیس فی

مثل میں خاص عہدہ داران کی خاص اس موقعہ پر تعیناتی کا کوئی ذکر نہیں ہوا۔ صرف لغرض
انتظام و گرفتاری مفسدان ناظم صاحبان و تھانہ داراں کو لکھا جاتا رہا۔ میر نیاز علی صاحب
نے جب ان لوگوں کو گرفتار کیا۔ اور اس کے بعد جن اصحاب کو بصلہ خدمات عطا انعامات
ہوا ہے۔ ان کی فہرست اوپر ~~پیش~~ گذارش کر دی گئی ہے۔ دراصل حادثہ مثل کے ابتداء
میں جو روبکار ۲۹ کا تک ۲۹ شامل ہیں۔ ~~[illegible]~~ اسی سے ہی واقع راست بیان ہو سکتی ہے
لہذا رپورٹ پیش ہے۔ معروضہ 4 5/22 دستخط بحروف انگریزی۔

از فارن ڈیپارٹمنٹ

جواب بذریعہ روبکار بھجوا دیا جاوے کہ اول وکیل صاحب لودیانہ کی طرف سے اطلاع آنے
پر تھانہ داران کے نام احکام جاری کئے گئے تھے۔ پھر زیادہ شورش ہونے پر ناظم صاحبان
کے نام بنابر انسداد احکام جاری کئے گئے تھے اور فوج بمقام کوٹلہ بھیجی گئی تھی۔ خاص
طور پر کسی افسر کی ماموری نہیں ہوئی تھی۔

المرقوم۔ ۵ مئی ۱۹۲۲ء

Sd/-
Foreign Minister
Patiala Government.

ATTESTED

Addl. Director of Archives.
Punjab, Patiala.

نقل مشمولہ مثل نمبر H-10-R سمت ۱۹۳۸ دفتر فارن منسٹر ریاست پٹیالہ بابت انتظام
متعلقہ گرفتاری کوکہ جات

- - - -

منمبر ۹ تا ۱۲۱

غریب پرور سلامت . جناب عالی . جو فدوی اصل مراسلہ مضمون شکریہ
ازاں سکندر صاحب ڈپٹی کمشنر ضلع انبالہ مرسولہ حضور والا نسبت مقدمہ سرزد ہو جانے جرم قتل محمد بوجران
واقع رائے کوٹ جو منجانب بندگان حضور انور پیش کوشش عمل میں آئی ہے معہ جزئیات بارجہہ
درباب گرفتار کئے جانے مجرم واردات بکلو روبرو لفٹ(?) صاحب کمانڈر چیف حاضر
ہوا . معرفت جمعدار ڈیوڑھی کے اطلاع کرائی . فوراً طلب فرمالیا جس وقت فدوی
باریاب ہوا . صاحب موصوف مع خاوندی و کرم نوازی و شادمانہ ہو کر نہایت اخلاق اور شفقت
سے پیش آئے اور دست مبارک سے اشارت کرسی فرمائی . فدوی سلام معمول بجا لاکر کرسی
بیٹھ گیا . پھر بجانب حضور والا سلام شوقیہ عرض کیا کہ بفضل خدا و عنایات حضور کے داد اقدس
خداوند نعمت موکل بہت خوش و خرم ہے . فرمایا کہ ہماری طرف سے بخدمت سری مہاراجہ صاحب
بہادر سلام شوقیہ بذریعہ عرضی خود تحریر کرنا عرض کیا گیا کہ نہیں . عرض کیا کہ سرکار خاوندی جو
واکسلنسی(?) معلے سٹار آف انڈیا بمقام کلکتہ تشریف لے گئے تھے بسو(?) سرکار آقائم کو حضور کی
تشریف آوری تا بمقام کلکتہ نہایت انتظار اور اشتیاق ملاقات از حد رہا . فرمایا کہ ہمکو
کچھ کام سرکاری ضروری تھا اس لئے اتفاق اوس موقع پر نہ ہوا . اور ہمکو بدل خوشی ہے کہ سری مہاراجہ
صاحب بہادر کو سٹار آف انڈیا اپنے ہاتھ سے دیں . لہذا اسکے فدوی نے جزئیات بارجہہ کو ملاحظہ
کرایا اور مضمون اصل مراسلہ حرف بحرف پڑھ کر سنایا اور زبانی گذارش کیا کہ جانب سرکار آقائم
سے اس مقدمہ میں نہایت سعی اور کوشش ہوئی ہے جس کہ بعد اطلاع اس واردات

This document gives information of murder of butcher at Amritsar, Raikot etc. to the Deputy Commissioner, Ambala and considering Baba Ram Singh to be a mischievous man suggests his exile to Kala Pani.

File No. H-10-R Samvat 1938, Office Foreign Ministry, ***Patiala.***

کی سرکار خاوندی سے جملہ تھانہ داران و نائب ناظمان و ناظم اناحد گذرہ و خصوص سردار دلواسنگہ صاحب
حاکم صدر عدالت جوڈیشیل کو بحال ابتداء سے سزاے مجرمان مرجعہ و اسطہ سزا و
گرفتاری مجرمان تاکید بلیغ فرمائی گئی۔ سو باقبال سرکار یہ مقدمہ ثابت ہوگیا اور مجرمان ماخوذ شدہ
نے جرم سے اقبال کیا۔ بلکہ بعض از قتل ضرب شمشیر ہا مدونہ حسب نشاندہیدا مجرمان برآمد کئے گئے
فرمایا کہ درست ہے۔ پھر فرمایا کہ یہ جو شرارت ہے رام سنگھ کی ہے جو کوکوں کا گورو ہے۔ اول میں وہ
ایک غریب آدمی تھا۔ اب وہ بہت مالدار اور متمول ہوگیا ہے۔ اور بظاہر بودہ خاموش ہے کچھ نہیں کہتا۔
لیکن باطن میں یہ سب اوسکی کارسازی ہے۔ اور نیز کوکے لوگوں کا مقولہ ہے۔ کہ جو کچھ دنیا میں ہے وہ
سب اپنا ہے۔ کس طرح کہ جب تلوار کرینگے سب اپنا کرینگے۔ سوائے ہمارے اور کوئی نہیں ہوگا۔
سو جبتک رام سنگھ کالے پانی نہیں بھیجا جاتا۔ تب تک اسکا انتظام نہیں ہوتا۔ عرض کیا گیا کہ
درست ہے۔ عرض کیا کہ پہلے ہماری فوج کے لوگوں نے بھی مذہب کوکا اختیار کیا تھا۔ جس وقت
سرکار موکلم کو یہ حال معلوم ہوا تو اون لوگوں کو نوکری سے برخاست کی سزا دی گئی۔ جو لوگ
پٹیالہ میں اونکو بھی اور جس قدر علاقہ میں [illegible] بھی معلوم ہوئے سب کو سزا واقعی دی گئی۔ اور ان
ان لوگوں کا مذہب کا طریقہ خلاف مذہب سکھان کے ہے اور بعد سزا دینے سرکار موکلم کے پھر
کوکا فوج یا علاقہ متعہ ظاہر معلوم نہیں ہوا۔ پھر عرض کیا کہ حضور غور فرماویں کہ پہلے اس قسم کی
واردات مقام امرتسر وقوع سرزد ہوئی ہے۔ ابھی حسب آجتک کوئی پتہ نشان نہیں ملا۔
سرکار خاوندی سے لیو بیہوری ہوکر اسکا تدارک عمل میں آیا۔ فرمایا کہ شک
مالم کچھ ان پر طور سے رہا ہے۔ اور تمام مقام بلسعی اور کوشش سری مہاراجہ صاحب
سے رضامند اور خوشنودی ہے۔ فرمایا کہ ان مجرمان گرفتار شدہ سے ایک مقدمہ

جرم لبرٹ مہر سے اقرار کیا ہے ۔ غرضیکہ ایسا ذکر اذکار فرماتے رہے ۔ بعد اسکے فرمایا
کہ سری مہاراجہ صاحب بہادر کب تشریف لاویں گے ۔ عرض کیا گیا کہ ابھی تو مجھے خبر معلوم
نہیں ہے ۔ شاید بماہ ستمبر تشریف لاویں ۔ پھر فرمایا ۔ تم نے مہاراجہ صاحب کو پہلے ہی کہدیا ۔
اور ہم مہاراجہ صاحب بہادر کو دیکھ کر بہت خوش ہونگے ۔ خداوندا جو کہ گزارش کرنا اسکا
واجب اور مناسب تھا ۔ لہذا عرض کیا گیا ۔ [illegible] گشت شد ۔

عرضی
محمد علی وکیل گورنمنٹ

ATTESTED
[signature]
Addl. Director of Archives,
Punjab, Patiala.

No. of words. 3908. one copy Pages 1 to 27

Name of the applicant........Mrs. Surjit Kaur Jolly
2. Date of receipt of application...20-11-79
3. Date of return of application for deposit of fees ....—
4. Date of Deposit ....—
5. Search fee Rs ....nil
Copying fee Rs 9-81
Attestation fee Rs 2-45
6. Date when ready for delivery...4-12-79
7. Date of Posting or delivery ..5-12-79

No. Roc-2/79-80/2010 dt/5-12-79

نقل منشور اسل نمبر Mad. No. I-86 of 1923 محکمہ تاریخ شستری ریاست پٹیالہ .

بابت عرضداشت چندیداس وکیل انبالہ بدرخواست انتظام فرمانے جانے اقوام سکھان جنہوں نے

مذہب کوکا جدید ایجاد کیا ہے ..

— — —

صفحہ ۲۵ .

گرامی قدر چندیداس مسرور باشند

عرضی تمہاری معروضہ اسوج سدی ۱۲ سمت حال اطلاع ارشاد فرمائی صاحب ڈپٹی کمشنر بہادر واسطے

انتظام کوکہ موصول ہوا . حال معلوم ہوا . جوکہ اہلکاران سرکار سے بابت اشتمال کوکہ

یہ انتظام کیا ہے کہ جملہ کوکہ جو ملازم سرکار تھے موقوف کئے گئے اور سندجات لی گئی .

اور آئندہ کے واسطے یہ بندوبست کیا گیا کہ جو کوکہ ہوگا اسکا نام کاٹا جاوے گا اور سررشتہ

محکمہ عدالت سے اشتہار عام اس مضمون سے دیا گیا ہے چونکہ یہ مذہب خلاف مذہب

سکھی سکھ ہے . لہذا جو کوئی یہ مذہب اختیار کرے گا . اوسکو عدالت سرکار سے سزا

دی جاوے گی نیز کہ یہ انتظام واسطے اہلکاران کے قابل تشفی ہوگا . لہذا اللہ تمکو

مکمل ہوا توجہ سرکار اینجانب المرحوم — کاتک سدی ۴ سمت ۱۹۲۳ .

This document deals with the arrangement s which were made to suppress the Kukas. Chandidas Vakil of Patiala State informs the Maharaja of Patiala that Deputy Commissioner Ambala wants to dismiss all Kukas from the Government Services. This order was to be notified to the public through posters on behalf of the Court because Kukas were against the Sikh religion and whosoever would embrace this religion would be punished by the Court.

Mad No. I-86-1923, Katak Sudi H 1923 B. Parwana, Patiala Govt.

APPENDIX—V (ii)

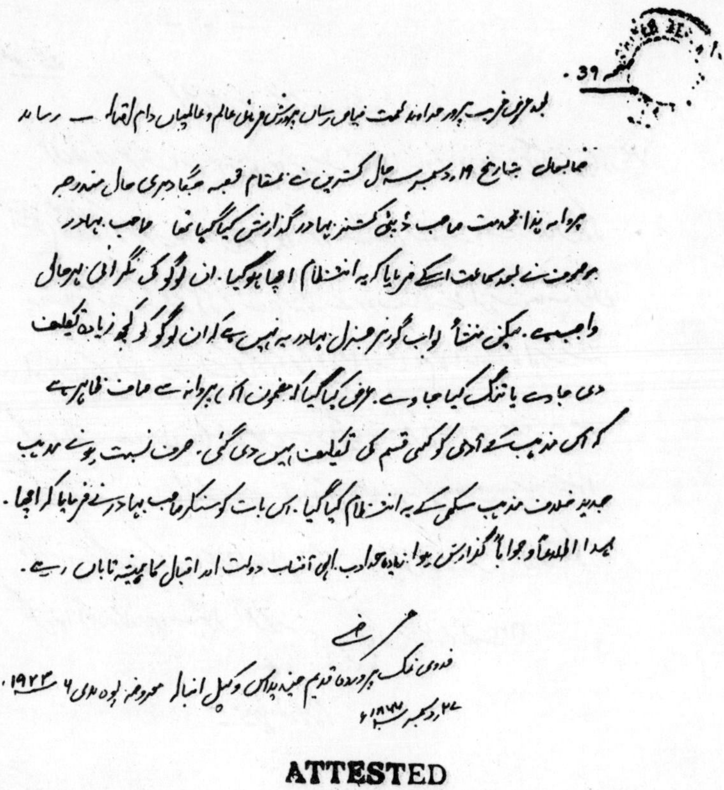
39

بعد عرض غریب پرور خداوند نعمت فیاض رساں پرورش فرمای عالم و عالمیاں دام اقبالہ ـــ رساند

حسب الحال بتاریخ ۱۹ دسمبر سال کمترین نے بمقام قصبہ جگادھری حال مندرجہ

پروانہ بندا بخدمت صاحب ڈپٹی کمشنر بہادر گذارش کیا گیا تھا صاحب بہادر

موصوف نے بعد سماعت اسکے فرمایا کہ یہ انتظام اچھا ہو گیا۔ ان لوگوں کی نگرانی ہر حال

واجب ہے۔ لیکن منشاء نواب گورنر جنرل بہادر یہ نہیں ہے کہ ان لوگوں کو کچھ زیادہ تکلیف

دی جاوے یا تنگ کیا جاوے۔ عرض کیا گیا کہ مضمون اکابر پروانہ سے صاف ظاہر ہے

کہ اس مذہب کے آدمی کو کسی قسم کی تکلیف نہیں دی گئی۔ صرف نسبت ہونے مذہب

جدید خلاف مذہب سکھ کے یہ انتظام کیا گیا۔ اس بات کو سنکر صاحب بہادر نے فرمایا کہ اچھا۔

لہذا الملتمس و جواباً گذارش ہوا زیادہ حد ادب۔ الہی آفتاب دولت اور اقبال کا ہمیشہ تاباں رہے۔

فدوی نمک پروردہ قدیم ... ۱۹۲۳

۲۷ دسمبر

ATTESTED

Addl. Director of Archives.
Punjab, Patiala.

This conveys the order of Governor-General to the Government of Patiala that Kukas should not be tortured, troubled or harassed in any way because British Government only wants to keep them under restrain.

Mad No. I-86-1923

PLATE I

Idol of Ganesh to be seen at the main gate of the residence of the Chief Priest of Harmandir Sahib (Golden Temple. Amritsar)

PLATE II

Photograph of Baba Dayal—Founder of Nirankari Movement.

PLATE III

Multi-coloured Flag of the Nirankaris was to be hoisted alongwith the Khalsa Flag of saffron colour.

PLATE IV

Parwana of Sahib Rattaji (reproduction of the manuscript)

PLATE V

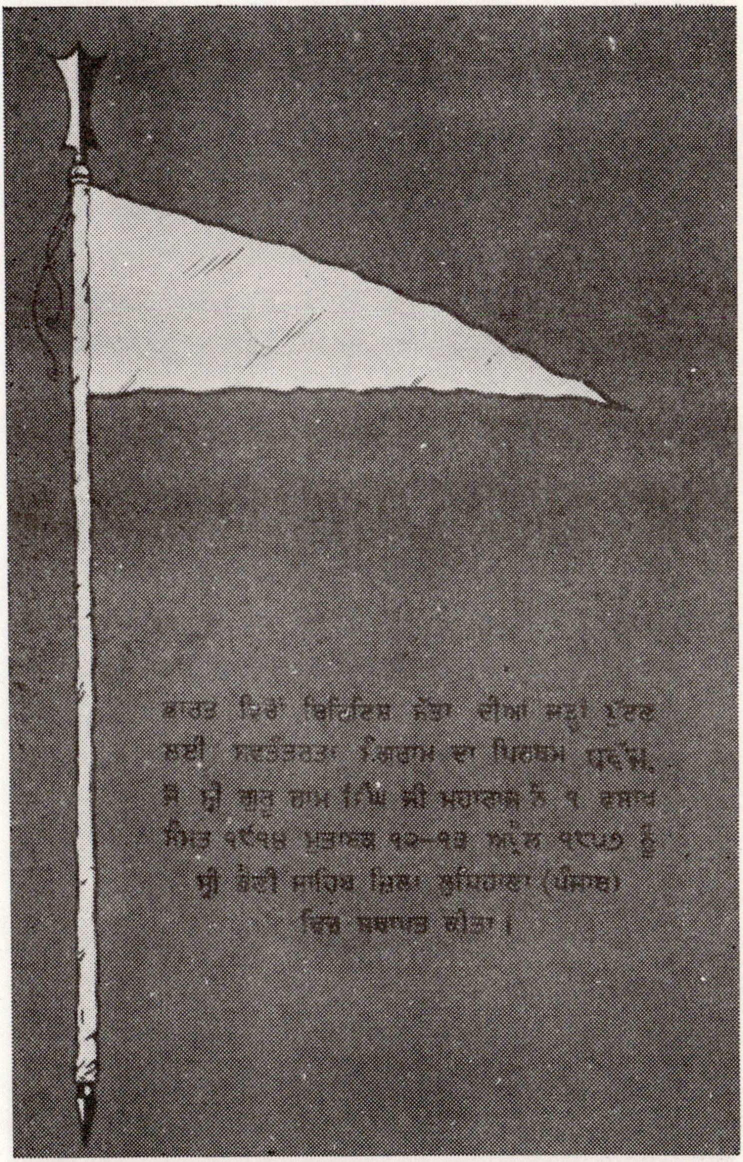

Plain white Namdhari Flag hoisted by Baba Ram Singh on 13th April 1857 at Bhaini Sahib.

PLATE VI

Har Mandir Sahib Sri Nirankari Darbar Rawalpindi.

PLATE VII

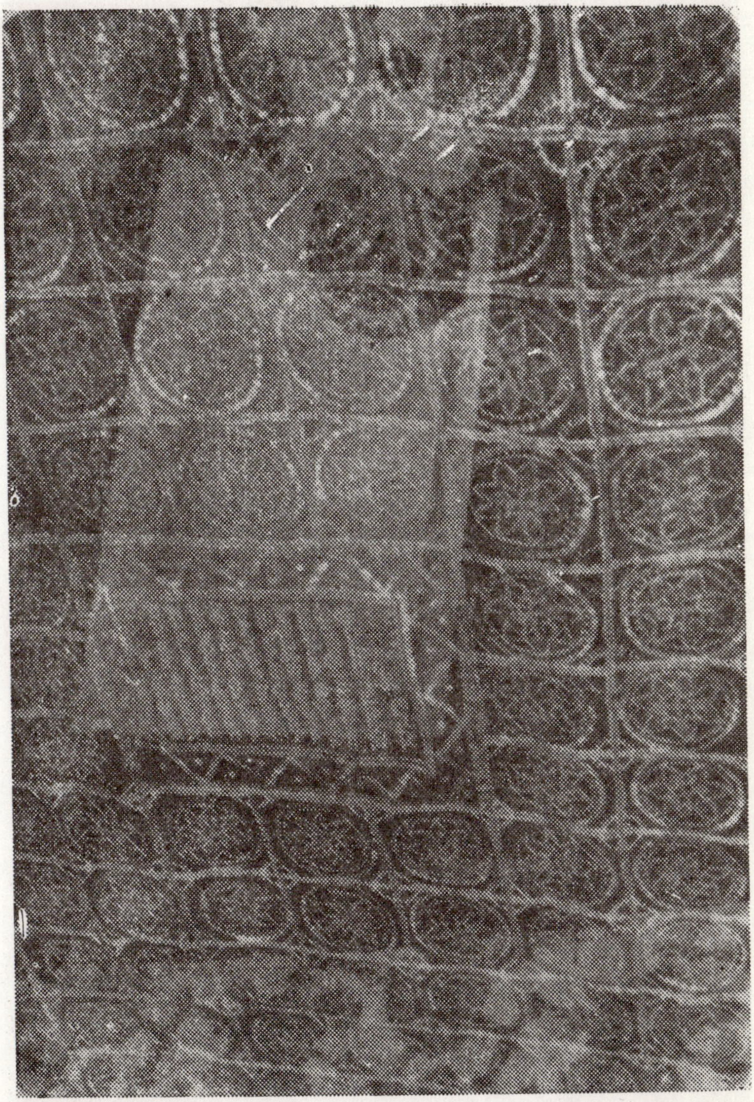

Reproduction of an origional Nirankari Rumala (a piece of cloth to cover Adi-Grunth) of 1865 A.D., quite contrary to the Namdhari who use only white covers. Nirankaris use costly, beautifully embroidred silkan covers for the Adi-Grunth.

PLATE VIII

Photo showing Baba Ram Singh riding on a famous horse—Chini, accompanied by his followers. It also illustrates their dress and the order of the procession

PLATE IX

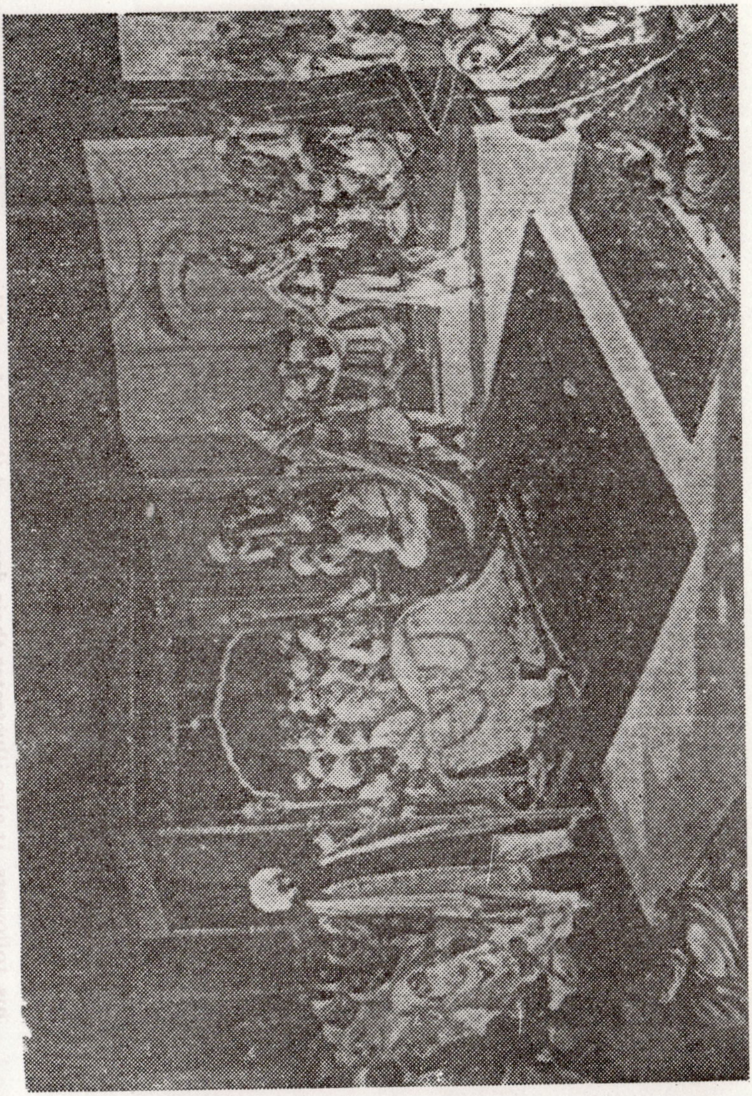

A scence of First Anand Mrriage, being performed by Baba Darbara Singh in 1855 A.D., at Shri Nirankari Darbar, Rawalpindi.

PLATE X

Gurudwara Sri Dayalsar Ji Rawlpindi.

Bibliography

I Primary Sources

(i) *Bakshikhana and Munshikhana Files of Foreign Department, Patiala*

(1) Mad No. 1-86 of 1923 B.K.

(2) File No. H-9-R Office Bakshikhana Records

(3) File No. H-10-R, 1938 B.K. Foreign Ministry

(4) File No. H-92-M Foreign Ministry (Political)

(5) File No. H-67-G 1873 A.D.

(ii) *Papers of Sangin Munshikhana Jeend States*

(1) File No. 741 and 781

(iii) *Mutfarka Munshikhana Jeend State*

(1) Papers No. 1362

(iv) *Malerkotla State Papers*

1. FFIA Mirasla Malerkotla State
2. F. FIB Mirsala Malerkotla State
3. FF 3 A Mirasla Malerkotla State

(v) *Proceedings of Foreign Department Political A National Archives of India, New Delhi and India Office London British Museum, London*

1. 10th August 1828 (Case No. 3) 16th August, 1828 (Case No. 6)
2. 14th November 1828 (Case No. 4) 22nd November 1828 (Case No. 7)
3. 2nd July 1830 (No. 65-70)
4. 4th July 1833 (No. 28-29) 17th September 1832 (51-52) 31st December 1832 (52).

5. 2nd January 1839 (No. 41)

6. 31st December 1847 (2511)

7. 22 March 1850 (103-104) 26th April 1850 (70-76) 6th September (123-124)

8. 13th February 1832 (37-40)

9. 7th January 1853 (218-220) 21st January (224-225)

10. 27th March 1857 (245-47) 12th June (252-255) (54)

11. 16th July 1858 (3) 29th October (54)

12. 1st April 1859 (141-143)

13. February 1867 (154-157) March (111-112)

14. February 1868 (202-203) September (383-85) October 1868 (No. 197)

15. February 1872 (39, 43, 44)

(vi) *Proceedings Foreign Department Political B*

16. February 1872 (132-133)

(vii) *Consultation Foreign Department Political*

17. September 1881 (101-105 general B)

18. May 1882 (327-333).

19. October 1882 (43-45).

(viii) *Proceedings of Foreign Department Secret*

20. 15th August 1845 (34).

21. 26th December 1846 (983-84).

22. 5th April 1881 (688).

23. January 1882 (568, 572, 574, 589, 591, 592).

24. January 1882 (578 Enclosure 9, 571 Enclosure 2 and 572 Enclosure 3).

25. Foreign Department Secret Proceeding F August 1889 (114-115).

(ix) *Confidential Foreign Department K.W. Secret F*

26. August 1889 (114-115).

(x) *Home Department Judicial A Proceedings*

27. 13th January 1871 (52-53) 29th July (45-61)

28. 30th January 1872 (55-71) February (57-58)

29. March 1872 (235) June (11, 107-111, 112-132)

30. July 1872 (208, 11, 12-220)

31. August 1872 (246, 272-284)

32. June 1872 (279-395)

(xi) *Proceedings Home Department Judicial B*

33. August 1879 (257-259)

34. September 1880 (232-236)

35. October 1881 (188-195)

(xii) *Proceedings Home and Foreign Record*

36. February 1854 (52-54)

(xiii) *Legislative/Parliamentary Papers*

37. East India Kuka Outbreak Volume 45 Call No. 422 p. 23 Debates

38. Kuka Outbreak Parliamentary Paper

No. 356 1872 (Reply to the Address in the House of Commons, July 22, 1872)

39. Act 7 of 1839 of papers regarding Anand Marriage Act (All the Volume)

40. Hansard's Parliamentary Debates

41. Kukas : Papers Relating to the Kuka sect (Selections from the Record s of the Government of Punjab) Lahore, 1872.

(xiv) *Microfilms and Manuscripts*

1. *Caste and Class among the Sikhs of North West India* Columbia University, Ph.D. 1963. Ph.D. dissertation Microfilm No. 377 Teen Murti.

2. *The Punjab Province and the Lahore Distt. 1849-1872.*
(A case of study British Colonial Rule and Social Change in India). Volume I & II University of Minesote Ph.D. 1975 Microfilm A.C. No. 1009.

3. *Punjab Politics and the Disturbance of 1907.*
Ph.D. dissertation Duke University Microfilm A.C.C. No.2.

4. *Religious and Social Organization in Northern Indian Village.*
Lapoint N. No. 21.

5. *Native Opinion,* North West Frontier Province Microfilm 1871-72-73, A.C.C. No. 94.

6. *Pioneer,* November 13, 1871 to February 5, 1872 A.C.C. No. 1455.

7. *Bhagwat-I-Kuka.* (*Kuka* insurrection at Malerkotla) M/804 Punjab Archives, Patiala (Manuscript).

8. Kavi Sant Dass Chibber and Narain Kav, *Ustat Sri Amritsar Ji Ki,* (Sikh Reference Liberary, Amritsar).

9. Pooran Singh, *Sri Amritsar Ji Ki Ustat* (1880 Samuat), (Sikh Reference Library Amritsar).

10. Bhai Roop Singh, *Nirankari Chalan da Chitha* (Hukumnama Akal Purakh Ji Ka Sabh Sikhan Prati, Rawalpindi 1857 AD (Nirankari Darbar Chandigarh)

11. Bhai Manna Singh, *Hukumnamo Sri Satguru Sahib Ratta Ji Maharaj* (Parwana Likhiya), Rawalpindi 1873 AD (Nirankari Darbar Chandigarh).

12. *Will of Sahib Ratta Ji,* Rawalpindi 1906 (Nirankari Darbar Chandigarh).

13. *Satguru Bilas,* Santokh Singh Sirsa.

14. Bhai Kala Singh Namdhari, *Singhan Namdharian da Sahib Bilas* 1913 AD (Sirsa).

15. *Singhan Namdharian da Panth Parkash,* 1914 AD (Sirsa).

16. Kavi Sodha, *Sri Amritsar Mahma* (Village Kala District Amritsar) (Sikh Reference Library).

17. Text written on Shri Nishan Sahib of the time of Baba Darbar Singh (Nirankari Darbar Singh Chandigarh).

18. Text written on the old Rumala of Sahib Ratta Ji's time (Nirankari Darbar Chandigarh).

19. *Bhai Balak Singh Di Ardas Saain Jawahar Mal de Naum* (Sikh Reference Library Amritsar).

(xv) *Private Papers*

1. *Majithia Papers* (Sunder Singh) Teen Murti.

2. *North Book Collection Papers* dated 1872-90 MSS Eur C 144 India Office Library, London.

3. *Dowdall Collection Papers* dated 1866-1922 (during this service on the North-West Frontier) Province MSS Eur D 848 India Office Library, London.

4. *Edwards Collection Papers,* dated 1847-62 Sir Edwards Commissioner of Peshawar, Commissioner of Ambala 1862-65, M. SS Eur E 211 India Office Library, London.

5. *Marquis of Salisbury Papers,* Secretary of State for India (1874-78) No.1596-1613 National Archives.

6. *Harlien Manuscripts Regarding,* India Affairs 18th-19th Centuries. No. 148-149 National Archives, New Delhi.

7. *North Brook Papers,* Early of North Brook as Viceroy (1872-76) (Microfilm) A.C.C. No. 1957-66 (10-Rolls).

II Secondary Sources

(i) *Books (English)*

1. Ali, Malik, Ikram, *A Bibliography of the Punjab and its dependencies,* Lahore—1968.

2. Ahmed Quammuddin, *The Wahabi Movement in India,* Calcutta—1966.

3. Ahluwalia, M.M., *Kukas the Freedom Fighters of the Punjab,* New Delhi-1965.

4. Ahluwalia, M.L., Kirpal Singh, *The Punjab's Pioneer Freedom Fighters,* Calcutta—1964.

5. Bali, A.N. *Glimoses of Punjab History,* Delhi—1969.

6. Bajwa Fauja Singh—*A brief Account of Freedom Movement in Punjab,* Punjab University Patiala—1972.

7. Military System of the Sikhs, Delhi—1964.

8. Bajwa Fauja Singh, *Kuka Movement,* New Delhi—1966.

9. Banerjee, I.B., *Evolution of the Khalsa.* Volume II, Calcutta, 1947.

10. Bingley, Captain A.K., *Hand Book for Indian Army Sikhs,* 1899.

11. Besant, Annie, *India A Nation,* Madras. 1925.

12. Bose, N.S., *The Indian Awakening and Bengal,* Calcutta—1960.

13. Choudhary, Bal Mukand, *History of the Freedom Movement in India,* Ambala—1957.

14. Chhabra, G.S., *Advanced History of the Punjab* Volume II, Ludhiana—1960.

15. Desai, A.R., *Social Background of Indian Nationalism,* Bombay—1966.

16. Dowson. J., *Classical Dictionery of the Hindu Mythology and Religion,* London 1928.

17. Davey, Cunningham Joseph, *A History of the Sikhs,* New Delhi—1966.

18. Deva Singh, *Colonisation in the Rachna Doab* Lahore, 1929.

19. Douie, Sir J.M., *The Punjab, North West Frontier Province and Kashmir,* Cambridge, 1916.

20. Desh Sewak—*Gurudwara Reform Movement and Sikh Awakening,* Jullunder, 1922.

21. Eismie, G.R.—*Thirty Five Years in the Punjab* Edinburgh, 1908.

22. Edward, Herbert—*A Year on the Punjab Frontier in 1848-49,* London 1851.

23. Field, *Religion of the Sikhs*—1901 (Reprint).

24. Forsyth—Sir Thomas Doughlas—*Autobiography and Reminiscences ...ed. by his daughter-Forsyth, Ethel*—London, 1887.

25. Forquhar, J.N. ...*Modern Religious Movement in India,* London, 1929.

26. Furneauk, R.—*Massacre at Amritsar,* London, 1963.

27. Ganda Singh—*Bhai Jodh Singh Abinandan Granth* ed. Khalsa College, Patiala, Punjab Sahit Academy, Ludhiana.

28. Gargi, Balwant Singh—*Nirankari Baba,* Delhi—1973.

29. Ganda Singh—*A Bibliography of the Punjab,* Patiala—1966.

30. Garewal, J.S. and Indu Banga—*Early 19th Century Punjab*—Amritsar—1975.

31. Gustafron W—Esic and Kenneth W. Jones—*Sources on Punjab Hisatory,* Delhi—1975.

32. Garewal, J.S., *In the Bylanes of History,* Simla 1975.

33. Ganda Singh—*Sikhism and the Nirankari Movement,* Patiala.

34. *Guru Nanak's Impact on History*—Publication Division Ministry of Information and Broadcasting, New Delhi—1969.

35. Gandhi, S.S.—*History of the Sikh Gurus,* New Delhi—1978.

36. Henry, Cox Holled Wallace—*The Punjab and North Western Frontier of India by an old Punjabee,* London, 1878.

37. Henry Cotton—Indian and Homes Memories, London—1911..

38. Khushwant Singh—*The Sikhs,* London—1953.

39. *A History of the Sikhs,* (Second Print) USA—1965.

40. Kaur Dr. Rajender—*Why Social Bycott of Nirankaries,* Delhi—1979.

41. Karunaan K.P.—*Religion and Political Awakening in India,* Meerut—1965.

42. Latif, Sayed Mohammed—*History of the Punjab,* Calcutta—1891.

43. Mecleod—*Evolution of the Sikh Community,* Oxford—1975.

44. Marinco, Ethne K.—*The Transformation of Sikh Society* New Delhi—1976.

45. Majumdar R.C.— *History and Culture of the Indian People,* Bombay—1965.

46. Mohinder Singh—*Akali Movement,* New Delhi, 1978.

47. Macauliff—*The Sikh Religion,* Vol. II, Oxford—1909.

48. Malcolm John—*Sketches of the Sikhs*—London, 1812.

49. Mehta, H.R.A., *History of the growth and Development of Western Education in Punjab,* 1846-1884, Lahore—1929.

50. Narang, Sri Gokal Chand—*Glorious History of Sikhism,* New Delhi—1972.

51. *Transformation of Sikhism,* Lahore—1946.

52. Nahar Singh—*Guru Ram Singh and the Kuka Sikhs Documents* in Three Volumes (1963-71) New Delhi—1955.

53. Natrajan S. —*A Century of Social Reform in India* Bombay—1969.

54. Nirankari, Baba Surinder Singh—*Nirankari Gurmat Prarambhta*—Chandigarh—1974.

55. Payne—*A short History of the Sikhs,* London, 1883 (Reprint) by the Department of Languages, 1970, Punjab University, Patiala.

56. Princep, H.T.—*The Origin of the Sikh Power in the Punjab,* Calcutta—1834.

57. Rose, H.A.—A Glossary of the Tribes and Castes of the Punjab and North West Frontier Province—Volume—III, Lahore—1914.

58. Royal Asiatic Society, London, *The Sikh and their History,* 1917.

59. Scott—*Religion and Short History of the Sikhs*—1930.

60. Smith—Punjab—*The Punjab being a brief account of the country of the Sikhs*—London—1845.

61. Shri,Sohan Lal—*Umdat-Ut-Twarikh,*5 Volumes, Lahore, 1889 (Translated by V.S. Suri), Delhi—1961.

62. Singh H. and Singh T.—*Tales from Sikh History of the Rawalpindi,Attack and Peshawar Distt.*, Rawalpindi—1915.

63. Sanehai, Sawaran Singh—*Foremost Freedom Fighters*—Maiden lead—1972.

64. Singh, Gurmeet—*Sant Khalsa*—Sirsa,1978.

65. Smith, Marian—*Synthesis and other processes in Sikhism*—1948.

66. Sher Singh—*History of the Nirankari Movement,* Chandigarh—1972.

67. Sinha, N.K.—*Rise of the Sikh Powers,* Calcutta—1946.

68. *Ranjeet Singh,* Calcutta,1933.

69. Sahni Ruchi Ram—*Struggle for Reform in Sikh Shrines* ed.Ganda Singh, Amritsar,1965.

70. Thorburn, S.S.—*The Punjab in Peace and War,* Published 1883, Reprinted—1970.

71. Teja Singh,*Sikhism,its Ideas and Institutions,* Lahore,1938.

72. Thorton (Thomas)—*A History of the Punjab and of the rise, Progress Present Conditions of the sect and Nation of the Sikhs,* London—1846.

73. Thomas, F.U. Dea—*The Sociology of Religion,* New Delhi—1969.

74. Tripathi—*Rise and Rall of the Mughal Empire,* Allahabad, 1956.

75. Water, H.A.—*The Ahmediya Movement,* Calcutta—1918.

76. Vincent A. Smith—*Oxford History of India.*

(ii) Urdu/Persian

1. Abul Fazal—*Akbaruama* (Persian), Volume II.

2. Jahangir Emperor, *Tuzuk-I-Jahangir* (Tr.), Volume I.

3. Mufti Ghulam Sarwar Quereshi—*Tarikh-I-Makhjan-I-Punjab*,Lahore,1877 AD.

4. Maulvi Ghulam Bhikh Jullundri, *Tarikh-I-Wakri.*

(iii) *In Gurmukhi*

1. Avtar Singh—*Horna Dharma Nalon Khalsa Dharm which ki Vdai Hai,*Amritsar,1895.

2. Amar Bharti—*Sikh Itihas Te Kuke*—New Delhi—1964.

3. Ashok Shamsher Singh, *Punjab Dian Lahran Athwa Sikhan di Navin Jagrity,* 1954.

4. Bhanu Datta—*Guru Singh Itihas,* Lahore—1883.

5. Bhagat Singh Namdhari—*Suri Guru Govind Singh Ji Ki Bhavisat Bani* Part-I, Patiala—1940.

6. Charan Singh—*Atal Prakash* (Life of Baba Atal Rai Amritsar—1892.

7. Dhyan Singh—*Sri Satguru Bilas,* Bhaini Sahib—1942.

8. Ganda Singh—*Sikh Itihas Bare,* Amritsar, 194

9. " —*Sikh Itihas Val,* Lahore—1945.

10. " —*Punjab Dian Varan*—1945 42.

11. " —Kukiyan-di-Vithya, Amritsar—1946.

12. Gyani Ishar Singh Nara—*Itihas Baba Sri Chand Ji Sahib* are Udasin Samparday—Delhi—1975.

13. Hira Singh Dard—*Bahu Mule Ithihasik Lekh Sikh Sudharak Lahran.*

14. " Gurmat Modhi Sri Baba Dayal Ji—Chandigarh—1979.

15. Sain Jawahar Mal ate Balak Singh—*Jeewan Priti*—1061.

16. Joginder Singh—*Nahin Tudh Jehva,* Delhi.

17. Jaswant Singh Das—*Baba Ram Singh Namdhari,* Amritsar—1962.

18. Kahan Singh—*Gur Shabad Rotnakar Mahan Kosh* Encyclopaedia of Sikh Literature, 4 Vol. Patiala, 1931.

19. Kahan Singh—*Gurmat Prarambhta,* Lahore—1898.

20. Kartar Singh—*Sarkar Khalsa,* Amritsar 1916.

21. Karam Singh Historian—*Bahu Mule Itihasik Lekh* Amritsar—1930.

22. Kahn Singh Bhai—*Nirankari Prem Prakash,* Chandigarh, 1955.

23. Kapur Singh—*Sapt Sring*—1952.

24. Mehr Singh—*Bharat which Gurudwara* Parkashan Vibhag Soochna ate Parsaran Mantralya, April—1977.

25. Man Singh Nirankari—*Anand Viyah di Itihasik Kranti,* Chandigarh.

26. *Namdhari Itihas*—Pehla Hissa, Delhi—1956.

27. Nahar Singh—*Deshbhagat Varta,* lari No., 12, Delhi—1956.

28. Nidhan Singh Alam—*Jug Paltaoo Satguru,* Delhi-1947.

29. *Van-Su Vane Sardha Phul*—Nirankari Parchar Pustak No. 27, Chandigarh-1957.

30. *Gurmat Viyah Sabd Sangreh,* Chandigarh-1979.

31. Namdhari Bhai Balak Singh—*Pothi Sardha Puran,* 1957.

32. Partap Singh Gyani—*Sikh Itihasik Lectures,* Amritsar-1944.

33. " *Nakali Nirankari,* Amritsar, 1967.

34. Randhir Singh Ithias Khojee—*Udasi Sikhan di Vithya* S.G.P.C. 1958.

35. Santokh—*Gur Pratap Suraj Granth,* Lahore—1883-84.

36. Sradha Ram—*Sikhan de Raj di Vithya,* Vol. I & II, Ludhiana—1868.

37. Shamsher Singh Ashok—*Sikhi te Sikh Itihas,* Ludiana—1951.

38. " —*Punjab dian Lahran,* Patiala-1954.

39. Surinder Singh Kohli—*Amritsar Anoop Ramdasspur* Amritsar—1978.

40. Inder Singh Chakrverty—*Kukian Bare,* Delhi—1957.

41. Ardas Bhagwati Ke Nirankar—*Youngman's Nirankari,* Association, Chandigarh—1979.

42. Bhai Jodh Singh—*Gurmat Nirnay.*

(iv) *Hindi*

1. Babu Sivaprasad—*Sikhon ka Uday aur ast,* Benaras—1851.

2. Nahar Singh—*Namdhari Itihas Pratham Bhag,* Delhi—1956.

3. Sant Nidhan Singh Alam,—*Krantikari Satguru* Delhi—1947.

4. Thakur Desraj—*Sikh Itihas,* Prakashak Gramouthan Vidyapth Sangariya.

III. Gazetteers and Reports

1. *The Twentieth Annual Report of the Lodiana Mission.* Including stations at Lodhiana, Sharnpur, Sabathu, Jalandor, Ambala, Lahore, Dehra for the year ending September 30th June 1854.

2. *The Census of Punjab* taken on 17th February 1881 Volume I, Calcutta 1883.

3. The Punjab and its Feudatories Part I. *The Report of the Census of India,* Volume XIX 1891.

4. *Gazatteer of Rawalpandi District,* 1893-94 Punjab Government, Lahore.

5. *Punjab Gazatteer Ludhiana* 1888-89, Lahore.

6. *Imperial Gazatteer of India,* Provincial series Punjab, Volume II, 1881-82.

7. *Encyclopedia Brittanica,* Chicago University 1946 Book 20.

8. *Gazatteer of Hoshyarpur district,* 1883-84 Punjab Govt. Press (Lahore).

IV. Journals

(i) *English*

1. *The Calcutta Review,* September 1859, Vol LXV.

2. *The Illustrated Weekly of India*, Vol. XLII 43, Sunday October 24, 1971.

3. Indian Historical Records Commission Proceedings Vol. XXXIV, Part-II.

   Trivandrum, December 1958.

4. *The Tribune*, dated 11th May, 1957.

5. *The Tribune,* dated 15th August, 1957.

6. The Punjab Past and Present Volume I and II Part No. I and II 1967, 1970, 1973, 1976.

(ii) *Hindi*

Samaj Sudhar Patrika 4th December, 1941.

(iii) *Gurumukhi*

1. Sat Jug Basant Ank 8 Magh 1980 BK (1923 AD)
2. " 25 Magh 1981 " (1924 AD)
3. " 22 Magh 1983 " (1926 AD)
4. " 10 Magh 1985 " (1925 AD)
5. " Magh 1984 " (1927 AD)
6. " 22 Magh 1985 " (1929 AD)
7. " Magh 1985 " (1928 AD)
8. " Magh 1994 " (1994 AD)
9. Sat Jug Sant Ank 9 Chaitra 1996 (1939 AD)
10. " 20 Bhadron 1998 (1941 AD)
11. Sat Jug Hola Ank Chaitra 2012 (1955 AD)
12. Phulwari Ank Masik Ithasik No. July 1928.
13. Phulwari Sikh Itihasic No. 1930.
14. Sachitar Kaumi Ekta June 1978.

Tracts :

15. Nirankari (*Pahli Kiyari*) Youngmen Association Rawalpandi 31st January, 1932.
16. Nirankari Sunehera, 1931.
17. Nirankari Ekta Sandesh, 1940.
18. Nirankari Gurmat Sandesh, 1934.
19. Nirankari, 1932.
20. Nirankari Prem Sunhera, 1935.

Index